A History of the World in Seven Cheap Things

A History of the World in Seven Cheap Things

A Guide to Capitalism, Nature, and the Future of the Planet

RAJ PATEL
AND JASON W. MOORE

VERSO
London • New York

This paperback edition published by Verso 2020
First published in the UK by Verso 2018

1 3 5 7 9 10 8 6 4 2

Verso
UK: 6 Meard Street, London W1F 0EG
US: 20 Jay Street, Suite 1010, Brooklyn, NY 11201
versobooks.com

Verso is the imprint of New Left Books

ISBN-13: 978-1-78873-774-6
ISBN-13: 978-1-78873-215-4 (EBK)

British Library Cataloguing in Publication Data
A catalogue record for this book is available from the British Library

Printed and bound by CPI Group (UK) Ltd, Croydon, CRO 4YY

To Phil McMichael

Teacher, Mentor, Jester, Shark

Contents

Acknowledgments

In a book that seeks to understand how we have come to where we are, our acknowledgments must begin with our families and the extended webs of kin, love, intellect, and reciprocity that made it possible for us to be cared for as we wrote, made us care about what we wrote, and helped us understand far better what we were doing. We worked in the hope that our children might one day live within a different web of life.

The communities that made this book possible were vast, from the supporting colleagues seen and unseen at our respective institutions to those whose work made the page—or screen—on which you read these words. At University of California Press, no reparation would be too great for Kate Marshall's championing of the book, the board's decision to accept it, our reviewers' invaluable suggestions, or the toil of Bradley Depew, Dore Brown, and the design team. We're particularly grateful for the editorial choices that allowed us to work with Juliana Froggatt, who made this book far more sensible.

We wouldn't have had the chance to collaborate with the press had it not been for Caroline Eisenmann, Karolina Sutton, and Kris Dahl at ICM. And we wouldn't have had occasion to approach them had it not been for Mark Metzler, who in his time at the University of Texas at Austin brought Jason to Raj's door, making it possible for us to meet, plot, and ultimately write this book.

Raj: Again, thanks to Mark Metzler for the gift of getting to meet, and learning to see the world anew through, Jason—and then for providing us such valuable insights into our work at the University of Texas History Department seminar. Elsewhere on the forty acres, Eric Tang, Sharmila Rudrappa, Jason Cons, Bob Jensen, Billy Chandler, Karen Engle, and their colleagues in black studies, Asian American studies, anthropology, radio, television, film, and law were deep sources of inspiration. At the Lyndon Baines Johnson School of Public Affairs, Erin Lentz and Jamie Galbraith were kind enough to entertain strange ideas over beer, and Sydney Briggs suffered an early draft with grace and acuity. My terrific students indulged a semester of successive iterations of the arguments in this book, and I'm pleased to recognize how much I owe Bryce Block, Leo Carter, Lucia Gamboa, Caitlin Goodrich, Jose Guzman, Ben Hirsch, Brian Jackson, Tim Knoedler, Josh Meuth Alldredge, Alex Payson, Bobak Reihani, Scott Squires, and Mary Vo. I owe a particular debt to the magnificent staff at the University of Texas at Austin Libraries, especially at the Benson Latin American Collection and Perry-Castañeda Library.

Conversations with Steven Tomlinson, Eugene Sepulveda, Tom Philpott, Rebecca McInroy and David Alvarez, Tim and Karrie League, Shawn Sides, and Graham Reynolds have always improved a project conceived in the academy. Malik Yakini,

Kandace Vallejo, Bianca Bockman, Yotam Marom, Deirdre Smith Shabaaz, and the Wildfire Project board and team always asked the right questions, and the UC Berkeley geography shock troops, with brilliant graduate students ably directed by Gill Hart, Nathan Sayre, Richard Walker, Michael Watts, Comrade Boal, and the Retort collective, knew where to look for answers.

Versions of this book were shared with participants in a few venues, from the Unit for Humanities at Rhodes University (UHURU) seminar (at the University Currently Known as Rhodes University), always benefiting from Richard Pithouse, Vashna Jagarnath, and Michael Neocosmos, to two "Initiatives in Critical Agrarian Studies" conferences, through which Jun Borras made it possible to imagine completing this book. At the International Studies Association, Andrej Grubačić led a merry panel, including Christopher K. Chase-Dunn, Barry Keith Gills, and Denis O'Hearn, in fine conversation.

An embarrassing list of people have read or heard slices of the book and shared how it might be improved. Deep thanks, then, to Kolya Abramsky, Rachel Bezner Kerr, Jun Borras, Zoe Brent, Chris Brooke, Harry Cleaver, Josephine Crawley-Quinn, Silvia Federici, Harriet Friedmann, Leland Glenna, Sam Grey, Shalmali Guttal, Friede Habermann, Naomi Klein, William Lacy, Phil McMichael, Daniel Moshenberg, Joe Quirk, Jackie Roth, Olivier De Schutter, Daniel Bowman Simon, John Vandermeer, and Ken Wilson for their time and wisdom.

Jason: My thanks go first to my always gracious and ever insightful coauthor, Raj, for his vision that world-ecology's relevance extends far beyond the university—and that it needs *this* book to do that. This book is possible only because of the care, love, and support of Diana C. Gildea and Malcolm W. Moore, who sustained our small family through the many weekends and evenings filled with writing. Marge Thomas, as ever, helped me to put this book into a wider vision and personal practice of planetary healing. The world-ecology conversation to which this book contributes has been nourished by a wonderfully gracious and intellectually generative community of scholars, including A. Haroon Akram-Lodhi, Fredrik Albritton Jonsson, Elmar Altvater, Martin Arboleda, Gennarro Avallone, Luke Bergmann, Henry Bernstein, Jun Borras, Neil Brenner, Gareth Bryant, Terry Burke, Bram Büscher, Jennifer Casolo, Daniel Aldana Cohen, Sam Cohn, Hanne Cottyn, Sharae Deckard, Treasa De Loughry, Marion Dixon, Barbara Epstein, Henrik Ernsston, Sam Fassbinder, Harriet Friedmann, Clodagh Gannon O'Malley, Diana C. Gildea, Bikrum Gill, Andrej Grubačić, Daniel Hartley, Aaron G. Jakes, Gerry Kearns, Steve Knight, Zahir Kolia, Markus Kröger, Benjamin Kunkel, Nick Lawrence, Emanuele Leonardi, Sasha Lilley, Larry Lohmann, Peter Marchetti, Justin McBrien, Laura McKinney, Phil McMichael, Fred Murphy, Michael Niblett, Andrzej Nowak, Denis O'Hearn, Kerstin Oloff, Christian Parenti, Michael Paye, Stephen Shapiro, Beverly Silver, David A. Smith, Marcus Taylor, Eric Vanhaute, Richard Walker, Immanuel Wallerstein, Michael Watts, Tony Weis, and Anna Zalik.

My graduate students at Binghamton University and elsewhere have been an enormous reservoir of hope and inspiration: Kushariyaningsih Boediono, Alvin Camba, Giuseppe Cioffo, Christopher R. Cox, Daniel Cunha, Joshua Eichen, Luis Garrido de Soto, Kyle Gibson, Çağrı İdiman, Benjamin J. Marley, Roberto J. Ortiz, and Fathun Karib Satrio. So too my students in successive undergraduate seminars at Binghamton, especially Dayne Feehan.

I also thank the scholars and activists who invited me to talk at research centers, academic programs, bookstores, and social justice centers over the past three years. They—and the audiences who came to see me speak—pushed me to think all the more deeply about the countless lacunae in the world-ecology conversation. Even—and especially—when we have disagreed, my thinking has sharpened and evolved.

Together: We offer this book not as a series of closed formulations, of truth handed down from on high to be damned or praised, but as a contribution to an ongoing conversation about the fate of this planet and how we will live—and die—on it. It is our hope that the challenges of this conversation, the discomfort it will bring, and the destabilization of age-old verities that come with it will be outweighed by the joy and love of a collective project to create a just and emancipatory world for its humans and critters. For all this book's imperfections, we hope the reader will evaluate its merits with this in mind: we must think and act as if our lives depend on it.

May 25, 2017

Austin, Texas, and Vestal, New York

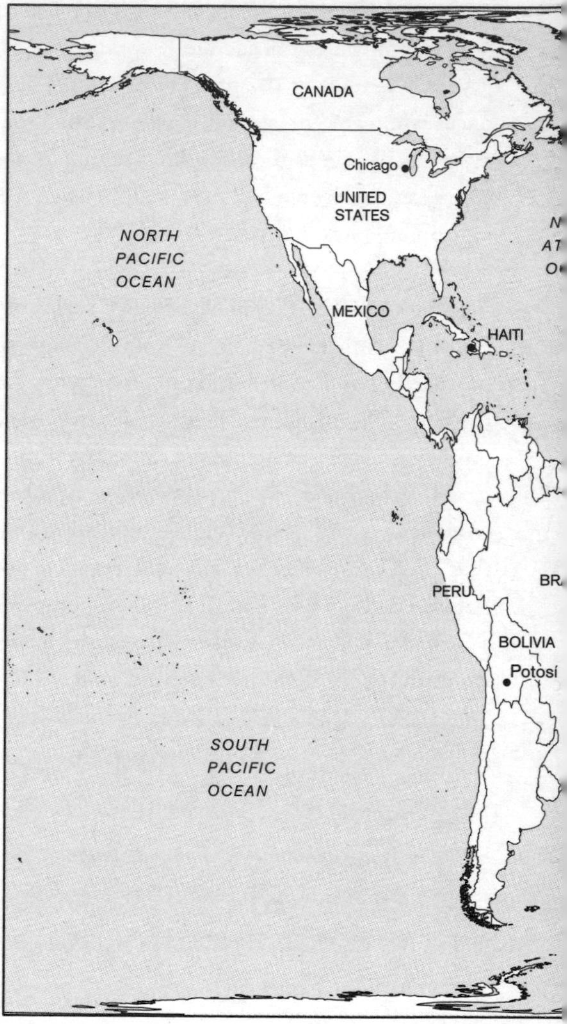

Map 1. Key locations in world-ecology, shown in the Gall-Peters projection, which distorts country shapes in order to preserve relative area sizes.

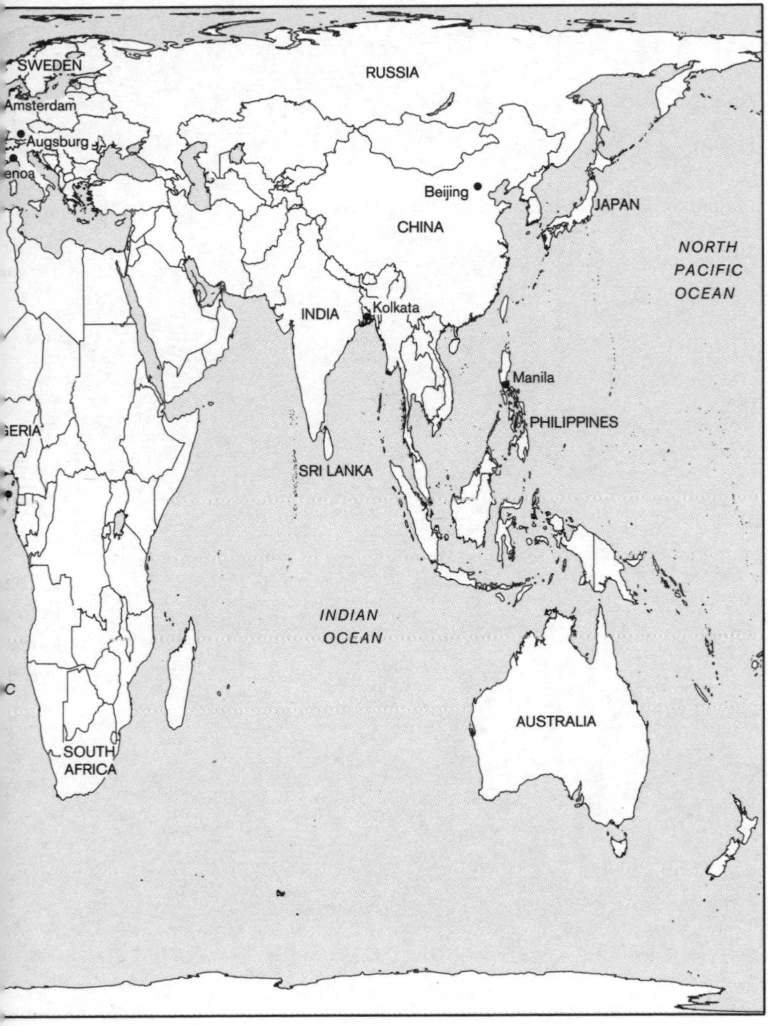
SWEDEN
RUSSIA
Amsterdam
Augsburg
enoa
Beijing
JAPAN
CHINA
NORTH
PACIFIC
OCEAN
INDIA
Kolkata
Manila
GERIA
PHILIPPINES
SRI LANKA
INDIAN
OCEAN
C
AUSTRALIA
SOUTH
AFRICA

Introduction

> Lightning and thunder need time, the light of the stars needs time, deeds need time, even after they are done, to be seen and heard. This deed is as yet further from them than the furthest star, and yet they have done it!
>
> Friedrich Nietzsche, "The Madman," in *The Gay Science*

Settled agriculture, cities, nation-states, information technology, and every other facet of the modern world have unfolded within a long era of climatic good fortune.[1] Those days are gone. Sea levels are rising; climate is becoming less stable; average temperatures are increasing. Civilization emerged in a geological era known as the Holocene. Some have called our new climate era the Anthropocene. Future intelligent life will know we were here because some humans have filled the fossil record with such marvels as radiation from atomic bombs, plastics from the oil industry, and chicken bones.[2]

What happens next is unpredictable at one level and entirely predictable at another. Regardless of what humans decide to do, the twenty-first century will be a time of "abrupt and irreversible" changes in the web of life.[3] Earth system scientists have a rather dry term for such a fundamental turning point in the life of a biospheric system: state shift. Unfortunately, the ecology from which this geological change has emerged has also produced humans who are ill equipped to receive news of this state shift. Nietzsche's madman announcing the death of god was met in a similar fashion: although industrial Europe had reduced divine influence to the semicompulsory Sunday-morning church attendance, nineteenth-century society couldn't imagine a world without god. The twenty-first century has an analogue: it's easier for most people to imagine the end of the planet than to imagine the end of capitalism.[4]

We need an intellectual state shift to accompany our new epoch.

The first task is one of linguistic rigor, to note a problem in naming our new geological epoch the Anthropocene. The root, *anthropos* (Greek for "human"), suggests that it's just humans being humans, in the way that kids will be kids or snakes will be snakes, that has caused climate change and the planet's sixth mass extinction. It's true that humans have been changing the planet since the end of the last ice age.[5] A hunting rate slightly higher than the replenishment rate over centuries, together with shifting climate and grasslands, spelled the end for the Columbian Plains mammoth in North America, the orangutan's overstuffed relative the *Gigantopithecus* in east Asia,[6] and the giant Irish elk *Megaloceros giganteus* in Europe.[7] Humans may even have been partly responsible for tempering a global cooling phase twelve thousand years ago through agriculture-related greenhouse gas emissions.[8]

Hunting large mammals to extinction is one thing, but the speed and scale of destruction today can't be extrapolated from the activities of our knuckle-dragging forebears. Today's human activity isn't exterminating mammoths through centuries of overhunting. Some humans are currently killing everything, from megafauna to microbiota, at speeds one hundred times higher than the background rate.[9] We argue that what changed is capitalism, that modern history has, since the 1400s, unfolded in what is better termed the Capitalocene.[10] Using this name means taking capitalism seriously, understanding it not just as an economic system but as a way of organizing the relations between humans and the rest of nature.

In this book, we show how the modern world has been made through seven cheap things: nature, money, work, care, food, energy, and lives. Every word in that sentence is difficult. *Cheap* is the opposite of a bargain—cheapening is a set of strategies to control a wider web of life. "Things" become things through armies and clerics and accountants and print. Most centrally, humans and nature don't exist as giant seventeenth-century billiard balls crashing into each other. The pulse of life making is messy, contentious, and mutually sustaining. This book introduces a way to think about the complex relationships between humans and the web of life that helps make sense of the world we're in and suggests what it might become.

As a teaser, let's return to those chicken bones in the geological record, a capitalist trace of the relation between humans and the world's most common bird, *Gallus gallus domesticus*.[11] The chickens we eat today are very different from those consumed a century ago. Today's birds are the result of intensive post–World War II efforts drawing on genetic material sourced freely from Asian jungles, which humans decided to recombine to produce the most profitable fowl.[12] That bird can barely walk, reaches maturity in weeks, has an oversize breast, and is reared and slaughtered in geologically significant quantities (more than sixty billion birds a year).[13] Think of this relationship as a sign of Cheap Nature. Already the most popular meat in the United States, chicken is projected to be the planet's most popular flesh for human consumption by 2020.[14] That will require a great deal of labor. Poultry workers are paid very little: in the United States, two cents for every dollar spent on a fast-food chicken goes to workers, and some chicken operators use prison labor, paid twenty-five cents per hour. Think of this as Cheap Work. In the US poultry industry, 86 percent of workers who cut wings are in pain because of the repetitive hacking and twisting on the line.[15] Some employers mock their workers for reporting injury, and the denial of injury claims is common. The result for workers is a 15 percent decline in income for the ten years after injury.[16] While recovering, workers will depend on their families and support networks, a factor outside the circuits of production but central to their continued participation in the workforce. Think of this as Cheap Care. The food produced by this industry ends up keeping bellies full and discontent down through low prices at the checkout and drive-through. That's a strategy of Cheap Food. Chickens themselves are relatively minor contributors to climate change—they've only one stomach each and don't burp out methane like cows do—but they're bred in large lots that use a great deal of fuel to keep warm. This is the biggest contributor to the US poultry industry's carbon footprint.[17] You can't have low-cost chicken without abundant propane: Cheap Energy. There is some risk in the commercial sale of these processed birds, but through franchising and subsidies, everything from easy financial and physical access to the land on which the soy feed for chickens is grown—mainly in China, Brazil, and the United States[18]—to small business loans, that risk is mitigated through public expense for private profit. This is one aspect of Cheap Money. Finally, persistent and frequent acts of chauvinism against categories of animal and human life—such as women, the colonized, the poor, people of color, and immigrants—have made each of these six cheap things possible. Fixing this ecology in place requires a final element—the rule of Cheap Lives. Yet at every step of this process, humans resist—from the Indigenous Peoples[19] whose flocks provide the source of genetic material for breeding through poultry and care workers demanding recognition and relief to those fighting against climate change and Wall Street. The social struggles over nature, money, work, care, food, energy, and lives that attend the Capitalocene's poultry bones amount to a case for why the most iconic symbol of the modern era isn't the automobile or the smartphone but the Chicken McNugget.

All this is forgotten in the act of dipping the chicken-and-soy product into a plastic pot of barbeque sauce. Yet the fossilized trace of a trillion birds will outlast—and mark the passage of—the humans who made them. That's why we present the story of humans, nature, and the system that changed the planet as a short history of the modern world: as an antidote to forgetting. This short book isn't, however, a history of the whole world. It's the history of processes that can explain why the world looks the way it does today. The story of these seven cheap things illustrates how capitalism expanded to yield maps like the one below, showing how small a portion of the earth has lain outside the scope of European colonial power.

We'll explain precisely what we mean by *cheap* below. First we need to make the case that it's not just some natural human behavior but rather a specific interaction between humans and the biological and physical world that has brought us to this point.

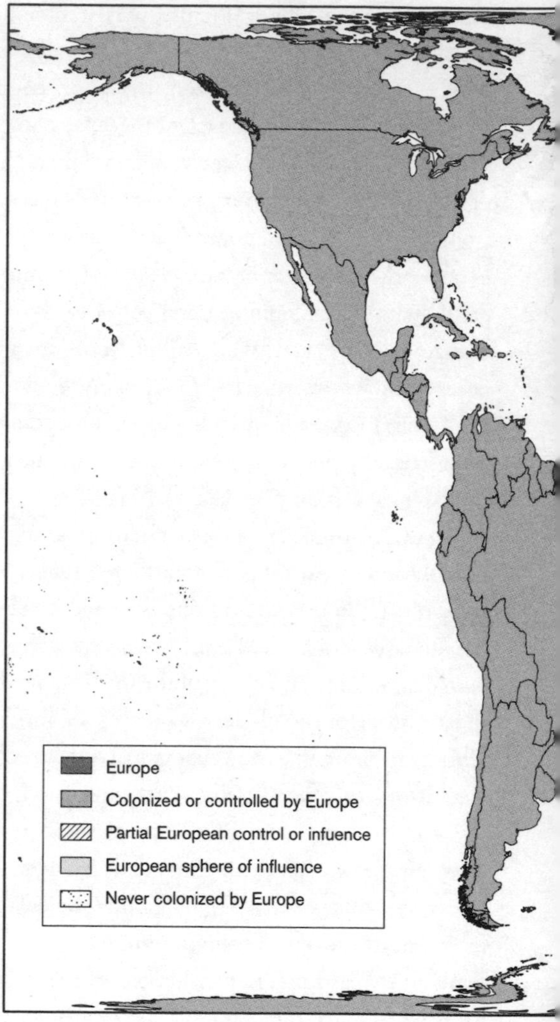

Map 2. Parts of the world colonized by Europe.

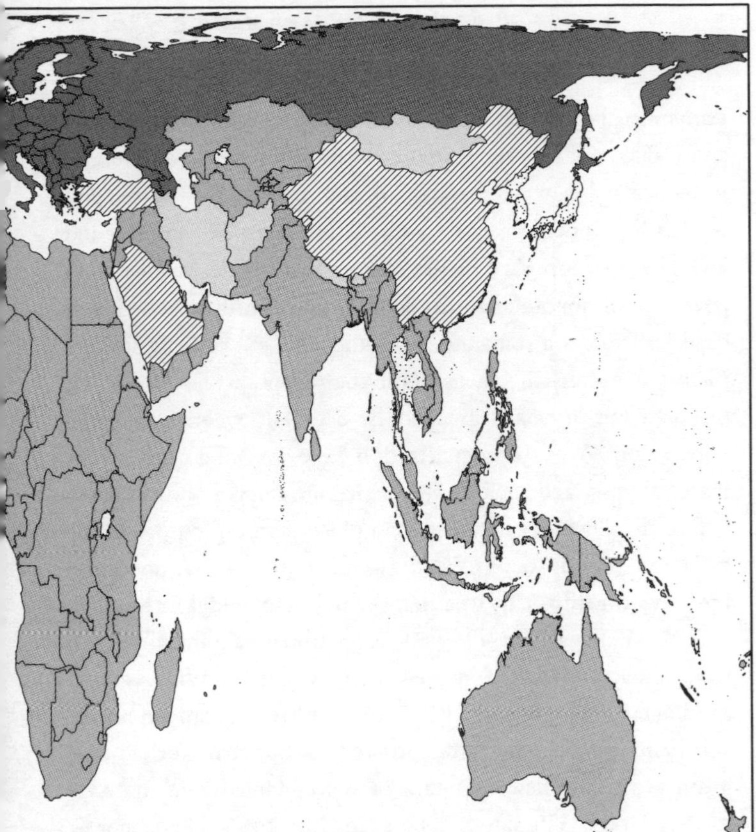

A BRIEF GUIDE TO HUMANS AND NATURE BEFORE CAPITALISM

Lamenting how poorly humans treat the natural world is ancient sport. Plato did it in the *Critias*, describing a time nine thousand years before his, when the area around Athens was forested and tended by a noble people who held property in common and loved nature more than Plato's contemporaries. As he told it, his peers had dishonored nature and allowed the hills to be stripped bare.[20] Plato's is a romanticized—and almost certainly false—history of periurban Athens.[21] Our analysis points not to a deficit of honor but to what happened, by accident, when a marginal tributary of West Asian civilization experienced a crisis of climate, disease, and society. We begin our story a few centuries before the dawn of capitalism, in a place with aspirations to the riches and civilizations of Central and East Asia but poorer by far,[22] in a time made by weather. We begin in feudal Europe.

The Medieval Warm Period was a climate anomaly that ran from about 950 to 1250 in the North Atlantic.[23] Winters were mild and growing seasons were long. Cultivation spread northward and upward: vineyards sprouted in southern Norway, and grain farms climbed mountains and highlands from the Alps to Scotland.[24] Human numbers in Europe swelled, nearly tripling—to seventy million—in the five centuries after 800.[25] England's population peaked around 1300 and wouldn't reach that level again until the end of the seventeenth century.[26] The agricultural surplus grew even faster. Towns sprang up everywhere, and by 1300 a growing share of the population—perhaps a fifth—worked outside agriculture. Such relative prosperity also fueled expansionary appetites. The Crusades are an example: highly commercialized and militarized operations that targeted the wealth of the eastern Mediterranean, beginning in 1095. They were accompanied by other movements of conquest, two of which loomed large in the shaping of the modern world four centuries later. The first was the Christian Reconquista of Iberia, in what are today Portugal and Spain. The Castilians and Aragonese began to roll back Islamic power on the peninsula through the first wave of Crusades—and the Crusaders made conquest pay through tribute, in what would become a characteristic of colonial capitalism. The second movement was subtler and more powerful. Feudalism's most important feature was its capacity to sustain massive and ongoing settler expansion without centralized authority. To do this, it relied on cultivation—the greatest conqueror of all. By the fourteenth century, agriculture took up a third of all European land use, a radical, sixfold increase over the previous five centuries, much of it realized at the expense of forests.[27]

Feudal Europe rode the Medieval Warm Period until its peak around 1250, when the climate turned colder—and wetter. After centuries of relative food security, famine returned, and with a force all the greater for smashing against a civilization used to altogether different weather. In May 1315, massive rains struck across Europe, possibly as a result of the eruption of New Zealand's Mount Kaharoa.[28] They did not relent until August, when the deluge ended with an early cold snap. Harvests had been weak in previous years, but 1315's was disastrous—and so was the next year's. Europe's population contracted by up to 20 percent over the next few years.[29] The continent did not escape from the Great Famine—as historians call it—until 1322.[30]

Although contemporaries did not know it, they had entered the Little Ice Age, a period that would end only in the nineteenth century. The Little Ice Age laid bare feudalism's vulnerabilities.

Its food system, for instance, worked well only while the climate remained clement. This was chiefly because that system ran through a particular class arrangement, in which lords enjoyed formal control over the land and peasants cultivated it. Lords oversaw a rising peasant population, which was able to generate a rising surplus, with a tendency toward diminishing returns. Soil fertility was slowly exhausted over the centuries, a decline partially concealed by a rising population of peasants wringing the last out of fixed areas of land. When the climate turned, it created a cascade of failures, propagated through a class system that enforced soil exhaustion and starvation, killing millions.

One explanation for this civilizational crisis lines up well with the warning in Robert Malthus's *Essay on the Principles of Population:* there were too many people and not enough food. To use more modern language, climate change affected Europe's carrying capacity, reducing the number of people who could be sustained on the degraded land under feudalism. But carrying capacities swell or shrink depending on who rules. The issue—then as now—was really one of power. In fact, Malthus has less to offer this story than Karl Marx. Feudal lords wanted cash or grain, which could be easily stored and marketed, and they overwhelmingly consumed the modest surpluses wrung from the soil, leaving precious little to reinvest in agriculture.[31] Absent the lords' power and demands, peasants might have shifted to crop mixes that included garden produce alongside grains, perhaps solving the food problem. As for the number of people, family formation and population growth are not determined by an eternal procreational drive but rather shaped by a host of historical conditions turning on culture, class, and land availability. As Guy Bois notes in his classic study of Norman feudalism, a transition to different ways of working land, with more peasant autonomy and power over what and how to grow, would have allowed medieval Europe to feed up to three times as many people.[32] But that transition never happened, and feudal arrangements staggered on until receiving a final coup de grace in 1347: the Black Death.[33]

Europe emerged from the Medieval Warm Period in poor shape. The structures that had produced sufficient food to nourish peasants and cities from the beginning of the second millennium weren't able to cope with the changing climate, casting a growing layer of the population into malnutrition.[34] Eleventh-century bodies exhumed from English cemeteries show better health than those from the thirteenth century.[35] The food shortages at the end of the Medieval Warm Period made European bodies more vulnerable to disease, and the Black Death turned this vulnerability into an apocalypse. Wiping out between one-third and one-half of Europe's population, it took advantage of the medieval world's version of globalization. Nearly everywhere, urbanization and commercialization were bringing more people into cities and more cities into trade networks. Arteries of trade that carried goods and money from Shanghai to Sicily also unified Asia and Europe into a supercontinental "disease pool."[36]

Once the Black Death reached Europe—Sicily by October 1347 and Genoa just three months later—feudalism unraveled. That unraveling can tell us something important about how great crises occur and how they entangle dynamics such as climate and population with power and economy. Feudalism, like many agrarian civilizations, tended to exhaust its agroecological relations. As population increased under feudal class arrangements, farming became more labor intensive, with more people working the land, reducing predation and weeds, nurturing crops with more care. Throwing people into fields didn't address feudalism's class structure—it merely managed its decline. In England, signs of feudalism's exhaustion were evident from 1270. In the half century before the Great Famine, peasant diets, already exceedingly modest, sharply deteriorated. Grain yields fell, and per capita consumption of grain—the mainstay of the peasant diet—declined by 14 percent.[37]

Civilizations don't collapse simply because people starve. (Since 1970, the number of malnourished people has remained above eight hundred million, yet few talk of the end of civilization.)[38] Great historical transitions occur because "business as usual" no longer works. The powerful have a way of sticking to time-honored strategies even when the reality is radically changing. So it was with feudal Europe. The Black Death was not simply a demographic catastrophe. It also tilted the balance of forces in European society.

Feudalism depended on a growing population, not only to produce food but also to reproduce lordly power. The aristocracy wanted a relatively high peasant population, to maintain its bargaining position: many peasants competing for land was better than many lords competing for peasants. But with the onset of the Black Death, webs of commerce and exchange didn't just transmit disease—they became vectors of mass insurrection. Almost overnight, peasant revolts ceased being local affairs and became large-scale threats to the feudal order. After 1347 these uprisings were synchronized—they were system-wide responses to an epochal crisis, a fundamental breakdown in feudalism's logic of power, production, and nature.[39]

The Black Death precipitated an unbearable strain on a system already stretched to the breaking point. Europe after the plague was a place of unrelenting class war, from the Baltics to

Iberia, London to Florence.[40] Peasant demands for tax relief and the restoration of customary rights were calls that feudalism's rulers could not tolerate. If Europe's crowns, banks, and aristocracies could not suffer such demands, neither could they restore the *status quo ante,* despite their best efforts. Repressive legislation to keep labor cheap, through wage controls or outright reenserfment, came in reaction to the Black Death. Among the earliest was England's Ordinance and Statute of Labourers, enacted in the teeth of the plague's first onslaught (1349–51). The equivalent today would be to respond to an Ebola epidemic by making unionization harder. The labor effects of climate change were abundantly clear to Europe's aristocrats, who exhausted themselves trying to keep business very much as usual. They failed almost entirely. Nowhere in western or central Europe was serfdom reestablished. Wages and living standards for peasants and urban workers improved substantially, enough to compensate for a decline in the overall size of the economy. Although this was a boon for most people, Europe's 1 percent found their share of the economic surplus contracting. The old order was broken and could not be fixed.

Capitalism emerged from this broken state of affairs. Ruling classes tried not just to restore the surplus but to expand it. East Asia was wealthier, so although its rulers also experienced socioecological tribulations, they found ways to accommodate upheaval, deforestation, and resource shortages in their own tributary terms.[41] One solution that reinvented humans' relation to the web of life was stumbled upon by the Iberian aristocracy—in Portugal and Castile above all. By the end of the fifteenth century, these kingdoms and their societies had made war through the Reconquista, the centuries-long conflict with Muslim powers on the peninsula, and were so deeply dependent on Italian financiers to fund their military campaigns that Portugal and Castile had in turn been remade by war and debt. The mix of war debt and the promise of wealth through conquest spurred the earliest invasions of the Atlantic—in the Canary Islands and Madeira. The solution to war debt was more war, with the payoff being colonial profit on new, great frontiers.[42]

THE EARLIEST FRONTIERS

Early modern colonialism used frontiers in an entirely new way. Always before, rising population density in the heartlands had led to the expansion of settlement, followed by commerce. This pattern turned inside out in the two centuries after 1492. Frontiers were to become an organizing principle of metropolitan wealth. The demographic and geographical logic of the resulting civilization would radically invert patterns established millennia earlier. Financial wealth—as we will see in chapter 2—made these conquests possible. And it was in an experiment on an early Portuguese colonial outpost that many of the features of the modern world were first convened, in the manufacture of one of the first capitalist products: sugar.

One of the earliest flares of the modern world was lit on a small northern African island, where in the 1460s a new system for producing and distributing food took shape. In 1419, Portuguese sailors first sighted an island less than four hundred miles (644 kilometers) west of Casablanca, which they called Ilha da Madeira, "Island of wood."[43] The Venetian traveler and slaver Alvise da Ca' da Mosto (Cadamosto) reported in 1455 that "there was not a foot of ground that was not entirely covered with great trees."[44] By the 1530s it was hard to find any wood on the island at all. There were two phases in the clear-cutting of Madeira. Initially, the trees had been profitable as lumber for shipbuilding and construction. The denuded forest became acreage for wheat to be sent back to Portugal starting in the 1430s. The second, more dramatic deforestation was driven by the use of wood as fuel in sugar production.

Humans, primates, and most mammals love the taste of sugar.[45] Since the discovery of sugarcane in New Guinea in 6000 BCE, humans have understood the biological necessities of its treatment.[46] There is a peak time to harvest the cane, when it is turgid with sweet juice—but then the grass is thick and difficult to cut. Once chopped, the cane can be coaxed to yield its greatest quantity of sugar for only forty-eight hours.[47] After that, the plant starts to rot.

The botany of sugarcane thus calls for speedy production, which for millennia made it hard to produce in large amounts. This is why Sidney Mintz reports that "in 1226, Henry III requested the Mayor of Winchester to get him three pounds [1.4 kilograms] of Alexandrine sugar if so much could be had at one time from the merchants at the great Winchester Fair."[48] Increasing the amount that "could be had at one time" was not easy. One had to surmount the limits of what a single family might produce. One had to invest in new techniques and technology. Persians and North Africans in the great Muslim civilizations had, for instance, discovered that potash (potassium carbonate) could produce clearer sugar crystals: the best sugar was from Alexandria in Egypt, hence Henry III's specific hankering for it.[49] But it took new experiments in work, nature, and commerce to invent ways to produce far, far more.

Sugar had arrived in Iberia by the fourteenth century, brought by King Jaume II of Aragón (1267–1327), who also brought a Muslim slave expert in the art of sugar production. By 1420 it was being grown commercially, funded by German banking houses like the Ravensburger Handelsgesellschaft and cultivated on rented plots near Valencia by a mixture of slaves and free workers.[50] But sugar remained rare—and there was a ready market for it. In the 1460s and 1470s, farmers on Madeira stopped growing wheat and started growing sugar exclusively. A lot more sugar. The sugar frontier quickly spread, at first to other islands in the Atlantic, then on a massive scale to the New World.[51] Like palm and soy monocultures today, it cleared forests, exhausted soils, and encouraged pests at breakneck speed.[52]

To reach such speeds, production had to be reorganized, broken into smaller, component activities performed by different workers. It simply isn't possible to get good returns from workers who are exhausted from cutting cane and then spend the night refining it. New management and technologies helped move sugar manufacture from edge runner mills (big pestle-and-mortar machines) and small holdings to two-roller mills and large-scale slave production in São Tomé.[53] Centuries before Adam Smith could marvel at the division of labor across a supply chain that made a pin, the relationship between humans, plants, and capital had forged the core ideas of modern manufacturing—in cane fields. The plantation was the original factory. And every time the sugar plantation found a new frontier, as in Brazil after São Tomé and the Caribbean after that, that factory was reinvented—with new machines and new combinations of plantation and sugar mill. The only thing missing from this story, of course, is the humans who did the work. In Madeira, they were Indigenous People from the Canary Islands, North African slaves, and—in some cases—paid plantation laborers from mainland Europe.

The plantations were irrigated by *levadas,* water channels forged of trees, mud, sweat, and blood. Today, thirteen hundred miles (twenty-one hundred kilometers) of levadas remain on an island thirty-seven miles (sixty kilometers) across at its widest point. Hydraulic engineers deployed slaves, sometimes dangling on ropes, to carve small canals through rock faces to channel streams to the cane fields.[54] Many workers died in rockslides and dam breaches, but the engineers transformed flows of water in Madeira so effectively that Afonso de Albuquerque, the first duke of Goa and the second governor of Portuguese India, asked that Madeirans be sent "to change the course of the River Nile."[55] Financed by Flemish and Italian capitalists, masters from Portugal oversaw cane's planting, watering, harvest, and transformation into crystalized sugar. Turning cane stalks into sugar used prodigious amounts of fuel. At least fifty pounds (twenty-three kilograms) of wood was needed to boil and distill enough sugarcane juice to return a single pound (0.45 kilograms) of sugar. To turn the cane, heavy with water, into molasses and loaves of sugar, mills were built around Madeira's capital, Funchal, to which slaves transported the cane. At its zenith, Madeira's industry used five hundred hectares (1,236 acres) of forest each year to feed the boilers that kept the tributes of sugar flowing to Europe's courts. Yet after the boom, the bust. Output peaked in the first decade of the sixteenth century, and the furnaces sputtered out by the 1530s, the trees having been stripped from the island. Production crashed, and investors found greater returns from large-scale slave-planted sugar whose processing was fueled by forests in the New World.[56] Europe's wealthy ate the sugar, and sugar ate the island.

Capitalism didn't leave Madeira—it reinvented itself.[57] With no affordable fuel (the island's only remaining trees were in the interior highland, too inaccessible to be efficiently felled), new strategies emerged to wring profit from the devastated land. After sugar came wine, grown in the ashes of the cane industry.

Grapes demand less labor, water, and fuel than cane. But wine needs casks, so for centuries the wood for Madeira barrels was brought from the most economical source: the cheap forests of the New World. Commodities flowed the other way too, as Madeira was a conduit for the Atlantic slave trade until the eighteenth century.[58] In a more recent act of reinvention, the island today uses that grim history as a source of revenue through tourism.[59] Yet as the sugar frontier closed in Madeira, new frontiers opened elsewhere, and forces less obvious than a craving for sweetness shaped the island, and soon the planet.[60]

FRONTIERS AND CHEAPNESS

This sketch of a colonial frontier gives us a glimpse of how capitalism was to work beyond Madeira. Before analyzing the story of sugar and the island more thoroughly, we need to explain why we think it's important to analyze frontiers. Often in visualizations of the spread of capitalism, the image that offers itself is an asteroid impact or the spread of a disease, which starts at ground or patient zero and metastasizes across the planet. Capitalist frontiers require a more sophisticated science fiction. If capitalism is a disease, then it's one that eats your flesh—and then profits from selling your bones for fertilizer, and then invests that profit to reap the cane harvest, and then sells that harvest to tourists who pay to visit your headstone.[61] But even this description isn't adequate. The frontier works only through connection, fixing its failures by siphoning life from elsewhere. A frontier is a site where crises encourage new strategies for profit. Frontiers are frontiers because they are the encounter zones between capital and all kinds of nature—humans included. They are always, then, about reducing the costs of doing business. Capitalism not only *has* frontiers; it exists only *through* frontiers, expanding from one place to the next, transforming socioecological relations, producing more and more kinds of goods and services that circulate through an expanding series of exchanges. But more important, frontiers are sites where power is exercised—and not just economic power. Through frontiers, states and empires use violence, culture, and knowledge to mobilize natures at low cost. It's this cheapening that makes frontiers so central to modern history and that makes possible capitalism's expansive markets. This gives us a precious clue to how productivity is understood and practiced. While much has been made of its gory and oppressive history, one fact is often overlooked: capitalism has thrived not because it is violent and destructive (it is) but because it is productive in a particular way.[62] Capitalism thrives not by destroying natures but by putting natures to work—as cheaply as possible.

Through its frontiers, capitalism taps and controls a wider set of relations of life-making than appear in an accountant's balance of profit and loss. There isn't a word in English for the process of making life, though such words are found in a range of other languages. The Anishinaabeg, whose original lands extended widely across northeastern North America, have *minobimaatisiiwin,* which means "the good life" but also "a continuous rebirth" of reciprocal and cyclical relations between humans and other life.[63] Southern African Bantu languages have *ubuntu,* human fulfillment through togetherness, and the Shona language has the further idea of *ukama,* a "relatedness to the entire cosmos," including the biophysical world.[64] Similar interpretations exist of the Chinese *shi-shi wu-ai* and the Maori *mauri.*[65] Absent a decent term in English, we use the idea of *oikeios. Oikeios* names the creative and multilayered pulse of life making through which all human activity flows, shaped at every turn by natures that consistently elude human efforts at control. It is through the oikeios that particular forms of life emerge, that species make environments and environments make species. Likewise, the pulse of human civilization does not simply occupy environments but produces them—and in the process is produced by them.[66]

Everything that humans make is coproduced with the rest of nature: food, clothing, homes and workplaces, roads and railways and airports, even phones and apps. It's relatively easy to understand how something like farming mixes the work of humans and soils, and also mixes all sorts of physical processes with human knowledge. When the processes are larger in scale, it becomes easier to think about "social" and "natural" processes as if they were independent of each other. It is somehow easier to grasp the immediate relationship to soil and work of a farmers' market than a global financial market. But Wall Street is just as much coproduced through nature as that farmers' market. Indeed, Wall Street's global financial operations involve it in a web of planetary ecological relationships unimaginable in any previous civilization. History is made not through the separation of humans from nature but through their evolving, diverse configurations. The "human" relations of power and difference, production and reproduction, not only produce nature; they are products of nature. There is, for example, a variety of mosquito (*Culex pipiens*) that has made its home in the London Underground and adapted to the dark world of the British commuter to such an extent that it can no longer interbreed with its topside counterparts—hence the new species *Culex pipiens molestus*.[67] This new species, made through human activity, is a small karmic counterbalance to those species destroyed by the work done in the City of London (Britain's Wall Street) by these commuters, off whose blood the mosquito feeds.

The relationship between the wider web of life and capitalism is the subject of this book. Capitalism's frontiers always lie firmly within a far larger world of life making. For capitalism, what matters is that the figures entered into ledgers—to pay workers, to supply adequate food to workers, to purchase energy and raw materials—are as low as possible. Capitalism values only what it can count, and it can count only dollars. Every capitalist wants to invest as little and profit as much as possible. For capitalism, this means that the whole system thrives when powerful states and capitalists can reorganize global nature, invest as little as they can, and receive as much food, work, energy, and raw materials with as little disruption as possible.

Economists might at this point mutter "Externalities" and wonder why we haven't read the original scholars of externalities, Arthur Cecil Pigou or James Meade.[68] We have, which is why we're writing this book. In economics, an externality is a cost or a benefit, private or social, that doesn't appear in the calculus of production. We're arguing that the modern world emerged from systematic attempts to fix crises at the frontier, crises that resulted from human and extrahuman life inserting itself into that calculus. The modern world happened because externalities struck back.[69]

Capitalism is not a system where cash is everywhere but rather one in which islands of cash exchange exist within oceans of cheap—or potentially cheap—natures. Reproducing life within the cash nexus is expensive, and it grows more expensive over time. Workers' wages can be frozen, even rolled back, but in the end inequality precipitates crises of the kind we've recently seen bring about populist protests in the United States and the United Kingdom. Workers demand dignity, and their labor becomes expensive. Production processes burn through an island, and energy is no longer cheap. The climate changes, and crops can no longer grow as abundantly as they once did. Frontiers are so important in these processes because they offer places where the new cheap things can be seized—and the cheap work of humans and other natures can be coerced.

We come, then, to what we mean by *cheapness:* it's a set of strategies to manage relations between capitalism and the web of life by temporarily fixing capitalism's crises. Cheap is not the same as low cost—though that's part of it. Cheap is a strategy, a practice, a violence that mobilizes all kinds of work—human and animal, botanical and geological—with as little compensation as possible. We use *cheap* to talk about the process through which capitalism transmutes these undenominated relationships of life making into circuits of production and consumption, in which these relations come to have as low a price as possible. Cheapening marks the transition from uncounted relations of life making to the lowest possible dollar value. It's always a short-term strategy. And cheapness has always been a battleground. Looking at these seven cheap things helps us see the horizon of what is possible. It helps us grasp the stakes in social conflicts today and the reparations that need to be made for solidarity to be meaningful. In examining money, work, care, energy, food, lives, and above all nature, we argue for a new way to understand what we call capitalism's ecology, the blend of relations that explains how the modern world works. Why these seven? We couldn't do fewer, and while there might be more, each of them was present at the dawn of capitalism's ecology. They're a useful start to the project of both interpreting and changing the world—and it's now time to explore how each of them mattered in Madeira.

Nature

When settlers landed on Madeira, they brought along invasive species. On one of the smaller islands, Porto Santo (whose first lord was Columbus's father-in-law), rabbits quickly escaped captivity and devoured local flora. Other invasions followed. A snail indigenous to Madeira, *Caseolus bowdichianus,* was extinct within a century of colonization. But the record suggests that the majority of the extinctions on Madeira happened over the past two centuries—not under the initial colonial onslaught but later, as successive waves of foreign species and agrarian capitalism snuffed out millions of years of evolution.[70]

The trees, water, soil, fauna, and flora on Madeira and the sea around the island were treated as "free gifts," transformed into a series of inputs or hindrances to production.[71] In a seminal paper on overfishing, "Reefs since Columbus," Jeremy Jackson notes how humans have extinguished life from the time that young Columbus arrived on Madeira.[72] Humans under capitalism abuse the ecosystems of which we are part—and on which we depend. Capitalists are, for instance, happy to view the ocean as both storage facility for the seafood we have yet to catch and sinkhole for the detritus we produce on land. The balance of food and trash will soon tip. By 2050, two years after the last commercial fish catch is projected to land, there will be more plastic in the sea than fish.[73] The intellectually slack explanation here is that humans bring destruction in their wake. But nature is more than a resource pool or rubbish bin.[74] A central reason for beginning our story at the frontier of the Portuguese empire is that Madeira so clearly demonstrates what happens when the metabolism of humans in the web of life becomes governed by the demand for profit.

If profit was to govern life, a significant intellectual state shift had to occur: a conceptual split between Nature and Society. This was a momentous shift but usually pales alongside the birth of the world market, the conquest of the Americas, and the dispossession of peasants. No less important, however, was the transformation in how some humans understood, and acted upon, nature as a whole. It's important to be clear that this was always the work of *some* humans—those in charge of conquering and commercializing a world that counts only dollars. We may all be in the same boat when it comes to climate change, but most of us are in steerage. Our qualification here is important for two big reasons. First, it helps us place responsibility and look to those classes and relationships that profit from this separation. Second and more significant, the human "separation from nature" took shape around a truly massive exclusion. The rise of capitalism gave us the idea not only that society was relatively independent of the web of life but also that most women, Indigenous Peoples, slaves, and colonized peoples everywhere were not fully human and thus not full members of society. These were people who were not—or were only barely—human. They were part of Nature, treated as social outcasts—they were *cheapened.*

The cleaving of Nature from Society, of savage from civilized, set the stage for the creation of our other cheap things, as we argue in chapter 1. Nature was remade, reinvented, and rethought many times over the next five centuries. Capitalism's practices of cheap nature would define whose lives and whose work mattered—and whose did not. Its dominant ideas Nature and Society (in uppercase because of their mythic and bloody power) would determine whose work was valued and whose work—care for young and old, for the sick and those with special needs, agricultural work, and the work of extrahuman natures (animals, soils, forests, fuels)—

was rendered largely invisible. It achieved all this through the circulation of money, whose price in turn depended on global conquest and subjugation. Successive eras saw the control of food to sustain workers and of energy to make them more productive. Cheap things are thus not really things at all—but rather strategies adopted by capitalism to survive and manage crises, gambits made to appear as real and independent entities by the original sin of cheap nature.[75]

Money

Money is the medium through which capitalism operates, a source of power for those able to control it. That control isn't just about people and wealth. It's about how such control entwines with nature. Consider how tightly linked are American dollars and barrels of Saudi Arabian oil or, in an earlier era, Dutch rixdollars and New World ingots of silver. If modernity is an ecology of power, money binds the ecosystem, and that ecosystem shapes money. Money depends on culture and force to become capital. It divides and connects worker and capitalist, rich and poor regions—the Global North and the Global South in today's lexicon. It fosters nation-states and empires; it disciplines and depends upon them. To look at history this way moves away from seeing the modern world as a collection of states and toward seeing it as a world-system of capital, power, and nature. And it compels us to consider these processes over the span of centuries—not decades.[76]

Elements of this approach were initially offered in the 1970s by Immanuel Wallerstein, who showed how capitalism emerged through a cascading series of political and economic transformations in which a new, and grossly unequal, division of labor was forged. Among his chief insights were two with special relevance to this book. First, global inequality is a class process made possible by political as well as market forces. Second, production and accumulation have been remade through a radical remaking of nature.[77] If subsequent scholars dropped Wallerstein's insistence on capitalism as an ecology, we build on his thinking to show how work and power unfold within planetary nature—in wholesale transformations that constitute an ecology. And because we're interested in the forces that condition socioecological relationships over distance, it should be clear why money matters so much.

With a world-historical eye, trivial historical details become vital. One example: the relationship between fifteenth-century Genoese banking, Madeira's ecology, and today's planetary crisis. Humans like the taste of sugar. Sugar needs water. Irrigation on Madeira needed work, which needed to be funded. Slaves weren't cheap to buy, transport, or maintain, and it took a full season for the water to feed the cane and the cane to be harvested, processed into sugar, and sold in mainland Europe, exchanged for silver that then bought spices from Asia. In between all these were credit and debt and the flow of money into commodities, in which the Italian city-state of Genoa was central.

Money isn't capital. *Capital* is journalism's shorthand for money or, worse, a stock of something that can be transformed into something else. If you've ever heard or used the terms *natural capital* or *social capital,* you've been part of a grand obfuscation.[78] Capital isn't the dead stock of uncut trees or unused skill. For Marx and for us, capital happens only in the live transformation of money into commodities and back again. Money tucked under a mattress is as dead to capitalism as the mattress itself. It is through the live circulation of this money, and in the relations around it, that capitalism happens.

The processes of exchange and circulation turn money into capital. At the heart of Marx's *Capital* is a simple, powerful model: in production and exchange, capitalists combine labor power, machines, and raw material. The resulting commodities are then sold for money. If all goes well, there is a profit, which needs then to be reinvested into yet more labor power, machines, and raw materials. Neither commodities nor money is capital. This circuit *becomes* capital when money is sunk into commodity production, in an ever-expanding cycle. Capital is a process in which money flows through nature. The trouble here is that capital supposes infinite expansion within a finite web of life. Marx chides economists who believe that their profession explains markets through supply and demand, when those are precisely what need to be explained. To understand those forces requires an examination of markets through the "organic whole" of production and exchange.[79] That organic whole robs life from the worker just as it exhausts the soil of the capitalist farmer.[80]

This cycle of money into commodities and then back into money isn't just a way of looking at capital. It is an optic through which to see far longer rhythms in the rise and fall of empires and superpowers, the span of the *longue durée*.[81] Remember that after making a commodity and selling it, capitalists ideally have a profit. The permanent demands of profit making require those profits to themselves generate profitable returns. That causes a problem, because the amount of capital tends to grow faster than the opportunities to invest it advantageously. That's why financial bubbles—episodes when large sums of capital flow into a particular economic sector, like home mortgages before the 2008 crisis—recur throughout the history of the modern world. Empires help fix this problem. Over the long run, empires open new frontiers. Over the short run, when profitability slows they go to war—and borrow to do it. Bankers are happy to lend because other opportunities for profit making are relatively slight and states are typically good credit risks. They also have armies ready to go to war, at the state's expense, to defend a safe and valuable currency. The relations between bankers and governments lead in the short term to reinvestment, in the medium term to the concentration of wealth and returns in the financial sector, and in the long term to the rise and fall of commercial power centered on a city, state, or international regime.[82]

In that arc, some people benefit a great deal, while others merely get by—or worse. Thomas Piketty's ideas on how investment return has outstripped GDP growth in the Global North have generated much interest recently, but they belong to an older class of insights about how finance relates to the rest of capitalism's ecology under successive state regimes.[83] Capitalism is not just the sum of "economic" transactions that turn money into commodities and back again; it's inseparable from the modern state and from governments' dominions and transformations of natures, human and otherwise. Financial capital's paroxysms of expansion and collapse are central to understanding how capitalism has developed, as we discuss in chapter 2. Through the advance of financiers, who have aimed to shape and profit from their investments, capitalism's ecology now affects every tendril of the planet's ecology.[84] The story of how money came to rule not just humans but a good chunk of planetary life begins with the invasion of the New World's wealth. The unholy alliance of European empires, conquerors, and banks would turn New World natures into commodities and capital. Centrally, capitalism's ecology needed new ways of managing humans, their bodies and the resources they required to survive. Because money doesn't just turn into commodities by itself: for that you need labor.

Work

Initially, the Portuguese, Genoese, and Flemish sugar plantation owners on Madeira brought Guanches, people indigenous to the Canary Islands, to work their land. A few fifteenth-century wills show that owners bequeathed Guanches to their heirs.[85] Indigenous workers succumbed to European disease and brutality. They were supplemented and replaced with a mix of wageworkers and North African slaves, humans whose recent ancestors had made a living in subsistence agriculture but who themselves arrived in Madeira as a consequence of either enslavement or exclusion from the land they once worked. Madeira was a field site for experiments in the limits of human endurance and strength but also for the trial of new technologies of order, process, and specialization that—centuries later—would be used in England's industrial factories. We don't know nearly enough about the ways that workers on Madeira—slaves and freedmen alike—resisted their masters and employers. There's little recorded about how they fought the regime that both worked them to death and exhausted the soil on which they labored.[86] But we do know that they resisted and that their attempts to combat the conditions of their exploitation generated crises sufficient for authorities to forbid slaves from living alone or with freedmen in 1473.[87]

The story of cheap things and the crises that follow their cheapening is not one of inevitability. Humans can and do fight back. Capitalists then try to address that resistance with a range of cheap fixes. These too inevitably generate their own crises and, in turn, more and more sophisticated mechanisms of control and order.[88] This class struggle is a vital engine of change in capitalist ecology. Although we know little about slave rebellion in Madeira, we do know that by the end of the sugar boom, the technologies of slavery and plantation had been refined and were being exported across the Atlantic, first to São Tomé, where runaway slaves called Angolares scorched the island's sugar mills and besieged its capital for two weeks in 1596.[89] We also know, as we discuss in chapter 3, that it is in workers' opposition to their exploitation that some of the most potent challenges to capitalism can be found.

Slavery remains, as does resistance to it. There are more humans in forced labor in the twenty-first century than were transported by the Atlantic slave trade.[90] The International Labor Organization found than there were nearly 21 million people in forced labor in 2012, of whom 2.2 million were in labor forced upon them by the state (prison work) or rebel military groups. Of the remaining 18.7 million, 4.5 million were involved in commercial sexual exploitation and 14.2 million in forced economic exploitation.[91] For comparison, 12.5 million Africans were enslaved and transported through the Middle Passage.

Slavery didn't begin in Madeira, but *modern* slavery did. The modern difference lies in slaves' being put to work in agricultural mass production and in their expulsion from the mythic domain of Society. Although slaves had always been at the bottom of the social order, in the centuries after Madeira's boom and bust they were kicked outside that order, stripped of anything that resembled citizenship. For Indigenous and African slaves, modernity meant not only actual death but also "social death."[92] Treating slaves as part of Nature rather than Society was a successful move for investors. For that success to multiply, more workers needed to be found, their broken bodies cared for, and their communities supported by work that was forever unpaid. In other words, capitalists needed more labor and needed it to be educated and maintained as cheaply as possible. From this imperative emerged an entire regime of cheap care, one so vital to capitalism's ecology that its history has been all but erased.

Care

The part of Madeira's early history about which the least is known, yet without which it would have been impossible, is the work of what social scientists call social reproduction.[93] The work of care, for young and old, infirm and sick, learning and recovering, makes capitalism possible. Where else do humans come from but from other humans? How else are they socialized than through communities? How else are they cared for and nurtured than through networks of support? The demands for this care to be performed cheaply helped to refashion older patriarchies and produced modern categories of sex and gender difference in capitalism's ecology.

We know that by the time the Brazilian sugar industry was trading in slaves, women were 20 percent cheaper than men.[94] In Europe, a generalized wage cut in the sixteenth and seventeenth centuries affected all workers but women especially, who received just a third of the already "reduced male wage."[95] They were also still expected to tend to labor at home, and indeed the domestic sphere was a conscious invention of early capitalism.[96] Burdens of work, care work, and community support fell increasingly on women, whose social position came to be policed, just as work in the cane fields was.[97] The burning of witches was a form of discipline for those women who resisted their confinement in this domestic sphere, as we discuss in chapter 4. Patriarchy isn't a mere by-product of capitalism's ecology—it's fundamental to it. So crucial was "women's work" to the rise of capitalism that by 1700 it had been radically redefined. Women's labor became "non-work"[98]—rendered largely invisible, the better to cheapen it.

In 1995, researchers hazarded a dollar value for women's unpaid work. A United Nations team suggested that all unpaid reproductive labor, if compensated, would be valued at sixteen trillion dollars. Of that, eleven trillion represented women's unpaid work.[99] This was about a third of the world's total economic activity—a figure that would have been higher had banking not already taken a larger and larger share of the world's economy. In the United Kingdom, more recent studies have suggested that reproductive labor is worth more than the taxes from London's mighty financial services sector.[100] Still others have argued that the UN estimate was too low and that "household nonmarket activity" is the equivalent of 80 percent of the gross world product: nearly sixty trillion dollars in 2015.[101]

Duties of care are poorly waged, if paid at all, and social reproduction needs more than labor to be effective. As the planet's workers moved from rural to urban areas, one thing came to matter above all in the new cash nexus: the ability to secure sufficient nutrition on one day in order to labor on the next. Hence the emergence of a regime of cheap food.

Food

In the story of Madeira, the cheap food isn't sugar. Sugar was still a luxury in fifteenth-century Europe. The food that needed to be cheap was what the slaves ate. Cane workers then, as now, will have stolen the odd stalk of ripe cane to chew, its watery, sweet juice providing a few extra calories and little nutrition. Brazilian slavers sometimes gave their sick slaves meat and eggs so that their property would recover and go back to work, though the food was strictly accounted, a debit in the ledger of profit and loss.[102] There are few records of the diets of slaves under Portuguese rule in Madeira, though it is likely that they brought with them the rice, millet, and sorghum that they had cultivated in Africa, and which their descendants would pocket in their violent passage to the New World.[103] No matter the menu, a constant of capitalism is that food needs to be available, cheaply, for workers to consume—for both profits and social order to be maintained, as we show in chapter 5.[104]

There's a long tradition of rulers recognizing that one of the best routes to securing the consent of workers and the poor is through their stomachs. The Roman philosopher and landowner Cicero saw his house attacked by a hungry crowd, and a century later the emperor Claudius was pelted by stale bread crusts in another food rebellion.[105] Cheap food has been central to the maintenance of order for millennia. In capitalism's ecology, that order has been maintained by tamping down workers' costs of feeding themselves and their families. This may seem trivial today, when transportation and housing account for larger shares of household income than the cost of food. But the relative unimportance of food is historically novel—it is cheap because it has been made so. From 1453 to 1913, the percentage of English builders' wages spent on food fell from 80 to 77.5 percent.[106] It is a far more recent phenomenon for British food consumption to have fallen to 8.6 percent of household expenditure (as of 2014; in the United States it was 6.6 percent, in Italy 14.2 percent, in China 25.5 percent, and in Nigeria 56.6 percent).[107] These numbers are kept low through strategies that, in the United States, for instance, foster dollar burgers and the buckets of cheap chicken with which we began.

The irony of our Madeira example is that sugar has since become a cheap commodity crop precisely through the relations pioneered there. From being an occasional treat, English sugar consumption rose fourfold toward the end of the seventeenth century and doubled again in the eighteenth, closing that century at around 13 pounds per person. Today, sweetener consumption in the United States is 76 pounds per person per year—of which 41 pounds is refined sugar and 25 pounds is high-fructose corn syrup.[108] From 2005 to 2010, the average daily calorie intake from added sugars was 355 for men and 239 for women in the United States, about 13 percent of total daily calories (recent research suggests an intake of more than 2–3 percent will have negative health effects).[109] Sugar isn't, however, humans' only energy source. The other commodity whose price has been kept low in order for the US working class to survive is the second greatest expenditure for English builders over seven centuries: fuel.

Energy

The subtropical laurel forests on Madeira, the "Island of wood," weren't fuel to start off with. Initially they were used as timber—the material out of which the Portuguese fleet was hewn, the stuff for construction projects in metropolitan Lisbon.[110] But wood stops being the thing that keeps out the water when it becomes more valuable as the thing you burn to fire the boilers that make sugar.[111] These trees weren't naturally a fuel—they became so under specific conditions.

Almost every other civilization has harnessed fire and found material that can sustain flame. But on Madeira the arc of boom to bust, which happened in just seventy years, was limited by the number of trees on the island. In other words, the speed and scale of consumption of fuel under capitalism are unusual. Wood's cheapness in Madeira was cause and consequence of the rise and fall of the sugar industry there, the crisis precipitated by the depletion of a finite combustible stock. Fuel does triple duty under capitalism. It is not only its own industry and force for scaling production in other industries but also provides a substitute for labor power and serves to keep that labor power affordable—and *productive.* Cheap fuel is both an antagonist for workers put out of jobs by wood-, coal-, oil-, and other-energy-powered machines and a necessary input for the work of cheap care, central to the maintenance of order, as we show in chapter 6.

We are—need it be said?—living with the consequences of a civilization built on cheap energy, a reality verified by climate change. The global political economy of cheap fuel has not only wrought immense human suffering in its extraction but also, of course, remade planetary ecology. Climate change's effects have not, however, been distributed evenly. There is a calculus that allows us to map where the bodies most affected by past climate change are buried and where future casualties are likely to be. To see that map, we need first to understand a final strategy in capitalism's ecology: cheap lives.

Lives

Christopher Columbus was born in Genoa in 1451. He was for a time a resident of Porto Santo, off the main island of Madeira. He first arrived there in 1476 and in 1478 was commissioned to trade sugar back to Genoa for Ludovico Centurione, a scion of Genoese capital.[112] When Columbus arrived in Madeira, he saw slaves and learned how the law treated them. Slaves were legally different from other humans. In court, they could never be witnesses or victims—they were only allowed to be defendants, standing accused of crimes but never able to see or suffer one.[113] This jurisprudence informed Columbus's colonial apprenticeship. Between his departure from Madeira in 1478 to serve the Spanish crown and his return to Funchal for six days in 1498 as the viceroy of the Indies, Columbus inaugurated a genocide in the Caribbean that would see the death of many of the humans—and civilizations—living there.[114]

A century after Columbus's birth, the scale of the extermination, under the flag of the Spanish royal family and the Catholic cross, troubled some of its executors to such an extent that they went to the trouble of giving the enslavement and brutalization of other humans firm intellectual foundations. The 1550 "Valladolid Controversy" was where the boundary between the civilized and the savage was prosecuted. Over the course of a few weeks in Valladolid, Spain, two sides debated the treatment of humans across the Atlantic. On one side sat Bartolomé de Las Casas, the Dominican friar whose 1542 treatise *A Short Account of the Destruction of the Indies* testified to the violence he'd witnessed in the New World. On the other was Juan Ginés de Sepúlveda, an orthodox defender of Spain's right to conquest. In Valladolid, the two argued over whether natives were people or beasts. At stake was the encomienda system, the technology of colonial landownership that apportioned groups of Indigenous People among landowners, who "kept them in deposit" for the duration of two lifetimes: that of the deposited native and that of their children. Landlords agreed to care for these depositees by providing them with Spanish classes and schooling in Catholicism, and to pay a tax to the state for the right to have this labor pool.[115] At the end of the debate, after Las Casas had appealed to universal humanism and Sepúlveda had cited Aristotle in defense of the idea that Indians were "slaves by nature, uncivilized, barbarian and inhuman,"[116] both sides claimed victory. But while encomiendas were governed by slightly stricter laws afterward, conquest continued and Indian lives continued to be devalued. Sepúlveda's practices carried the day.

So why the debate? The philosophical disagreement over the humanity of Indigenous People was both about their place in a world cleaved between Nature and Society and about how they might be governed. It was a debate, in other words, about *cheap lives,* a term we use to refer to how the order of other cheap things—labor and care in particular—is policed and maintained through force and ideology. This is, we admit, a slightly different use of *cheap* than that in other chapters. We argue for its necessity in chapter 7, because without the power to decide whose lives matter and whose do not, it would not have been possible to suppress Indigenous Peoples or members of rival religions and states and appropriate their knowledge, resources, and labor power.

Modern equivalents abound in current debates around such topics as security, the status of immigrants and refugees, states' insistence on order while licensing the extraction of the natural resources on top of which so many Indigenous Peoples inconveniently live, oil wars, and the "existential threats" of modern terrorism.[117] Again, that humans should need to find safety and shelter from threats is not new. But since capitalism grows through its frontiers, the domestic and international deployments of force through nature to secure money, work, care, food, and fuel are accompanied by ideologies of race and state and nation, together with the appropriations and devaluations that these deployments involve. Cheap lives are made through the apparatus of the modern social order. They're absolutely necessary to capitalism's ecology. The power of these narratives of human community and exclusion has a particular salience today, as the tilts of Donald Trump's America, Vladimir Putin's Russia, Recep Tayyip Erdoğan's Turkey, and Narendra Modi's India suggest.

INTRODUCING WORLD-ECOLOGY

Our views of capitalism, life making, and the seven cheap things are part of a perspective that we call world-ecology.[118] World-ecology has emerged in recent years as a way to think through human history in the web of life. Rather than begin with the separation of humans from the web of life, we will ask questions about how humans—and human arrangements of power and violence, work, and inequality—fit *within* nature. Capitalism is not just part of an ecology but *is* an ecology—a set of relationships integrating power, capital, and nature. So when we write—and hyphenate—*world-ecology,* we draw on older traditions of "world-systems" to say that capitalism creates an ecology that expands over the planet through its frontiers, driven by forces of endless accumulation. To say *world-ecology* is not, therefore, to invoke the "ecology of the world" but to suggest an analysis that shows how relations of power, production, and reproduction work through the web of life. The idea of world-ecology allows us to see how the modern world's violent and exploitative relationships are rooted in five centuries of capitalism and also how these unequal arrangements—even those that appear timeless and necessary today—are contingent and in the midst of unprecedented crisis.

World-ecology, then, offers something more than a different view of capitalism, nature, and possible futures. It offers a way of seeing how humans make environments and environments make humans through the long sweep of modern history. This opens space for us to reconsider how the ways that we have been schooled to think of change—ecological, economic, and all the rest—are themselves implicated in today's crises. That space is crucial if we are to understand the relationship between naming and acting on the world. Movements for social justice have long insisted on "naming the system" because the relationships among thought, language, and emancipation are intimate and fundamental to power. World-ecology allows us to see how concepts we take for granted—like Nature and Society—are problems not just because they obscure actual life and history but because they emerged out of the violence of colonial and capitalist practice. Modern concepts of Nature and Society, as we shall see in chapter 1, were born in Europe in the sixteenth century. These master concepts were not only formed in close relation to the dispossession of peasants in the colonies and in Europe but also themselves used as instruments of dispossession and genocide. The Nature/Society split was fundamental to a new, modern cosmology in which space was flat, time was linear, and nature was external. That we are usually unaware of this bloody history—one that includes the early modern expulsions of most women, Indigenous Peoples, and Africans from humanity—is testimony to modernity's extraordinary capacity to make us forget.

World-ecology therefore commits not only to rethinking but to remembering. Too often we attribute capitalism's devastation of life and environments to economic rapaciousness alone, when much of capitalism cannot be reduced to economics. Contrary to neoliberal claptrap, businesses and markets are ineffective at doing most of what makes capitalism run. Cultures, states, and scientific complexes must work to keep humans obedient to norms of gender, race, and class. New resource geographies need to be mapped and secured, mounting debts repaid, coin defended. World-ecology offers a way to recognize this, to remember—and see anew—the lives and labors of humans and other natures in the web of life.

THE AFTERLIVES OF CHEAP THINGS

There is hope in world-ecology. To recognize the webs of life making on which capitalism depends is also to find new conceptual tools with which to face the Capitalocene. As justice movements develop strategies for confronting planetary crisis—and alternatives to our present way of organizing nature—we need to think about the creative and expanded reproduction of democratic forms of life. That's why we conclude this introduction, and this book, with ideas that can help us navigate the state shift that lies ahead.

A wan environmentalism is unlikely to make change if its principal theory rests on the historically bankrupt idea of immutable human separation from nature. Unfortunately, many of today's politics take as given the transformation of the world into cheap things. Recall the last financial crisis, made possible by the tearing down of the boundary between retail and commercial banking in the United States. The Great Depression's Glass-Steagall Act put that barrier in place to prevent future dealing of the kind that was understood to have knocked the global economy into a tailspin in the 1930s. American socialists and communists had been agitating for bank nationalization, and Franklin Roosevelt's New Dealers offered the act as a compromise safeguard.[119] When twenty-first-century liberal protestors demanded the return of Glass-Steagall, they were asking for a compromise, not for what had been surrendered to cheap finance: housing.

Similarly, when unions demand fifteen dollars an hour for work in the United States, a demand we have supported, a grand vision for the future of work is absent. Why should the future of care and food-service workers be to receive an incremental salary increase, barely enough on which to subsist? Why, indeed, ought ideas of human dignity be linked to hard work? Might there not be space to demand not just drudgery from work but the chance to contribute to making the world better?[120]

Although the welfare state has expanded, becoming the fastest-growing share of household income in the United States and accounting for 20 percent of household income by 2000,[121] its transfers haven't ended the burden of women's work. Surely the political demand that household work be reduced, rewarded, and redistributed is the ultimate goal?

We see the need to dream for more radical change than contemporary politics offers. Consider, to take another example, that cheap fossil fuel has its advocates among right-wing think tanks from India to the United States. While liberals propose a photovoltaic future, they can too easily forget the suffering involved in the mineral infrastructure on which their alternative depends. The food movement has remained hospitable to those who would either raise the price of food while ignoring poverty or engineer alternatives to food that will allow poverty to persist, albeit with added vitamins.[122] And, of course, the persistence of the politics of cheap lives can be found in the return to supremacism—from Russia and South Africa to the United States and China—in the name of "protecting the nation." We aren't sanguine about the future either, given polling data from the National Opinion Research Center at the University of Chicago which found that 35 percent of baby boomers feel blacks are lazier/less hardworking than whites and that 31 percent of millennials feel the same way.[123]

While maintaining a healthy pessimism of the intellect, we find optimism of the will through the work of organizations that see far more mutability in social relations. Many of these groups are already tackling cheap things. Unions want higher wages. Climate change activists want to revalue our relationship to energy, and those who've read Naomi Klein's work will recognize that much more must change too.[124] Food campaigners want to change what we eat and how we grow it so that everyone eats well. Domestic-worker organizers want society to recognize the work done in homes and care facilities. The Occupy movement wants debt to be canceled and those threatened with foreclosure and exclusion allowed to remain in their homes. Radical ecologists want to change the way we think about all life on earth. The Movement for Black Lives, Indigenous groups, and immigrant-rights activists want equality and reparation for historical injustice.

Each of these movements might provoke a moment of crisis. Capitalism has always been shaped by resistance—from slave uprisings to mass strikes, from anticolonial revolts through abolition to the organization for women's and Indigenous Peoples' rights—and has always managed to survive. Yet all of today's movements are connected, and together they offer an antidote to pessimism. World-ecology can help connect the dots.

We do not offer solutions that return to the past. We agree with Alice Walker that "activism is the rent I pay for living on the planet"[125] and that if there is to be life after capitalism, it will come through the struggles of people on the ground for which they fight. We don't deny that if politics are to transform, they must begin where people currently find themselves. But we cannot end with the same abstractions that capitalism has made, of nature, society, and economy. We must find the language and politics for new civilizations, find ways of living through the state shift that capitalism's ecology has wrought. This is why in our conclusion we offer a series of ideas that help us recognize and orient humans' place in nature through the forensics of reparation. Weighing the injustices of centuries of exploitation can resacralize human relations within the web of life. Redistributing care, land, and work so that everyone has a chance to contribute to the improvement of their lives and to that of the ecology around them can undo the violence of abstraction that capitalism makes us perform every day. We term this vision "reparation ecology"[126] and offer it as a way to see history as well as the future, a practice and a commitment to equality and reimagined relations for humans in the web of life.

CHAPTER ONE

Cheap Nature

It only took a day from her crime to her execution. Yet court documents don't even record her name. She lived in Tlaxcala, New Spain, and on Sunday, July 18, 1599, she smashed crosses in a church, incited Chichimec Indians to rebel against the Spanish, and killed a Tarascan Indian using sorcery. The next day she was arrested. Six witnesses testified against her. As the sun set, she was permitted to speak in her defense. She recounted her deeds and then—according to the court record—recounted a dream

> of deer and they said to her not to turn away and that they were looking for her and that they did not want to appear to anyone else but her, because she was ill and they wanted to see her, and she said that she was very old the time she saw the figures and now she is young and healthy and they have taken away some cataracts that she had, and then these two figures went into a cave with her and they gave her a horse, which she has in said pueblo of Tlaxcala, and that one of the two figures was a deer that rode atop of a horse and the other deer had the horse bridled, and on that occasion she was crippled and after seeing the two figures she is well.[1]

Of the crimes she committed, her dream was the worst. She might have fueled insurrection, desecrated a church, and interfered with the flow of silver from Chichimec land, but most dangerous, she offered a vision of order and nature contrary to the colonizers'. The horse was ridden not by Spanish men but by a deer—the symbol of the Chichimec: not white men astride nature, but local life upon the colonizers' life. The dreamer of this dream was guilty of calling not just for a political insurrection but for a cosmic one. She dreamed the order of the world seditiously. She was hanged as a witch later that afternoon.

It's hard to speak of this woman without knowing her name. Her killers called her a witch. That is a name she may have used for herself, albeit without its colonial venom. Even though her name was set at so little that it didn't merit an entry in the conquistadors' paperwork, it is an act of memory against forgetting that her story is told. The dreamer of this radically different ecology had to be killed, swiftly. To allow her to live would sanction an alternative to capitalism's world-ecology.

Our Chichimec woman was killed by a civilized society because her natural savagery broke its rules. This transgression, this crime, was a relatively new idea. As recently as 1330, *savage* meant "intrepid, indomitable, valiant."[2] That positive use faded by the end of the fifteenth century, replaced with its modern one of "in a state of nature, wild."[3] This isn't an accident. At the time of the execution of the Chichimec witch, the terms *nature* and *society* were being produced.

At the very moment when Las Casas and Sepúlveda were debating the fate of Indigenous Peoples—were they "natural" slaves?—the meaning of our everyday word *society* experienced a momentous change. Beginning in the middle of the sixteenth century, *society* came to mean not just the company we keep but also a bigger whole of which individuals are a part.[4] The notion that individuals are part of collective units greater than themselves isn't new—humans have long given names to and established boundaries around social groups: being part of the polis, the city, the Middle Kingdom, Christendom, the chosen people, and so on. But modern *society* has a historically unique antonym: *nature.* On the other side of "society" are not other humans but the wild. Before nation came society. Before society could be defended, it had to be invented.[5] And it was invented through the policing of a strict boundary with nature.

In the English language, the words *nature* and *society* assumed their familiar meanings only after 1550, over the arc of the "long" sixteenth century (c. 1450–1640).[6] This was, as we shall see, a decisive period in England's capitalist and colonial history. It marked the rise of the Spanish and Portuguese empires and their construction of massive New World production systems, worked by coerced Indigenous and African labor. These transformations were key elements of a planetary shift in the global center of power and production from Asia to the North Atlantic. That shift did not come fast. Europe was technologically and economically impoverished compared to civilizations on the other side of Asia, and only after 1800 did that change.[7] China, recall, already had the printing press,[8] a potent navy,[9] gunpowder, and vibrant cities,[10] and it was marked by both wealth and environmental crisis.[11] Where European capitalism thrived was in its capacity to turn nature into something productive and to transform that productivity into wealth. This capacity depended on a peculiar blend of force, commerce, and technology, but also something else—an intellectual revolution underwritten by a new idea: Nature as the opposite of Society. This idea gripped far more than philosophical minds. It became the common sense of conquest and plunder as a way of life. Nature's bloody contradictions found their greatest expression on capitalism's frontiers, forged in violence and rebellion—as the witch killing demonstrates.

We take for granted that some parts of the world are social and others are natural. Racialized violence, mass unemployment and incarceration, consumer cultures—these are the stuff of social problems and social injustice. Climate, biodiversity, resource depletion—these are the stuff of natural problems, of ecological crisis. But it's not just that we think about the world in this way. It's also that we *make* it so, acting as if the Social and the Natural were autonomous domains, as if relations of human power were somehow untouched by the web of life.

In this book, we use these words—*Nature* and *Society*—in a way that's different from their everyday use. We're capitalizing them as a sign that they are concepts that don't merely describe the world but help us organize it and ourselves. Scholars call concepts like these "real abstractions."[12] These abstractions make statements about ontology—*What is?*—and about epistemology—*How do we know what is?* Real abstractions both describe the world and make it. That's why real abstractions are often invisible, and why we use ideas like world-ecology to challenge our readers into seeing Nature and Society as hidden forms of violence. These are undetonated words. Real abstractions aren't innocent: they reflect the interests of the powerful and license them to organize the world.

That's why we begin our discussion of cheap things with Nature. Nature is not a thing but a way of organizing—and cheapening—life. It is only through real abstractions—cultural, political, and economic all at once—that nature's activity becomes a set of things. The web of life is no more inherently cheap than it is wicked or good or downloadable. These are attributes assigned to some of its relationships by capitalism. But it has been *cheapened,* yanked into processes of exchange and profit, denominated and controlled. We made the case in the introduction that capitalism couldn't have emerged without the cheapening of nature; in this chapter we explore the mechanics and effects of this strategy.

EARLY COLONIALISM AND NATURE

To live is to alter one's environment. Hominin evolution proceeded through a series of biological transformations—not least those engendered by fire, which reduced the energy needed for digestion and radically expanded human capacities to make worlds. While humans are an environment-making species, our organizations are fragile. Over the long sweep of history, civilizations have emerged and expanded with more than a little help from the rest of nature, and when that help is withdrawn they can crumble. Rome boomed in the centuries following the onset of the Roman Climatic Optimum (c. 300 BCE–300 CE).[13] The Medieval Warm Period (c. 950–1250) gave a helping hand to new states across Eurasia, from Cambodia to France.[14] Feudal Europe got its assist from a climate anomaly, and its crisis—and the eventual transition to capitalism—was coproduced by another climate shift.

The unraveling of European feudalism was made possible by the Little Ice Age, but not by climate alone. Feudal Europe was highly dynamic. While weather unfavorable to cereal yields was a problem, feudalism had sophisticated agricultural technologies. Beginning in the ninth century, agricultural productivity soared, new fields were claimed from the forests, and human and animal populations grew fast. European population densities were quite high by the early fourteenth century, but feudalism's systemic weakness wasn't something as simple as soil exhaustion. Feudalism crumbled because of peasants' inability to produce a bigger economic surplus for their seigneurs. Left to their own devices, peasants could have shifted from rye and wheat monocultures to a diversified crop mix that included garden produce. In western Europe that could have doubled or tripled food production.[15] But this shift was impossible, given the seigneurs' demand for *marketable* produce that could readily be turned into cash. In an unsettling parallel with the present day, feudal lords reproduced an agricultural system that privileged short-run gains over meaningful adjustments that would have dented their income but sustained life. It is in this context that cheap nature becomes strategic. Nature and Society began to take shape in the throes of feudal crisis and the birth of early capitalism.[16]

The lords' refusal to adjust precipitated an epochal crisis. As we saw in the introduction, agroecological problems enforced by lordly domination fused with climate change and demographic catastrophe to produce not only death but formidable peasant resistance. The ruling classes tried—and failed—to reenserf peasants in western Europe. But the crisis was about more than class; it was the moment when feudalism's ecology of power, wealth, and nature stopped working. That meant something genuinely epoch making: states, lords, and merchants all had to scramble for novel solutions to restore their wealth.[17]

At the core of these novel solutions was global conquest, not just by guns but also by making new frontiers, at once cultural and geographical. Life and land between money and markets became ways to treat and fix crises across the span of capitalism's ecology. At the heart of this relation with nature lay profit, and its poster child is Christopher Columbus. Columbus, who crops up in every chapter as an early practitioner of each of the strategies of cheap things, came to the Caribbean with not just the conqueror's gaze but an appraiser's eye—one sharpened in Portuguese colonial adventures off the shores of North Africa. He launched a colonization of nature as pecuniary as it was peculiar. European empires, beginning with the Spanish and the Portuguese, obsessively collected and ordered Natural objects—including "savage" human bodies—always with an eye on enhanced wealth and power. Columbus's cataloging of nature to evaluate (put a price on) it was an early sign that he understood what Nature had become under early modern capitalism.[18]

Columbus channeled the strategy of cheap nature almost from the first moment that he saw the New World.[19] On the eighth day of his first voyage in the Caribbean, he found a cape he named "Cabo Hermoso [Beautiful cape], because it is so.... I can never tire my eyes in looking at such lovely vegetation, so different from ours. I believe there are many herbs and many trees that are worth much in Europe for dyes and for medicines but I do not know them, and this causes me great sorrow."[20] He was from the outset an assessor with a keen sense of cheapness and power, able to cast his eye on nature and be frustrated that he couldn't instantly see money.

Profit didn't come just from trade, however. Nature had to be put to work. An early practical use of the division between Nature and Society appeared in the colonial reinvention of the encomienda. Originally just a claim on land, the encomienda became a strategy to shift certain humans into the category of Nature so that they might more cheaply work the land. When the Spanish crown was battling for territory in Iberia, encomiendas were a way of managing its spoils. These were temporary land grants given by the king to aristocrats so that they might profit from estates previously occupied by Moors.[21] In the Caribbean, encomiendas were transformed from medieval land grants into modern labor grants, allowing not just access to the land but the de facto enslavement of the Indigenous People who happened to be there. Rights of dominion came to encompass not just territory but also flora and fauna; Indigenous People became the latter. Over time, the encomienda system came to comprise a diversity of labor arrangements, combining legal coercion with wage labor.[22] This meant that the realm of Nature included virtually all peoples of color, most women, and most people with white skin living in semicolonial regions (e.g., Ireland, Poland).[23] This is why in the sixteenth century Castilians referred to Indigenous Andeans as *naturales*.[24]

THE INVENTION OF NATURE AND SOCIETY

From the beginning, humans understood they were different from the rest of nature.[25] Capitalism didn't invent the distinction. Its innovation was to turn this distinction into a hard-and-fast separation—and into an organizing principle. This was a task to which intellectuals on both sides of the Atlantic contributed. René Descartes (1596–1660), about whom more below, learned basic philosophical reasoning by studying the Mexican philosopher Antonio Rubio (1548–1615). Some of the sixteenth century's most sophisticated anticolonial Christian intellectual activity, as Enrique Dussel argues, happened in the Americas.[26] The English, at the same time, were developing ideas of "the savage and the civilized" in Ireland—their first colonial frontier. It's no coincidence that English rule in Ireland intensified after 1541—at the very moment when Nature and Society were assuming their familiar, current meanings. England's colonial forces were concentrated on that notch of land on the Irish east coast around Dublin. The initial area of English colonial activity was known as the Pale. Those outside it were "savages."

The inventors of Nature were philosophers as well as conquerors and profiteers. In 1641, Descartes offered what would become the first two laws of capitalist ecology. The first is seemingly innocent. Descartes distinguished between mind and body, using the Latin *res cogitans* and *res extensa* to refer to them. Reality, in this view, is composed of discrete "thinking things" and "extended things." Humans (but not all humans) were thinking things; Nature was full of extended things. The era's ruling classes saw most human beings—women, peoples of color, Indigenous Peoples—as extended, not thinking, beings. This means that Descartes's philosophical abstractions were practical instruments of domination: they were real abstractions with tremendous material force. And this leads us to Descartes's second law of capitalist ecology: European civilization (or "we," in Descartes's word) must become "the masters and possessors of nature."[27] Society and Nature were not just existentially separate; Nature was something to be controlled and dominated by Society. The Cartesian outlook, in other words, shaped modern logics of power as well as thought.

While Descartes is usually thought of as French, his perspective might just as easily be characterized as English and Dutch. Born and educated in France, he wrote most of his major works in the Dutch Republic between 1629 and 1649, when the republic was the era's greatest superpower and home to its most dynamic capitalism. These decades also saw the crescendo of a planetary ecological revolution that had begun nearly two centuries earlier, laying waste to forests from Brazil to Poland to the Spice Islands, clearing wetlands from Russia to England, and mining the earth from the Andes to Sweden.[28] So pivotal were these environmental transformations, each delivering some form of cheap nature, that more than five hundred commodities were traded on the Amsterdam Bourse (the first modern stock market) by the 1650s. Descartes's revolutionary materialism was very much in step with the times.

Descartes had not stumbled upon his revolutionary philosophy all on his own. The second law of capitalist ecology, domination over nature, owed much to Francis Bacon (1561–1626), a philosopher widely credited as the father of modern science. (That gendered language will make sense in a moment.) Bacon was also a prominent member of England's political establishment, at different times a member of Parliament and the attorney general of England and Wales. He argued that "science should as it were torture nature's secrets out of her."[29] Further, the "empire of man" should penetrate and dominate the "womb of nature." Science must "hound nature in her wanderings, and you will be able, when you like, to lead and drive her afterwards to the same place again.... Neither ought a man to make scruple of entering and penetrating into these holes and corners, when the inquisition of truth is his whole object."[30]

Bacon was a major political figure at a time when the lives of European women were being threatened, surveilled, and dominated in new—and thoroughly modern—ways. The invention of Nature and Society was gendered at every turn. The binaries of Man and Woman, Nature and Society, drank from the same cup. Nature, and its boundary with Society, was "gyn/ecological" from the outset.[31] Through this radically new mode of organizing life and thought, Nature became not a thing but a strategy that allowed for the ethical and economic cheapening of life. Cartesian dualism was and remains far more than a descriptive statement: it is a normative statement of how best to organize power and hierarchy, Humanity and Nature, Man and Woman, Colonizer and Colonized.

Although the credit (and blame) is shared by many, it makes sense to call this a Cartesian revolution. Here was an intellectual movement that shaped not only ways of thinking but also ways of conquering, commodifying, and living. This Cartesian revolution accomplished four major transformations, each shaping our view of Nature and Society to this day. First, either-or binary thinking displaced both-and alternatives. Second, it privileged thinking about substances, things, before thinking about the relationships between those substances. Third, it installed the domination of nature through science as a social good.

Finally, the Cartesian revolution made thinkable, and doable, the colonial project of mapping and domination. Focusing on the anticolonial Quechua writer Felipe Guamán Poma de Ayala (1535?–1616?), Dussel reflects on how Guamán, anticipating Descartes, "discovers the process through which the *ego conquiro* [I dominate/subjugate]—this expanding, self-centered subjectivity—passes, wildly overcoming all limits in its arrogances, until it culminates in the *ego cogito* [I think] based on God himself, as his own mediation to reconstruct the world under his control, at his service, for his exploitation, and among these the populations of the South."[32]

Guamán's point was more than just rhetorical. Cartesian rationalism is predicated on the distinction between the inner reality of the mind and the outer reality of objects; the latter could be brought into the former only through a neutral, disembodied gaze situated outside space and time. That gaze always belonged to the Enlightened European colonist—and the empires that backed him. Descartes's *cogito* funneled vision and thought into a spectator's view of the world, one that rendered the emerging surfaces of modernity visible and measurable and the viewer bodiless and placeless. Medieval multiple vantage points in art and literature were displaced by a single, disembodied, omniscient, and panoptic eye.[33] In geometry, Renaissance painting, and especially cartography, the new thinking represented reality as if one were standing outside it. As the social critic Lewis Mumford noted, the Renaissance perspective "turned the symbolic relation of objects into a visual relation: the visual in turn became a quantitative relation. In the new picture of the world, size meant not human or divine importance, but distance."[34] And that distance could be measured, catalogued, classified, mapped, and owned.[35]

The modern map did not merely describe the world; it was a technology of conquest. The 1502 Cantino Planisphere, the earliest surviving map of Portugal's global reach, can be understood only in terms of that tiny country's outsized ambitions. Beginning in 1503, Portugal launched a series of invasions of the Indian Ocean world, seizing over the next decade the central hinges of the ocean's lucrative trade: Hormuz on the Persian Gulf, Goa in western India, and Malacca in southeastern Asia.[36]

Sixteenth-century maps like the planisphere and the portolan charts used by sailors quickly yielded to the modern world's most famous—and still most used—cartographic technology: the Mercator projection. Gerard Mercator, whose (invented) family name translates to "merchant," lived most of his life in Flanders, in present-day Belgium, one of his era's most commercially dynamic regions. Europe's greatest geographer, he made his living by selling not maps but globes—at the beginning of a time when it became possible to think of the planet as a sphere.[37] Mercator's project was revolutionary in fusing the new

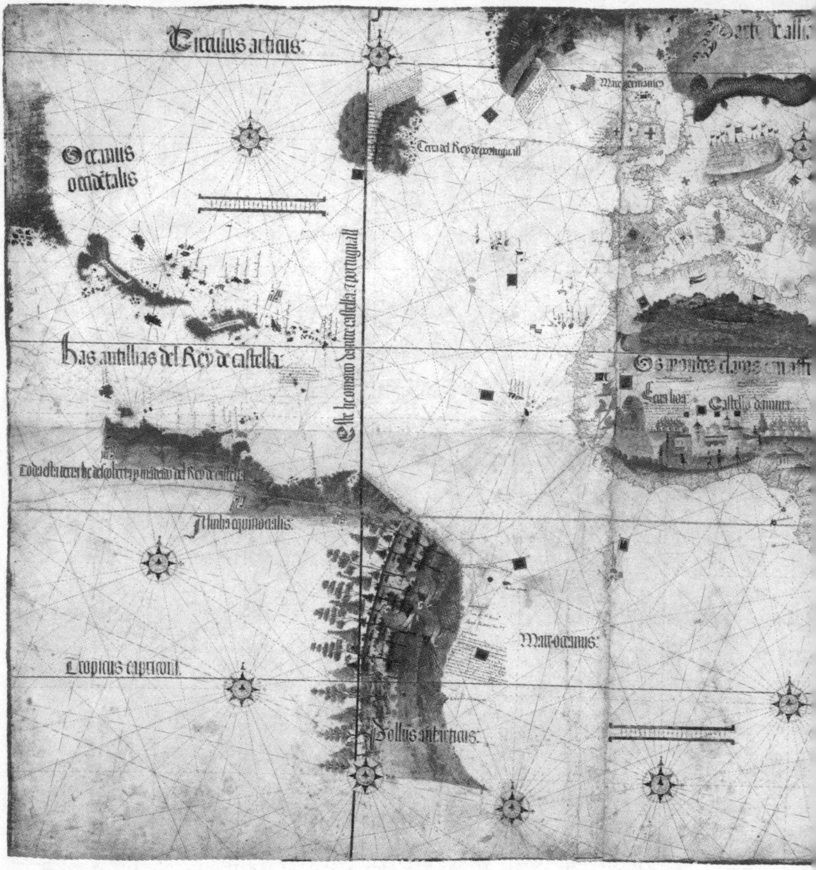

Map 3. Anonymous, Cantino Planisphere, 1502. Biblioteca Estense Universitaria, Modena, Ital

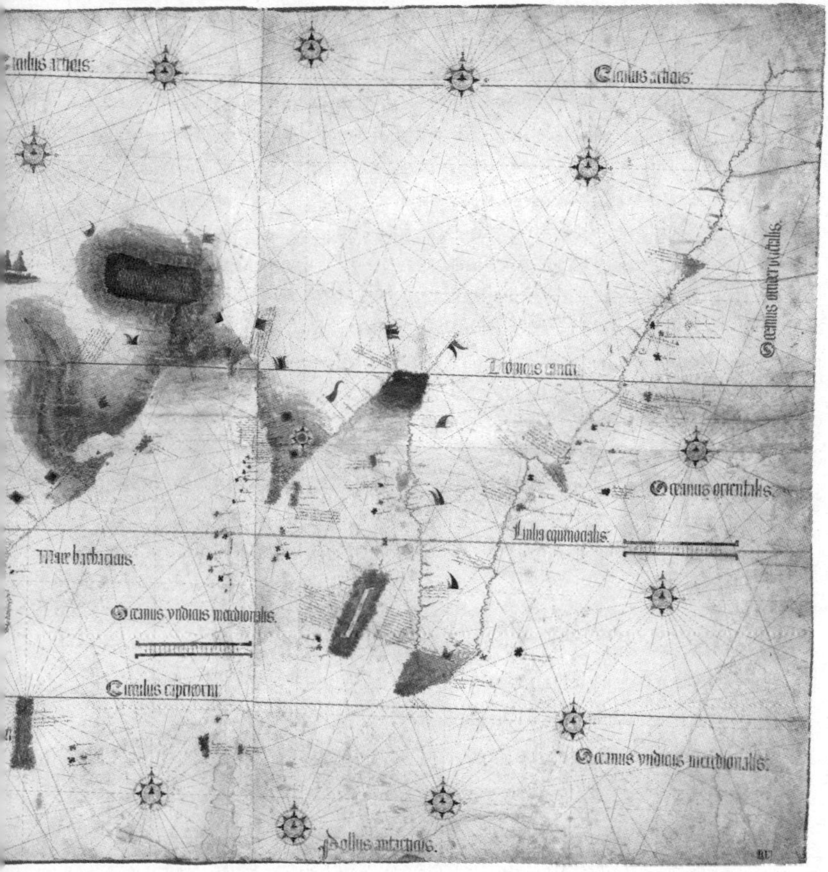
Circulus articus
Tropicus cancri
Oceanus orientalis
Linea equinocialis
Mare barbaricus
Oceanus yndicus meridionalis
Circulus capricorni
Oceanus yndicus meridionalis
Polus antarcticus

cartography with the demands of rapacious and militarized commercial expansion. As Jerry Brotton reminds us,

> The importance of Mercator's innovation in terms of accurate navigational practice and commercial profit was quite clear. Instead of taking awkward and imprecise bearings on board ship across the surface of a globe or a portolan chart, his new projection allowed for a line of bearing to be drawn accurately across the surface of a plane map, explicitly foregrounding ... its usefulness to the art of navigation.... With pilots and navigators in mind, Mercator went on to outline the mathematical procedure which allowed him to employ an accurate grid of straight lines across his map, whilst also retaining the relative geographical accuracy of the topography of the globe.[38]

To conquer and cheapen global life, in other words, one must be able to map it.

NATURE, PRIVATE PROPERTY, AND LABOR

For early modern materialism, the point was not only to interpret the world but to control it. In suggesting that we "make ourselves as it were the masters and possessors of nature,"[39] Descartes offered a manifesto for (some) human minds over a Nature that included most humans at the time. The Cartesian revolution went hand in hand with two other key historical processes. One was a range of interventions that made a growing number of humans dependent on the cash nexus for their survival. Social scientists call this "proletarianization," the transformation of human activity into something to be exchanged in the commodity system—what we today call the labor market.[40] Proletarianization was never narrowly economic; it was the product of a second historical process: the creation of new forms of territorial power that emerged after 1450. The old territorial power—the overlapping jurisdictions and personalized authority of medieval Europe—had crumbled in the long feudal crisis (c. 1315–1453). The new empires and the internal transformations of the Low Countries and England were made possible by power of a new type. At its core was the generalization of private property.

Although Portugal pioneered a capitalist ecology, the English story better demonstrates how capitalism transformed land and labor. As grain prices stagnated—and labor became more expensive—over the fifteenth century, English landlords took advantage of the demographic collapse to appropriate vacated peasant holdings. In a process that accelerated after 1500, a growing share of the land was removed from customary use, wherein the landlords' ability to increase rental fees was limited, to a leasehold sector, where rents could be adjusted to market forces.[41] Where this relatively peaceful means of land grabbing was not possible, landlords seized upon a loophole in feudal arrangements: they could impose "entry fines" upon inheritance.[42] If a peasant—often an eldest son—inherited the land but could not pay these fines, the land wasn't his. These and other loopholes proliferated, and competitive rents set by supply and demand were increasingly imposed—rents no longer had to be reasonable, as in earlier centuries.[43]

Landlords weren't simply grabbing land. They were transforming the way others could relate to nature. Placing customary lands under a system of competitive rents reduced the commons, the areas of land in which peasants had exercised some autonomy. Commoning involves the processes of managing access to land one doesn't own, covering a wide range of rights, including those of pasturing animals, collecting firewood and construction materials from a forest, and gleaning. In addition to these rights came responsibilities, such as stinting: refraining from collecting wood, for example, so as not to prejudice the ability to collect wood in the future. These rights and responsibilities were vital to peasant survival, allowing them to make up the difference between the season's crop and what they needed for their families to endure. As the commons receded and access to what remained became more difficult, peasants had to fill the gap some other way. Churches and other institutions for social support offered little. So peasants were forced either to leave the land or to offer the only thing they had left to sell: their labor. In this sense their labor was "free"—its sale was uncoerced by anything other than poverty and prison terms for vagrancy, the laws against poverty and vagabondage being motivationally harsh. Peasants had no choice but to sell their labor to survive.[44]

Peasants could and did resist.[45] The first half of the sixteenth century witnessed a series of agrarian and urban riots, culminating in Kett's Rebellion of 1549, when sixteen thousand rebels seized Norwich, then England's second largest city.[46] Peasants' anger was directed not only at the enclosure of the commons and the ongoing attack on their customary rights. It also targeted the idea of competitive rent, which was "relatively new and outrageous" in the century after 1450.[47]

Not for the last time, the outrageous quickly became normal. England's landlords would farm for cash or, more often, rent out their land to tenant farmers who did. This revolutionized production—differently from the sugar plantations of Madeira and the New World, but no less significantly. The remaking of English property transformed the relationship between humans and the ground beneath their feet. As a result, English agricultural productivity soared, and the country's nonagricultural population with it. Labor productivity on English farms grew 75 percent between 1600 and 1700, by which point more than half of the English population worked outside agriculture.[48]

The rise of private property was at once material, political, and symbolic. Cadastral surveys and state-sponsored bourgeois property relations were sites of struggle between classes and between ways of organizing humans and the rest of nature. For the English in sixteenth-century Ireland, surveying was an important "component in the triumph of civility over savagery."[49] Maps were a way to know and control nature. Alternative forms of knowledge about nature were seditious. This is why witchcraft and Indigenous knowledge constituted existential threats to capitalism, challenging both its epistemology and its ontology. Inca experiments in agriculture, Mesoamerican advances in soil enrichment, and Chinese medicine were forms of knowledge that had to be confined to the boundaries of folklore, if not extinguished outright.[50] Knowledge was enclosed too. If anything was to be known about nature and the world, European men would author and authorize it.

As we've seen, the enclosure of knowledge was central to a cultural revolution that explicitly cast colonized peoples—and nearly all women—as part of Nature, the better to discipline and manage them. As England intensified its rule in Ireland after 1541, imperial policy prioritized the relocation of "the wild Irish that dwell now dispersed in woods" into English-style towns.[51] The Spanish pursued a similar program at greater scale in colonial Peru after 1571, resettling Andeans—*naturales*—in agricultural villages based on the Spanish model. The Dutch did likewise in southeast Asia after 1620.[52] These were far from the only such initiatives in capitalism's formative centuries. They laid the foundation for a long colonial project that insisted on the expulsion of the colonized from civilized society and on the moral necessity of empire as a school for "backward" peoples. They even justified slavery as "a school for civilization," to paraphrase the early twentieth-century historian Ulrich B. Phillips.[53]

FAILING TO APPRECIATE THE CAPITALOCENE

The three processes of cultural apartheid through the Enlightenment, proletarianization, and the privatization of property were at the core of capitalism's cheap nature strategy, one that turned the work of human and nonhuman alike into cheap things. But there's nothing like an ecological crisis to remind civilization that nature is never cheap. Climate change makes it impossible to ignore planetary change in our daily lives. The intensity and frequency of "extreme weather events" in recent years have been inescapably clear. Droughts have devastated California agriculture. Residents of Basra, Iraq, saw the mercury hit 129°F (54°C) in July 2016, while parts of Iran experienced a heat index of 140°F (60°C) that month.[54] Iraq's economy may have shrunk by as much as one-fifth during its summer 2016 heat wave.[55] Indeed, rising heat stress—with lethal impacts on children and the elderly—is likely to render parts of the Middle East uninhabitable by the end of the century.[56] Unprecedented wildfires have shaken western Canada. Heat waves have killed thousands in India.[57] For Americans, the August 2016 flooding of Louisiana—driving thirty thousand people from their homes—capped off a statistically improbable run of extreme weather. The storm was a once-in-five-hundred-years event, according to the National Oceanic and Atmospheric Administration. The previous fifteen months had seen eight such storms.[58]

This is what it is like to live in the Capitalocene. Certainly, previous human civilizations altered their environments. But none were guided and governed by the strategy of cheap nature, which has allowed the transformation of the planet into Nature and Society through the subjugation of human and extrahuman life. Those who have opposed this transformation, like the Chichimec witch at the beginning of this chapter, have faced death. Indigenous People continue to resist, and continue to face slaughter—though the language of the Capitalocene tells us that such people aren't being annihilated. They're being *developed.*

Cycles of nature into money and then into capital have brought us to this moment in geological history. That's why we need to explore the thing that Columbus desperately wanted to see when he looked at New World natures, which has remained in the background of our account so far, yet without which modern capitalism would be unthinkable: cheap money.

CHAPTER TWO

Cheap Money

Poderoso caballero es Don Dinero:
nace en las Indias honrado,
donde el mundo le acompaña,
viene a morir en España,
y es en Génova enterrado.

Lord Money is a powerful knight,
born in the Indies, honored
where the world accompanies him,
coming to die in Spain,
and be buried in Genoa.

Francisco de Quevedo y Villegas,
"Poderoso caballero es Don Dinero"

And [the Inca Guaina Capac] asked the Spaniard [Candia, the first Spaniard to arrive in Peru] what it is that he ate; he responded in the Spanish language and with gestures indicating that he ate gold and silver. And [Capac] gave large quantities of gold dust and silver and gold plates.

Felipe Guamán Poma de Ayala, *El primer nueva corónica y buen gobierno* [The first new chronicle and good government]

Like many humans, Columbus understood money intimately and imperfectly. We know this because in 1478 he was hired to bring a boatload of sugar from Madeira to Genoa and fluffed the transaction so badly that he had to appear in court.[1] Ludovico Centurione, one of Genoa's wealthiest bankers, had paid a merchant, Paolo Di Negro, 1,290 ducats, and Di Negro had hired Captain Columbus to freight fifty thousand pounds (22,680 kilograms) of sugar, giving him 103 ducats and a cargo hold filled with wool.[2] There were no takers for the wool in Madeira. Columbus returned with a short consignment of sugar to Genoa, where he was forced to attest to his lack of commercial success in court, at the age of twenty-seven "or thereabouts."[3] Columbus quickly skipped town, never to return.[4] But Genoese finance was to follow him for the rest of his life.

Columbus headed to the Iberian Peninsula, where a newly—and barely—unified Spain was launching the first of three major military campaigns. In 1478, King Ferdinand II and Queen Isabella sent soldiers into Portuguese territory on Gran Canaria, the largest of the Canary Islands. But they ran out of cash, so beginning in 1480, a Genoese, Francisco Pinelo, bankrolled four more Spanish expeditions over three years. By 1483, Gran Canaria was subdued and the creditors had to be satisfied.[5] But there was a problem. As Helen Nader notes, "The only immediate returns were unprecedented numbers of war captives. The royal creditors [the Genoese above all] ... became the royal slave brokers."[6] The pattern was quickly repeated. The second great military campaign was launched in 1482, the final phase of the centuries-long Reconquista on the Iberian mainland, again financed by Genoese. And again, the only booty worth anything was captives. When the port city of Málaga fell in 1487—an event that Columbus witnessed—its Jewish and

Muslim inhabitants were enslaved. The "most important businessmen of Malaga, both before and after its fall," were the Genoese Centuriones.[7]

Many of the same men who financed the Canarian and Iberian campaigns financed the third—a proposed transatlantic crossing to Asia. In 1490, Pinelo became a joint treasurer of the Santa Hermandad, "Sacred brotherhood," a highly militarized police force tasked with suppressing internal dissent to Castile's fragile state-building efforts.[8] It was the brotherhood that was responsible for expelling the Jews from Spain by July 31, 1492, just three days before Columbus set sail for the Americas. The Santa Hermandad's *other* joint treasurer was Luis de Santángel.[9] He was also, since 1481, the Kingdom of Aragon's *escribano de ración,* in charge of royal finances. It was Santángel who persuaded Isabella, previously dismissive of Columbus's requests, to reverse herself. And though the usual story has Ferdinand and Isabella financing Columbus's voyage, this is only half true. The Two Kingdoms (Ferdinand's Aragon and Isabella's Castile) weren't financiers so much as insurers, guaranteeing a loan that came in large part from the Santa Hermandad.[10]

At the origins of capitalism's ecology is a cycle that goes beyond that of money into commodities and back again. A peculiar and very modern magic lies here. States wanted the loot of war but needed money to pay their soldiers. Without wars they couldn't acquire the riches that they needed in part to pay for the previous war. War, money, war. Bankers needed governments to repay them, and governments needed bankers to fund them. What's new about capitalism isn't the pursuit of profit but rather the relations among the pursuit, its financing, and governments. These relations were to remake the planet, and they are the subject of this chapter.

FINANCE AS ECOLOGY

For the past six centuries, planetary life has turned on the power of money.[11] Not just any kind of money: money as *capital,* as the power to command life, work, and resources. That capital circulates for two reasons. One is the modern world market, which first took shape in the era of Columbus. The other is modern imperialism, which—not coincidentally—emerged at the same time. Neither world market nor world power could exist without finance, at once indispensable to and powerless without imperial ambition and commodity exchange.

Money facilitates and compels action at a distance. The earliest uses of money, in the Fertile Crescent, relied on precious metal to facilitate agricultural trade and even manage a debt crisis in 1788 BCE.[12] Note the steps to make a currency: First you need to acquire a rare substance, usually metal from the earth. Next you take it to a mint, an instrument of a powerful organization that can vouch for metallurgical purity, that can literally stamp its authority onto the surface of a coin, plain as a fact. Under capitalism, this minted money is then exchanged for labor power, machines, and raw materials that become commodities that are then exchanged for money again.

World money, world nature, and world power—these form the peculiar trinity of environment making that shaped capitalism from the conquest of the Americas to the unfolding disaster of global warming in the twenty-first century. In the modern world, money *is* an ecological relation. It has become, in the capitalist era, a relation that shapes the conditions of existence not only for humans—but for all life.

This is why it makes sense to say that Wall Street is a way of organizing nature. We'll make the case that the capitalist world-ecology needs cheap money: a secure denomination of exchange that can be relied upon to facilitate commerce, controlled in a way that meets the needs of the ruling bloc at the time. Its cheapness includes two major dimensions. One is the appropriation of the base primary commodity (silver, gold, oil) and its regulation to keep interest rates—the price of money—low. The other is the control over the wider cash economy, which only states (cities, nations, and ultimately empires) can provide. As Fernand Braudel put it, finance capital "only triumphs when it becomes identified with the state, when it is the state"—a statement with special relevance for our times, when Goldman Sachs has treated the White House as a branch office.[13] In the sixteenth century, European colonialists discovered that they could expand the dominion of silver worldwide. Through the connections that followed, capitalists achieved a result that, with few interruptions, continues to today—a cheap money system that facilitates, protects, and expands frontiers in capitalism's ecology.[14]

Cheap money means one thing above all: low interest. Even in today's world of fast-moving container ships and high-frequency stock trades, credit is the lifeblood of capitalism. If cheap work, food, energy, and raw materials are the necessary conditions for capitalist booms, cheap credit makes them all possible.[15] Historically, there's been a virtuous circle of cheap money and new frontiers. When opportunities for profit making have contracted in established regions of production and extraction, capitalists have taken their profits and put them into money dealing. That's one reason why after each great boom in world capitalism—for the Dutch in the mid-seventeenth century, for the British in the mid-nineteenth century, and the American postwar golden age—there's been a process that scholars call financialization. In these periods, capitalists reorient from older and less profitable industrial and commercial pursuits to forms of money dealing. Instead of hiring troublesome workers, building expensive factories, buying raw materials, and making something, increasing numbers of capitalists turn to something simpler and (temporarily) more attractive: loaning money and making speculative bets on the future. Financialization in this sense is essentially a gamble on some future, more profitable, industrial revolution.[16] We're living in such a time at the moment, and history isn't reassuring about its likely outcome: such cycles of accumulation usually end in war, and with the rise of new financial powers, as we'll see below.

Two movements make financialization attractive and even useful to capitalism when the world's economic pie stops growing. One is the tendency of leading powers to go to war, or at a minimum to build up their war-making capacity. This is what happened after the economic stagnation of the 1970s, when the United States launched the largest military build-up in peacetime history. As we will see, modern states rarely self-finance their wars. They have to borrow money just like anyone else. The other thing that boosts financialization is that capital in the heartlands of the system begins to flow toward the frontiers. In the late nineteenth century, for example, gigantic sums of British capital, in the form of loans, flowed out of London and toward the rest of world, especially to build railroads—which in turn were central to the next century's extraordinary cheapening of food and raw materials.[17] Financialization's bet on the future has worked historically so long as there were bountiful frontiers, where humans and other natures might be put to work—or otherwise extracted—for cheap. When the long boom partly made possible by the global railway network went bust in the 1970s, a new era of financialization began. And though the neoliberal era originated in a crisis of expensive money—the 1979 Volcker Shock, in which interest rates crested 20 percent in a bid to control inflation—a protracted era of cheap money followed. As Anwar Shaikh explains, the neoliberal "boom"—such as it was—that began in the 1980s was "spurred by a sharp drop in interest rates.... Falling interest rates also lubricated the spread of capital across the globe, promoted a huge rise in consumer debt, and fueled international bubbles in finance and real estate."[18] The difference today is that the frontiers of cheap nature are fewer and the piles of cash on the tables of the global casino are higher than ever. In the twenty-first century, money masks and tries to postpone the underlying problems of socioecological crisis, but for most humans and planetary life, cheap dollars can no longer paper over these problems. As to what a cocktail of monetary, biological, climatological, and social upheaval might look like, history has some lessons.

THE MONETARY ORIGINS OF THE MODERN WORLD

The Black Death (1347–1353) sparked a fiscal crisis. One of its consequences was a fall in the number of people able to mine, and thus a dearth of cash. European aristocrats wanted Malaccan spices, Persian silks, and Chinese porcelain, and European industry needed raw materials—cotton from Egypt, alum from Syria. Europeans paid with coin they minted with rare metals from mines under their control. For that reason, European silver and gold (what little there was) swiftly flowed east and south. Although the trade balance was offset just a little with European animals and finished goods, John Day notes that "the pull of this deficit was all but irresistible. It drained Bohemia and Sardinia of silver almost as fast as it was mined; it captured a lion's share of Hungarian and Sudanese gold from the moment it entered the Mediterranean circuit; it contributed to—if it did not create—chronic balance of payments problems as far away as England and Flanders."[19]

The Little Ice Age was a global problem, most of all in one of the planet's thriving trading centers—China. Although climate had led to recession and fiscal crisis earlier, the consequences were different this time.[20] The mid-fifteenth-century climate upheaval combined in China with domestic turmoil in the imperial court. In response, the Ming dynasty closed its mints, which in turn contributed to a global shortage of silver. The Ming state also retreated from "its unprecedented involvement in international affairs, [and] no other government in the world was in a position to assume [China's] role as the engine of economic growth. Between the early 1440s and the mid-1460s, societies from one end of Eurasia to another found themselves in deep economic and political trouble."[21]

One result was an exacerbation of popular Chinese suspicion of paper currency. Gold and silver coins, which people trusted as stores of value, began to disappear from circulation.[22] The bad paper money drove out the good metallic money. In Malacca, on the southern half of the Malay Peninsula, currency was in such short supply that local traders resorted to making coins out of tin.[23] Florentine and Genoese bills of exchange circulated in Europe as some of the few trusted means of exchange, but without swelling vaults of silver or gold to back them up, they did little to alleviate the problem.

EUROPEAN SILVER

For medieval Europeans, the notion that money could take any form other than coin was nearly unthinkable. "Of all the strange customs" reported by the thirteenth-century Venetian explorer Marco Polo, "none seemed to astound him more than the power of the state to compel [the use of paper money] ... throughout the empire."[24] But Europe had no great empires of the kind Polo reported—only a few middling and hundreds of small states, nearly all of which were familiar with the debasement of coinage. When the class, climatic, and epidemiological crises of the fourteenth century fatally undermined the feudal order, Europe's monetary system went from bad to worse.

Trust between users of money was in short supply, with parties uncertain that the coin they received was unadulterated. Silver and gold—bullion—provided a crucial hedge against debasement and distrust.[25] But European mines flooded, and the money in circulation contracted—by two-thirds, maybe more, in the century after 1350.[26] While there was little mutual trust, there was even less silver.

European merchants needed trustworthy money, badly: not just metal from the ground, but networks through which that metal could become money, authorized by a power that could guarantee its circulation to meet the demand at the expanding frontier. The first solution lay in southern Germany, in Augsburg, where the Fugger family attended the birth of modern money.[27] They not only dominated European finance for nearly a century but also forged capitalism's first and most basic industry: metallurgy. It was from the silver-and-copper-rich Erzgebirge (Ore mountains), today a rough boundary between Czechia and Germany, that the material of modern money originally flowed. Indeed, the word *dollar* comes from the minted coins—thalers—of Joachimsthal (now Jáchymov), the era's greatest boomtown.

After 1450, the silver shortage began to ease. In that year, no European mine produced more than ten thousand marks (2.5

tons) of silver. But by 1458, eight mines produced more than fifty thousand marks (12.5 tons) a year.[28] European silver, and to a lesser extent African gold,[29] provided the crucial material basis for the extraordinary growth of commodity exchange starting in the late fifteenth century.[30] This first modern silver boom "either allowed merchants in distant centers to take up funds for commercial activity secure in the knowledge that their bills on these markets would be met when they fell due, or made abundant funding available to those proffering bills to finance their trade. In such circumstances money markets where commercial credit could be funded at relatively low interest rates drew trade towards them and effected a realignment of commercial activity in accordance with . . . central European mining activity."[31]

The silver boom didn't just make money—it also produced one of the first modern working classes, devastated landscapes, and provoked modernity's first great worker and peasant revolt, the German Peasants' War of 1525. By then there were one hundred thousand workers in central Europe engaged in mining and metallurgy—and countless more in auxiliary trades.[32] The environmental consequences were rapid and devastating. Georgius Agricola, the first modern geologist, observed, "The woods and groves are cut down, for there is need of an endless amount of wood for timbers, machines, and the smelting of metals. And when the woods and groves are felled, then are exterminated the beasts and birds, very many of which furnish a pleasant and agreeable food for man. . . . When the ores are washed, the water which has been used poisons the brooks and streams, and either destroys the fish or drives them away."[33]

Silver—along with copper and iron—devoured forests and threatened peasant livelihoods. As we saw in the previous chapter, woodlands were overwhelmingly common lands before the sixteenth century. They were, in Jack Westoby's phrase, "the poor man's overcoat," crucial to survival.[34] The poor fought against their enclosure, but by the time of the German Peasants' War,[35] access to commons had been sharply limited and forest acreages significantly reduced. Against these challenges to commoning, sixteenth-century peasants demanded the restitution of access to the forest in their Twelve Articles manifesto.[36] The radical cleric Thomas Münzer (a surname that translates as "Minter" or "Coiner") in 1524 denounced these forest enclosures, through which "every creature has been made into property: the fish in the water, the bird in the air, the off-spring of the earth—creation, too, must become free."[37] The worker and peasant revolt for which he gave his life interrupted European finance and might have provoked further revolutions had not financiers from a small Italian city-state funded a colonial solution.

GENOESE BANKING

By the middle of the fifteenth century, Europe had begun to shake off the impacts of the century and a half of disease, war, and famine that had decimated continental life since 1315. In 1453, the old Eastern Roman Empire met its end, with Constantinople falling to the Ottoman Turks, and England and France finally concluded their Hundred Years' War. The 1450s were eventful in other respects too: Columbus and his future patrons Isabella and Ferdinand were born (1451–52), Johannes Gutenberg's printed Bibles began to circulate, and the first sugar was cultivated on Madeira. This was also the decade when the Peace of Lodi (1454) ended the "Italian Hundred Years' War," a century or so of conflict among the four "great powers" of northern Italy: Venice, Genoa, Florence, and Milan.[38]

The Republic of Genoa was by far the weakest of these powers. Indeed, it was always more of a transnational holding company than anything resembling an empire.[39] This is not to say, however, that it was a bit player—its tax revenues in 1298 were greater than those of France, and its population larger than London's.[40] But it was a place of instability. Medieval Genoa was wracked by social revolt: between 1413 and 1453, fourteen revolutions turned the city upside down.[41] The "central theme" of Genoese history was "conflict, often waged with suicidal intensity, between the aristocracy and the upper-middle class."[42] Consider it a battle between the 1 percent and the 0.1 percent, waged financially. This continued until 1528, when the aristocrat Andrea Doria sealed the victory of the 0.1 percent by rewriting the republic's constitution.

Genoa's overseas territories were administered by the commune, the municipality itself. The commune's debts increased as its foreign territories fell to Ottoman expansion and Venetian competition in the east. A group of the commune's aristocratic creditors started the Casa di San Giorgio (the House—later the Bank—of Saint George) in 1407.[43] Within a year, this bank had negotiated control of territory from the commune so that the aristocrats could recoup their debts from the city, principally from its merchant class. The city ceded title of its assets (territories) as interest payments and collateral throughout the fifteenth century: "Lerici in 1479, Corsica in 1482, Sarzana in 1484."[44] In successive credit crunches, the city's 0.1 percent siphoned resources and islands in the Mediterranean away from its wealthy merchant class, held the revenues in their own bank, and kept their own books.[45] This tension, between the banks and the states on which they depend, has yet to subside.

Genoese merchants hunted for ways for the municipality to pay off its creditors. In 1417 the commune developed a state lottery system with a jackpot "equivalent to the annual salary of ten chancellors."[46] It sold its treasures, which is how the Holy Grail became a financial instrument: the cup from which Jesus allegedly drank at the Last Supper was brought to Genoa by Guglielmo Embriaco (in English, "William the Drunkard") after his invasion of Caesarea (now in Israel). In 1319 the city pawned the Grail to Cardinal Niccolò Fieschi to pay the bank. The resulting financial instrument was called *Compera Cardinalis*.[47] The city also trucked in horror, trading in slaves not just from its Iberian conquests but also from raids into western Asia and northern Africa. "Contracts by which slave owners rented out their slaves for profit [indicate] that the rate of return was about 7–10 percent on invested capital. This was a higher yield than San Giorgio paid on shares, and hence the Genoese … invest[ed] in human flesh."[48] One in every twenty inhabitants of the city was a slave in the fifteenth century. It is from this history that the Italian greeting and farewell *Ciao!* derives: "'(Vostro) schiavo,' '(your) slave.'"[49]

The Casa was a mighty economic and political force and became the municipality's sole source of credit, at times acting as an exclusive central bank for Genoa. It wasn't, however, always in charge. Moments of merchant and then proletarian insurrection loosened the bank's grasp on the commune. The municipality pushed back against its creditors, asking for discounts on its bond repayments—which stimulated a secondary market in bonds—and had Pope Callixtus III decree this legitimate in 1456. In the history of credit, capital, and the state, it's worth noting that capital doesn't always win.

Recent financial histories have ignored the Casa di San Giorgio, in part because of the obscurity of its manuscripts, in part because the Genoese weren't the showboaters that the Venetians were.[50] But their facility with credit lines and their connections to European aristocracies made it possible for them to access money at the lowest possible interest rates until the eighteenth century.[51] They were masters of cheap money, a mastery they achieved by financing, and reaping the rewards from, Spain's colonial exploits. The Genoese weren't alone in making the provision of credit pay, and other banking institutions followed in their footsteps, later in Amsterdam and then in London and the United States. But the Genoese story is significant because it brings together many of the key elements of cheap money: the need for profit, the capacity to fund colonies, and the requisite attitude to nature. It also has, as we noted at the beginning of the chapter, a link through Columbus to the violence at the New World's frontiers.

Genoa's financiers needed the New World. Its trade faltered throughout the 1400s, a result of both the previous century's long depression and military defeat, as the Venetians and Turks ousted the city's merchants from their lucrative outposts in the eastern Mediterranean.[52] Genoa's relatively narrow hinterland had been thoroughly deforested, forcing its shipbuilders to rely on imported timber.[53] Defeat and geographical necessity pushed Genoa west—and toward Spain and Portugal. What it lost in the eastern Mediterranean, it would gain back—and more—in the Atlantic.

After 1450, Genoese financial power penetrated the Spanish domains, from southern Italy to the New World. Settling in Córdoba, Cadiz, and Seville, Genoese merchants were seemingly in every profitable line: silk, sugar, olive oil, wheat, dyestuffs.[54] Outmaneuvering the Catalans, they soon controlled the lucrative trade in wool, Castile's greatest export.[55] But while the Genoese were savvy traders, it's in financing war that they changed the world.

THE MONETARY ORIGINS OF THE MILITARY

Financing war has always been difficult. Taxes trickle in slowly, waning and waxing with poor and good harvests. War making, in contrast, demands speed and liquidity. Soldiers must be armed, fed, housed, and—above all—paid reasonably quickly. Carthage learned this the hard way when its (yet unpaid) mercenaries sacked the great merchant city in 241 BCE.[56] Spain's Philip II learned it too when his mercenaries—again, unpaid—sacked Antwerp, at the time a part of the Spanish Empire, in 1576. Then, as now, wars were paid on credit. Governments may be happy to balance their budgets on the backs of the poor, but when workers are armed and organized, as soldiers have been trained to be, the calculus shifts. Pay the soldiers, owe the bankers, because the soldiers are armed. It was a sign of things to come.

In the late fifteenth century, European warfare experienced a fundamental transition: "the military revolution."[57] The size of armies grew—by a lot, and very fast. In 1470, Spain counted perhaps twenty thousand soldiers under arms; a century later, it had ten times as many.[58] If Spain was precocious, it wasn't by much. European armies grew tenfold between 1530 and 1710.[59] The costs of war rose even faster.[60] New cannons were expensive to make and even more expensive to use: by the seventeenth century, a single cannon shot "was about equal to ... a month's pay for an infantryman."[61] A single major battle—as when English forces besieged the French at Boulogne for fifty-five days in 1544—might involve 150,000 cannonades. Fortifications and town defenses across Europe were renovated at huge expense. Queen Elizabeth, for instance, spent 130,000 pounds—half the crown's annual revenue—to modernize the Berwick-upon-Tweed fortress, right on the English-Scottish border.[62]

Because modern war depends on a state's capacity to borrow, an empire's credit score largely determines its ability to win on the battlefield. Bankrupt empires have a way of folding—as when the Soviet Union went broke in the 1980s after competing in the arms race. In the sixteenth century, the tradition of kings borrowing money to pay for war was well established, but the scale of new war debt had novel consequences. Once again, the Spanish connection is important. It was Charles V (1500–1558)—a grandson of Ferdinand and Isabella, and the king of Spain, as Carlos I, from 1516—who led the way. By 1519 he was also the holy Roman emperor, ruling over a pan-European realm that stretched from the North Sea to the Caribbean, and his was a reign filled with conflict. He turned from the central European Fuggers and Welsers to the Genoese to fund his wars.[63] Advancing loans to Charles, the Genoese demanded as collateral a first claim—not always honored—on American silver. Based on genocide and colonial brutality, this agreement established an enduring, and very modern, relationship: credit as a way of organizing global nature, world power, and planetary work. For nearly two centuries the Genoese banking families—with names like Centurione, Pallavicino, Spinola, and Grimaldi—were intimately involved in "the most important political and military decisions of the Spanish kings," touching on virtually "all aspects of Spanish economic life."[64] Indeed, it was Francisco Pinelo who organized, in 1503, and led the Casa de Contratación—Spain's ministry of foreign trade.[65] No wonder that in 1617 the Spaniard Cristóbal Suárez de Figueroa lamented that Spain had become "the Indies of the Genoese."[66]

Charles never quite learned that by itself, military force in a capitalist ecology is a limited form of world power. He burned through cash and had blood and debt to show for it. When his armies besieged Metz, in northeast France, in 1552, he spent two and a half million ducats: equivalent to a decade of the crown's share of American silver and gold.[67] Borrowing tens of millions of ducats, he left his son Philip II massively indebted on the latter's accession in 1556. Philip declared bankruptcy the next year, only to borrow yet more: a debt valued at thirty million ducats in 1556 doubled to sixty million by 1575 and reached one hundred million by 1598.[68] By the beginning of the seventeenth century, two-thirds—in some years more—of Spain's budget was committed to military spending.[69] Legions of tax collectors made possible its armies of death. In an era when economic growth was measured in fractions of a percentage point, Spain's tax receipts increased nearly 12 percent per year in the three decades after 1474, from nine hundred thousand to twenty-six million reales.[70] Revenues doubled again in real terms from the 1520s to the 1550s.[71] Although, as Benjamin Franklin wrote in 1789, "in this world nothing can be said to be certain, except death and taxes," cheap money links the two.[72]

The modern art of war became a way to turn gold and blood into capital. States wanted expanded territory and power but needed money secure these. As the costs of war rose, they borrowed more money and taxed accordingly—if the size of armies grew tenfold in the sixteenth century, the cost of fielding them likely grew twentyfold. Between 1500 and 1700, major wars raged for all but twenty-eight years.[73] No matter the outcome, then, war was profitable for the financiers.

Money, loaned to states, became capital. There were risks involved; bankers sometimes went bust. But the overall trend was clear. In a modern world with one financial system and many states jostling for power, the states would keep fighting, and keep borrowing. Massively indebted Spain, for a time richer and more militarily powerful than its rivals, tried—and failed—to subdue the Dutch Republic for most of the late sixteenth and early seventeenth centuries. The Dutch Republic was endowed with neither the riches of the New World nor abundant natural resources nor a large population. But it had two things the Spanish didn't: a vigorous manufacturing and commercial economy, and the riches that went with it. The Spaniards had gold and silver bullion; the Dutch had *capital.* The Dutch Republic became the superpower of the seventeenth century, using financial power itself as a mercantile weapon to conduct war by other means,[74] while Spain commenced a long stagnation and settled uncomfortably into the middling ranks of European powers.

CAPITALISM'S ECOLOGY: A GLOBAL STORY

So far we have discussed territorial power in a strictly geopolitical sense. But the shift from military to financial power was accompanied by another feature: modern colonialism. While Europe's states were fighting one another to a standstill across the early modern centuries, they were also making global empires. There had been massive empires before capitalism—think of the Romans or the Mongols. But never before in world history had there been transoceanic empires that scoured the globe for profit-making opportunities.

If it were simply the case that states made capital and capital made states, the cycle of war making and capital accumulation would have broken down quickly. Waging war against powerful rivals is a lose-lose situation. But early modern empires were organized not only to fight other empires but also to appropriate the unpaid work of human and other natures. If the brutality of early Spanish imperialism suggests appropriation as theft and butchery, such plunder was necessarily short lived. The Spaniards had to find ways to turn their colonies into a regular stream of wealth—predominantly in the form silver—and then turn it into money, with the help of Genoese and other bankers.

The dearth of sound money in the fifteenth century sat atop a crisis in medieval mining. As the economic revival after 1450 gathered momentum, however, technological advances and new business organization coincided to make the old mines profitable again. If we're accustomed to thinking of this era as one of merchants and bankers, it's worth noting that the fivefold expansion of silver, copper, and iron output in the second half of the fifteenth century was deeply industrial. The Fuggers who bankrolled Charles V grew rich on mining and metallurgy characterized by cutting-edge technology—for instance, the *Saigerprozess,* capable of extracting silver from low-grade ores—and something resembling the modern firm. But of all these metals, silver required the most energy to smelt. Central Europe's kings, dukes, and princes all wanted a share of the profits, and forest access in nearly all of the German states became tightly regulated during the sixteenth century. As we've seen, the forests were enclosed and thinned, and peasant access to what remained was sharply limited. By the 1520s, the "battle for wood" met up with the grievances of a greatly expanded working class that labored in the mines and smelters. The German Peasants' War of 1525 and other forms of worker unrest resulted in higher wages in the mines. Together, resistance and depletion meant a profit squeeze for mine owners in Europe. The 1544 "discovery" of silver in Potosí (then in Peru, now in present-day Bolivia) couldn't have come at a better time.[75]

So important was American silver to Spain's strategic interests that Philip II dispatched the aristocrat Francisco de Toledo in 1568 to revive the Viceroyalty of Peru's lagging silver output. One of his earliest interventions was the repurposing of an Indigenous labor regime: the mita. Every community in the sixteen provinces around Potosí had to send one in seven men to work in the silver mines. These men, called *mitayos,* were required to work from dawn until dusk.[76] This stipulation, enforced by violence, was waived on Sundays and Christian holidays. Toledo had been in Valladolid when Las Casas and Sepúlveda had debated the status of Indigenous humans in the New World (see introduction), and duties of care for the soul and inculcation into Christianity featured in his labor draft system. He knew that Indigenous People were in the realm of nature but might redeem their souls through labor.

The demands on the mitayos didn't involve a direct expropriation of land. While paid minimal wages, they were also required to self-organize the journey to Potosí and forced to buy their own tools and food. This labor system demanded much less capital investment than slavery, whose entrepreneurs bore both the purchase price of slaves and the costs of their maintenance. Because the mita imposed the costs of reproductive labor on the mitayos' home communities, these groups had to trade with the Spanish to access funds and food to allow their migrant workers to survive both while they worked and while they weren't working. This system had apocalyptic effects on Indigenous workers, with some estimates suggesting an 85 percent drop in population between 1560 and 1590.[77]

The human cataclysm found its analogue in the forest. Initially, the silver pulled from Cerro Rico (Rich mountain) was smelted in wood-burning furnaces. On the mountainside, thousands of small windblown furnaces called *huayras* were lit at dusk, "turning night into day," according to one eyewitness, so that indigenous Andeans might smelt some of the mountain's silver to spend on their own survival.[78] Small furnaces weren't enough for the Spanish, however. Viceroy Toledo's other intervention at the frontier was the introduction of a new, fuel-saving technology to extract silver: mercury amalgamation. It operated at a scale that dwarfed huayra production, in vats containing five thousand pounds (2,268 kilograms) of crushed ore. Its success, like that of Madeira's sugar industry, depended on feats of hydraulic engineering—in this case the construction of some thirty dams. These frequently burst, killing hundreds of mitayos at a time and polluting the water for those left behind. Yet despite being a "cold" process compared to smelting, mercury amalgamation drove rates of deforestation *up*. It used less fuel for every pound of silver, but the sheer volume of output—a 600 percent increase between 1575 and 1590—expanded fuel consumption dramatically.[79] So voracious was the combination of small smelters and mercury amalgamation extraction that by 1590 wood had to be brought in from nearly three hundred miles (five hundred kilometers) away. By the early sixteenth century there was little sign that the mountain of Potosí had ever been home to any trees—or indeed a vibrant Indigenous civilization.[80]

Once again we can see cheapness at work. Cheap lives turned into cheap workers dependent on cheap care and cheap food in home communities, requiring cheap fuel to collect and process cheap nature to produce cheap money—and quite a lot of it. Potosí was the single most important silver source in the New World, and New World silver constituted 74 percent of the world's sixteenth-century silver production.[81] Silver does not make trade, but global trade can be traced from the mines of Potosí. Unless it forms part of circuits of exchange, silver is just shiny dirt. It's the fusion of commodity production and exchange that turns it into capital.

That's why some commentators have suggested that the birth year of global trade was 1571, when the city of Manila was founded.[82] Silver from the New World didn't stay in Europe but was propelled along the spice routes and later across the Pacific. Japanese silver flowed to China from 1540 to 1620 as part of a complex network of exchange and arbitrage.[83] Without the connection of exchange of silver for Asian commodities, money couldn't flow from the New World into East Asia. Because the Portuguese and then the Dutch controlled maritime silver flows through Europe to Asia, the Spanish short-circuited them, annually sending as much silver (fifty tons) across the Pacific and through Manila as they did across the Atlantic through Seville.[84] Similar volumes of silver found their way to the Baltic. In eastern Europe, silver combined with credit, quasi-feudal landlords, and enserfed labor to deliver cheap timber, food, and vital raw materials to the Dutch Republic. To remember this is to insist that, although Europe features in it, capitalism's story isn't a Eurocentric one. The rise of capitalism integrated life and power from Potosí to Manila, from Goa to Amsterdam.

As capitalism's ecology spread through international trade, so did its stowaways. If you've ever been troubled by fire ants, you can blame the international bullion trade—they were the first international stowaways of the silver circuit. From southwestern Mexico through Europe or Acapulco and Manila to Taiwan, just as the specie flowed, so did this species.[85] A new planetary ecology was in the making.

WHY BANKERS NEED GOVERNMENTS

Even before capitalism, bankers faced a problem that persists today. Although it is clear that governments need bankers to fund war, bankers need governments too. Those with money are necessarily vulnerable to those with guns—or in different eras, swords and spears. Premodern merchants could be—and were—subject to political confiscations. Even with the rise of capitalism, bankers were still vulnerable. As conflicts between European countries grew—and as armies and the money to field them grew even faster—the Genoese and others turned that weakness into strength. The demand for credit rose faster than the states' capacity to intimidate and confiscate funds.

The inverse of this problem was that while capitalists had power over states, they were powerless to perform one of the key tasks of states in the modern world: identify, map, and secure cheap nature. Joseph Schumpeter famously observed that "without protection from some non-bourgeois group," capitalists are "politically helpless."[86] When property conditions are established, populations subdued, flora and fauna mapped, and infrastructures built, capitalists do pretty well. But this all relies on credit and the militaries it can buy, and it's worth pressing the difference between banking and other kinds of capitalist activity.

The historian Fernand Braudel offered an explanation of the dynamics of change between finance and commerce: "I would even argue that in the past—in say Genoa or Amsterdam—following a wave of growth in commercial capitalism and the accumulation of capital on a scale beyond the normal channels for investment, finance capitalism was already in a position to take over and dominate, for a while at least, all the activities of the business world."[87] While money, credit, and financial speculation are often taken as "economic" processes, the truth is that modern money flows because state institutions secure exchanges and defend the underlying system of cheap nature against unruly human and other natures.

Financiers needed all the standard protection that European crowns and courts delivered, plus something extra: permission and cover from the government to create new means of payment. Banks make credit. They take an asset—such as metal, oil, a house, the Holy Grail—and turn it into more money. As long as these new means of payment circulate and are not cashed in, they are potential sources of pure profit. But whether those credits are Genoese *compere* backed by the Holy Grail or collateralized debt obligations backed by dodgy mortgages, some power is needed to endorse and encourage them, and the profits that follow. Hence the role of a credible "lender of last resort"—a state bank or, more recently, the International Monetary Fund (IMF)—an institution that, with hard currency and military connections, can guarantee a given hegemonic order.

This is a dynamic system. As we mentioned at the start of this chapter, the rhythms of world money and world power are deeply entangled. After an initial flurry of productive activity at new frontiers, Giovanni Arrighi argues, "decreasing returns set in; competitive pressures on the system's governmental and business agencies intensify; and the stage is set for the change of phase from material to financial expansion."[88] After a roughly century-long cycle of accumulation has generated profits and more liquid capital, the balance of power shifts in a moment of crisis away from the capitalists who organized the accumulation and into the hands of bankers. This happened in the Genoese, Dutch, and British Empires, and it's now playing out in the United States. But there's something very different about the era of financialization that began in the 1980s. Previous great financial expansions could all count on imperialism to extend profit-making opportunities into significant new frontiers of cheap nature. Recent bursts of "land grabbing," of public, peasant, and Indigenous land dispossession and privatization,[89] have been accompanied by ocean grabs[90] and even a new space race.[91] The extraordinary volatility of financial markets speaks not only to the dominance of finance capital but also to its weakness. At some point, bets on the future must pay off. And that's precisely what past centuries' frontiers of work, food, energy, and raw materials enabled. Today, those frontiers are smaller than ever before, and the volume of capital looking for new investment is greater than ever before. This unprecedented situation explains something of the extraordinary coupling of radical wealth inequality and profound financial instability that now shapes our world. War and violence drip from every pore of this coupling, but this time there's no meaningful promise of creative destruction—only destruction.

This explains not just why it is possible for Goldman Sachs to have its hands in everything but why, at this moment, it's inevitable that Goldman Sachs is everywhere. From the fifteenth- and late sixteenth-century Genoese financier diaspora to the Amsterdam banking societies that reaped the rewards of Dutch colonialism to the British merchant banks that invested in exploitation at home and abroad to today's global financial elite, the relationship among states, financiers, and other capitalists has led to the rise and fall of cycles of accumulation.

CONTEMPORARY THREADS

Armed with this world-ecological history of cheap money, we can place contemporary financial capitalism in a broader context. The ever-increasing sophistication of financial engineering emerges not as "the rise of the quants" but as the outcome of centuries of accumulation, each with its distinctive ways of organizing capital, power, and nature. Flash trading, and the ability to make millions from trading decisions that are executed in milliseconds, is an extension of the first Genoese accountant recording that a particular transaction happened in the morning rather than the afternoon. Public-private partnerships and the mortgaging of state resources to inside dealers look, yet again, like the sale of the Holy Grail to the right buyer.[92]

Analysis that stretches back to the fifteenth century is above all practical. Recently—and hardly for the first time—Greece has suffered the wrath of forces beyond its borders. Because of reasons well documented elsewhere, the country was compelled in 2015 to adopt a series of measures on terms that systematically siphoned away its wealth and guaranteed that it would never repay its debt.[93] This was not a neoliberal policy in the conventional sense.[94] Indeed, the IMF recommended debt relief "far beyond what Europe [had] been willing to consider so far" in the name of extracting money from Greece at a rate that wouldn't entirely destroy its economy.[95]

The IMF had pointed out that systemically big banks—ones "too big to fail"—already had governments in their pockets. It also reported that the public was being made to pay for lax regulation, which allowed banks to find new ways to sell the credit they created and rely on central government insurance when those bets caused systemic crashes.[96] Yet the imperative for Germany to secure fiscal hegemony over Europe was more important than the economics lesson offered by the IMF. Power was more important than doctrine. The imperatives of empire and finance in the fifteenth century are still with us in the twenty-first.

Inevitably, payments to banks happen by exploiting workers and appropriating the rest of nature's work as much as possible. In Greece, debts were paid by intensifying the sell-off of natural assets, despite the ruling government's touting of its environmental credentials.[97] You can still see Greek "nature," of course, but it's fenced in, accessible at resorts and compounds where tourists with money acceptable to the country's creditors can enjoy, at bargain prices, the countryside and sea as commodities, exchanging euros for service at the bar. Across their economy, Greeks report working longer hours than Germans, yet they still manage to attract stereotypes of laziness, unlike their Teutonic counterparts.[98] This isn't an error in reporting—it shows how the work of some people has been appropriated differently from that of others. To understand how this has happened and how it continues, we need to examine more fully the ways that human time and effort transform nature into money. The work of work is the subject of our next chapter.

CHAPTER THREE

Cheap Work

As he sailed through the Caribbean, Columbus lamented his ignorance about the potential commercial returns of its unfamiliar flora and fauna. But he could appraise one component of the fauna quite well: the humans. He knew how to control his Indigenous captives, hazarded a guess at their capacity for work, and ultimately encouraged their export to Europe. "Let us in the name of the Holy Trinity go on sending all the slaves that can be sold," he wrote to Ferdinand and Isabella after his second voyage.[1] How did he know their value?[2] Because slaves were part of the fabric of his life in Europe. Columbus's childhood in Genoa put him in proximity to slaves, slavers, and traders in human bondage. He was also caught up in longer circuits and histories of exploitation by the Spanish and Portuguese, whose familiarity with slavery stretched back centuries: in Madeira, the Portuguese had first used Canarian slaves to produce sugar.[3] The Iberians had acquired this workforce through colonial conquest and legal chicanery. We'll have cause to revisit the jurisprudence of misery and race in chapter 7, on cheap lives. For now, though, we need to establish the relationship between work, nature, and finance.

During the Crusades, military rules of engagement permitted the capture of Saracens (Muslims) as enemy combatants, and their enslavement. Humans were a spoil of war, seized in the expansion of territorial control, and a means of repaying debts owed to the bankers of the holy war.[4] There were, however, no Muslims on the Canary Islands. Yet the imperative to return a profit on colonialism remained. So the Portuguese crown requested and received permission from Rome for its subjects to capture and enslave *any* north or west Africans they encountered on their colonial adventures. It was widely known that many north and west African residents weren't Muslims and therefore weren't enemies of Christendom in the required theological sense, but in 1452, Pope Nicholas V wrote to King Alfonso V of Portugal to give his permission anyway:

> Justly desiring that whatsoever concerns the integrity and spread of the faith, for which Christ our God shed his blood, shall flourish in the virtuous souls of the faithful ... we grant to you by these present documents, with our Apostolic Authority, full and free permission to invade, search out, capture and subjugate the Saracens and pagans and any other unbelievers and enemies of Christ wherever they may be, as well as their kingdoms, duchies, counties, principalities, and other property ... *and to reduce their persons into perpetual slavery, and to apply and appropriate and convert to the use and profit of yourself and your successors,* the Kings of Portugal, in perpetuity, the above-mentioned kingdoms, duchies, counties, principalities, and other property and possessions and suchlike goods.[5]

Papal papers likewise became vital in amassing workforces in the New World. Since it was hard to argue that residents of the Americas harbored actual enmity toward Christianity, a new criterion emerged: ignorance. What people knew, and didn't know, became the proper subject of the state, for the purposes of acquiring and managing a labor force.[6] Indigenous People who were ignorant of Christ needed, first, to be told of him, and of his vicar on earth. If they refused to accept this news with an embrace of their new monarchs in Iberia and the pope in Rome, provisions of warfare similar to those of the Crusades could sanction their enslavement. The 1513 *Requerimiento,* a nine-paragraph document that was read aloud in Spanish, was written to inform Indigenous People of their choices. It begins with a brief introduction to Christianity and the people who had arrived in the New World before requiring acceptance of the sovereignty of Spain and the pope, or else

> I certify to you that with the help of God we shall powerfully enter [into your country], and will wage war against you in all the ways and manners that we can, and shall subject you to the yoke and obedience of the Church and of their Majesties; we will take your people and your wives and your children, and will make slaves of them, and as such will sell and dispose of them as their Majesties may command; and we will take away your goods, and will do you all the evils and damage that we can, as to vassals who do not obey and refuse to receive their master, and resist and contradict him; and we protest that the deaths and losses which follow are your fault, and not that of their Majesties, nor ours, nor of the men who come with us.[7]

To hear the sound of these words, read by metaled strangers in the tropical heat, was to hear your judgment in a language you might never understand. It was an order to die by work. The document and its protocols did the job, providing abundant labor and starting an apocalypse among Indigenous People.[8] Concerns that the process might not be entirely legitimate mounted to such an extent that Charles V temporarily suspended colonial activities in the spring of 1551 so that a panel of fourteen judges could determine whether the war against the Indians was just. If the Indians were unsinning and ignorant, the property scooped up by the Spanish conquest and the Indigenous labor applied to it were acquired illegitimately.[9] These were the stakes in the Valladolid debate, which we discussed in the introduction. In his debate against Sepúlveda before the panel, Las Casas conceded that there is a hierarchy of life, that some kinds of humans are superior to others. At issue was the position of Indigenous People in this hierarchy and the duties of Christian conquerors toward them. In the end, it was resolved that although Indigenous People aren't part of society, they might escape their place in nature through generations of labor.

Note the toxic chemistry of greed and piety.[10] If colonization was to proceed, God had to be okay with it. Ultimately, it was the duty of care for Indigenous souls that licensed the appropriation of their land and their labor to work it, in the service of civilization. The Valladolid controversy succeeded not just in drawing the line between European humans and "natural" savages elsewhere but in establishing the legitimacy of that line for the purposes of labor. Indeed, it was through labor and piety that Indigenous People might, over two generations, succeed in releasing themselves from the bonds of the *Requerimiento.* In that time they would be schooled not just in Christ but in the proper value of dividing humanity and nature through work, while the Spanish reaped the silver and their lives.

Here lies one of capitalism's most sinister accounting tricks. Putting most humans into the category of Nature rather than Society enabled an audacious act of frontier bookkeeping. The salaries of soldiers, administrators, and sailors were charged in and paid through a cash nexus. But the volume of work produced through the cash nexus depended on much greater flows of work outside that nexus—yet within reach of capitalist power. The appropriation—really, a kind of ongoing theft—of the unpaid work of "women, nature and colonies" is the fundamental condition of the exploitation of labor power in the commodity system. You can't have one without the other.[11] When we talk of cheap work, then, we're getting at the ways that capitalism sets in motion not just human work and not just agriculture and resources—but how they fit together, and the relations that bind human and extrahuman work at every turn.

Why is such boundary enforcing necessary to capitalism? Simply put, because paid workers are expensive and become more expensive over time. This happens for all sorts of reasons. Workers organize and struggle, and as capitalism develops, it stamps out alternative sources of income and care. And if wage-workers in this expanded sense bear the costs—often horrifically, in the case of the billion-plus informal workers whom Mike Davis calls "surplus humanity"[12]—so too must capitalists. Every act of producing surplus value depends on a greater act of appropriating human and extrahuman life beyond the cash nexus. This logic was applied to workers not just in the New World but also, increasingly, in Europe. The unfolding of this logic and the strategies and counterstrategies of cheap work are the subjects of this chapter.

THE TEMPORAL ECOLOGY OF WAGE LABOR

Work was never meant to be fun. Consider the etymology of the French *travail* and the Spanish *trabajo,* each a translation of the English noun *work:* their Latin root is *trepaliare,* "to torture, to inflict suffering or agony."[13] But the way work works, and works on nature, has changed. For millennia, most humans survived through more or less intimate relations with land and sea. Even those who didn't were closely connected to the tasks and objects of labor. Human survival depended on holistic, not fragmented, knowledge: fishers, nomads, farmers, healers, cooks, and many others experienced and practiced their work in a way directly connected to the web of life. Farmers, for instance, had to know soils, weather patterns, seeds—in short, everything from planting to harvest. That didn't mean work was pleasant. Slaves were often treated brutally, although not with the same genocidal recklessness that characterized life and death in the Americas after 1492.[14] Nor did it mean that the relations of work were equitable: guild masters exploited journeymen, lords exploited serfs, men exploited women, the old exploited the young. But work was premised on a holistic sense of production and a connection to wider worlds of life and society.[15]

Like work, nature was integral to life. Medieval Europe's sense of nature was one of mutual dependence, as we have seen. That didn't mean there was no distinguishing between humans and the rest of nature—only that these categories were conceived of and lived in a holistic way. Humans had long recognized a difference between themselves and the rest of the world.[16] But that difference was a distinction, and not—as it became after Columbus—an *organizing principle.*

The modern worlds of work and nature emerged simultaneously from the ashes of European feudalism in the long fourteenth century (c. 1315–1453). Feudal agriculture, while enormously varied, was a mix of sustainability and soil mining.[17] Soil exhaustion threatened lordly wealth and peasant livelihoods, but the lord-peasant relationship limited the surplus that might be reinvested into agricultural productivity. Meanwhile, rising population density masked faltering soil fertility—more toil could compensate for tired soil in any case, as feudal lords were more concerned with the size of the crop than with the labor involved in planting and harvesting it.

This began to change in the sixteenth century as *land* productivity became less urgent and lucrative a concern than *labor* productivity. The enterprising Dutch or English farmer—and the Madeiran, then Brazilian, sugar planter—was increasingly connected to growing international markets for a processed good and correspondingly more interested in the relationship between work time and the harvest. As we saw in chapter 1, land in England was consolidated though enclosure, which concurrently "freed" a growing share of the rural population from the commons that they had tended, supported, and survived on. These newly displaced peasants were free to find other work and free to starve or face imprisonment if they failed. Workers and new relations to land were thus produced simultaneously. In the seventeenth and eighteenth centuries, elite fears of the itinerant poor resulted in harsh laws against vagabondage and the development of charities to ameliorate the worst effects of enforced destitution.[18] Government-sponsored threats of imprisonment were a strategy to move the poor into waged work, an activity that took the intelligence, strength, and dexterity of humans and disciplined them to productive labor using another modern invention: a new way of measuring time.

If the practice of labor rather than land productivity shapes capitalism's ecology, its indispensable machine is the mechanical clock.[19] The clock—not money—emerged as the key technology for measuring the value of work. This distinction is crucial because it's easy to think that working for wages is capitalism's signature. It's not: in thirteenth-century England a third of the economically active population depended on wages for survival.[20] That wages have become a decisive way of structuring life, space, and nature owes everything to a new model of time.

By the early fourteenth century, the new temporal model was shaping industrial activity. In textile-manufacturing towns like Ypres, in what is now Belgium, workers found themselves regulated not by the flow of activity or the seasons but by a new kind of time—abstract, linear, repetitive. In Ypres, that work time was measured by the town's bells, which rang at the beginning and end of each work shift. By the sixteenth century, time was measured in steady ticks of minutes and seconds.[21] This abstract time came to shape everything—work and play, sleep and waking, credit and money, agriculture and industry, even prayer. By the end of the sixteenth century, most of England's parishes had mechanical clocks.[22] In the twentieth century, as assembly lines in Detroit churned out Henry Ford's Model T, "scientific managers" were measuring units of work called therbligs (an anagram of their developers' last name, Gilbreth): each one a mere one-thousandth of a second.[23]

The conquest of the Americas therefore involved inculcating in their residents a new notion of time as well as of space. Wherever European empires penetrated, there appeared the image of the "lazy" native, ignorant of the imperatives of Christ and the clock. Policing time was central to capitalism's ecology.[24] As early as 1553 the Spanish crown began installing "at least one public clock" in its major colonial cities.[25] Other civilizations had their own sophisticated temporal rules, but the new regimes of work displaced Indigenous tempos and relationships with extrahuman life. The Mayan calendar is a complex hierarchy of times and readings from the heavens, offering a rich set of arrangements of humans within the universe.[26] Spanish invaders respected it only to this extent: they synchronized their colonial assaults to sacred moments in the calendar.[27]

As Edward Thompson observes, the governance of time follows a particular logic: "in mature capitalist society all time must be consumed, marketed, put to use; it is offensive for the labour force merely to 'pass the time.'"[28] The connection of specific activities to larger productive goals didn't allow for time theft, and the discipline of the clock was enforced by violence across the planet.[29]

Teaching new subjects the value and structure of capitalist time was a key part of the colonial enterprise. One settler noted in 1859 that Aboriginal Australians "now ... have the advantage of dating from the 'Nip Nip,' or Settlers' yearly regular shearing time. This seems to supply them with a mode of stating years, which before they had not. Months or moons then satisfied them."[30] But the regulation of time was also a focus of resistance. Another settler diarized, "This evening there was a grand Korroberry [*sic* for *corroboree,* an exuberant, possibly spiritual, gathering]—I endeavoured to dissuade them, telling them that it was Sunday—but they said 'black fellow no Sunday.'"[31] Why the resistance? Because they knew full well that their labor was the object of theft, that colonists were appropriating their work.[32] Before colonialism, like members of many hunter-gatherer societies, Aboriginal Australians could find enough food for themselves in less than six hours a day, far less than the twelve hours of the workday that capitalism imposed to reach the same result.[33] Resistance to the new regime was racialized as "lazy," and this view persists: in the United States more than 30 percent of whites view blacks as lazier than whites.[34]

Aboriginal Australians weren't alone in suffering the colonial practice of governing people through a "good day's work," the application of work and time to deploy labor for profit. Indigenous People, African slaves, sharecroppers, and wage earners worked under a variety of regimes, each of which was subject to constant revisions, in response to rebellions and in embrace of ever-more-efficient mechanisms to make workers work. In late medieval Europe, the rulers failed to restore feudalism because workers and peasants wouldn't have it; in the New World, Indigenous People fought enslavement but succumbed to European disease.[35] Early labor experiments encompassed forced wage work (the Andean mita), debt peonage, and indentured servitude.[36] These continued well into the twentieth century through debt-enforced (and strongly racialized) systems of debt-disciplining factory towns and sharecropping.

Some of these forms of work are occasionally called premodern, but a deeper consideration suggests otherwise. A sugar plantation in 1630s Brazil, for example, would be easily recognizable as a modern industrial operation in, say, the Bangladeshi textile industry.[37] "The specialization by skill and jobs, and the division of labor by age, gender, [race,] and condition into crews, shifts, and 'gangs,' together with the stress upon punctuality and discipline," Sidney Mintz observes, "are features associated more with industry than with agriculture"—especially before the Industrial Revolution.[38] The sugar plantation was a forerunner not only of today's industrial agriculture but of today's modern factory. These early modern sugar plantations not only were highly mechanical, with large, fuel-intensive boilers and heavy-duty rolling mills to extract cane juice from stalks, but also served as powerful drivers of "simplification": of the work process, as workers (slaves) were given simplified tasks, and of the land itself, which was reduced to a cane monoculture. Just as autoworkers on the line assemble simplified, interchangeable parts and fast-food workers manufacture standardized burgers, so did African slaves work specialized jobs in a simplified landscape of sugar monoculture.

The connections among work, nature, and this modern logic of simplification give us a way of grasping a longer continuity. Early capitalism's great commodity frontiers—of sugar, silver, copper, iron, forest products, fishing, and even cereal agriculture—were zones of experimentation in strategies of labor control in Europe and its colonies, and always spaces of conflict. Every resistance by labor was a new reason to bring in machines to work on uncommodified or minimally commodified natures. Modern work regimes and technologies emerged from the crucible of experiments, strategies, and resistances of early modern workers. By 1600, we find weaponized sugar mills in the cane fields of Brazil, sawmills in thickly forested Norway, and a huge, brutal hydraulic silver-mercury production complex in the Andes. We also find not only everyday forms of peasant resistance but active rebellion and workers' searches for alternatives,[39] the greatest being the slave rebellion on the sugar plantations of Saint-Domingue—the colony that would become Haiti.[40]

FOR EVERY GLOBAL FACTORY A GLOBAL FARM

Remember that capitalism gets its name from the "value in motion"[41] that is the transformation of money into commodity production and back again. Let's look at that exchange closely. Value is a specific crystallization of "the original sources of all wealth": human and extrahuman work.[42] Marx is useful here because he's always reminding us that human activity is part of nature—it's the power of money that gets between us and the direct "knowing" of the rest of nature. Like most work under capitalism, we experience nature in a way that's highly alienated. (Nature becomes a place we visit, not where we live.) Work and nature are given to us as separate domains of reality, a perception that has shaped environmentalist as well as labor politics. Marx's main point was that peasants, artisans, and others lose their direct access to the "means of production" under capitalism: someone else owns the tools, workshops, land, and stores, and capitalists pay workers to apply their labor to these means. Marx wanted to show that capitalism sees reality through the dualism of work and nature; at the same time, he reminds us that no such separation is possible: what happens to workers affects "external nature" and vice versa. In 1875, Marx chided German socialists who had forgotten a basic point: "Labour is not the source of all wealth. Nature is just as much the source of use values (and it is surely of such that material wealth consists!) as labour, *which itself is only the manifestation of a force of nature, human labour power.*"[43]

The insight that human labor is a "force of nature" and, in turn, that the web of life performs useful and necessary work permits a fresh view of how the concerns of environmentalists and labor activists have been separated into different domains and their common ground obscured. Seeing "jobs" and "environment" in a zero-sum conflict is analytically mistaken.[44] In 1875, Marx warned that the German socialists had erred when they considered labor the only source of wealth. They had, he thought, attributed "supernatural powers" to labor. One is tempted to make a similar point about twentieth-century environmentalists: they have ascribed supernatural powers to Nature—above all, the supernatural power to make or break civilization.

Understanding that both jobs and environments are made through capitalism can help to find grounds for solidarity and an opportunity for both environmentalist and labor movements to revisit their fundamental assumptions. There persists a powerful tendency to understand the modern world of work as somehow independent of the countryside, but *all* work has owed and continues to owe its existence to those countrysides. Every great era of capitalism has forged a relationship with agriculture that has pushed millions—and since the 1970s, hundreds of millions—of people off the farm.

Consider the US agricultural revolutions of the 1940s to 1970s, which we discuss in chapter 6, and of the nineteenth century. Both were premised on fossil fuel and industrial work. The South's plantations pumped cheap cotton into Britain's textile factories—themselves incubators of a brutal labor regime—from plants coproduced by the Mississippi delta's cheap labor and fertile soils. Slave numbers in the new frontier states like Alabama and Mississippi grew more than twentyfold from 1790 to 1860, and there were nearly four million slaves in the American South by 1860.[45] Enslaved workers were prodigiously productive, not least because the great plantations of the Mississippi delta were built atop another frontier of cheap work: rich alluvial soils.[46] Slavery was the cost of cheap cotton, whose price plummeted by more than 70 percent between 1785 and 1835.[47] The Southern cotton enterprise rested upon the eviction and extermination of native peoples who, like Mississippi's slaves, were cast into the realm of Nature. The exclusions of US agriculture and its subsequent exports of cotton and food made British industrialization possible in turn. Six of every seven English workers were employed outside agriculture by 1870. They needed to be fed—cheaply—and American agriculture was prepared to do exactly that. American grain exports to Britain increased fortyfold in the three decades after 1846.[48] That prodigious increase depended on agrarian industrialization: massive on-farm mechanization, which began modestly with reapers and other simple farm machines in the 1840s and grew rapidly in the following decades. By 1870, a quarter of American machine production was devoted to farm machinery.[49]

In that decade, not only did American grain feed English workers, but it also made possible a new world of work by wreaking havoc with European peasants in southern and eastern Europe. As American grain exports surged, grain prices collapsed—falling by half between 1882 and 1896.[50] Industrial agriculture makes food cheap by substituting peasants with capital. Then as now—we discuss NAFTA in the next chapter—peasants responded to their redundancy by migrating. Many moved to the United States, where they worked in the new industries of the second industrial revolution.[51]

We have come to call the industrial system that grew out of late nineteenth-century factories "Fordism," after the automaker Henry Ford. But we often miss a crucial point: Fordism was born on the farm. Its innovations built directly and immediately on the industrialization of the nineteenth-century family farm, the displacements that such farming enabled, and the technologies developed in its downstream food-processing industries—perhaps above all meat-packing's "disassembly lines."[52]

The food system was a laboratory for the spectrum of worker-management practices from slavery to unionized wage work. But it also provided an opportunity for workers to imagine politics differently. On these lines, as Upton Sinclair wrote in *The Jungle,* immigrant workers organized not just for better working conditions but for new ways to control the world. Although *The Jungle* is now remembered in the United States as a stomach-churning story of animal and worker cruelty, it concludes with the speech of a street organizer:

> Organize! Organize! Organize! … Fifty thousand Socialist votes in Chicago means a municipal-ownership Democracy in the spring! And then they will fool the voters once more, and all the powers of plunder and corruption will be swept into office again! But whatever they may do when they get in, there is one thing they will not do, and that will be the thing for which they were elected! They will not give the people of our city municipal ownership—they will not mean to do it, they will not try to do it; all that they will do is give our party in Chicago the greatest opportunity that has ever come to Socialism in America! We shall have the sham reformers self-stultified and self-convicted; we shall have the radical Democracy left without a lie with which to cover its nakedness! … Chicago will be ours! CHICAGO WILL BE OURS![53]

Chicago's politicians remain sham reformers, and the city has yet to turn Socialist. This has been in no small part because just as workers imagined a world in which their labor couldn't be cheapened, their bosses had different ideas.[54] The gambits that capitalists have used to keep work cheap and to forestall the radical solutions for which workers have organized were first developed in agriculture. In the cotton industry, for instance, a number of distinct tactics emerged. Cotton workers, who demanded too many concessions, were systematically displaced on both sides of the Atlantic by technologies that reduced the need for their labor (some industrial cotton-worker militants were themselves displaced handloom weavers).[55] Workers in one part of the world were pitted against those in another, with new trade routes opening up cheaper sources of cotton (saving time, money, and land for other more profitable uses).[56] Resources were spent developing alternative fibers (just as cotton replaced wool, so new textiles have threatened the negotiating power of cotton workers). And union power was smashed directly, by strike-breaking private police and through legislation aimed at keeping restive workers in their place.

The cotton industry was the site of some of the earliest workers' strikes on both sides of the Atlantic. In *Empire of Cotton,* Sven Beckert reports cotton worker protests in Britain in 1792 and handloom weaver petitions for a minimum wage in 1807 supported by 130,000 signatures.[57] The first US strike was led by women in 1824, when they walked away from a Rhode Island cotton mill. It's hardly a coincidence that at the other end of the industry, in the fields from which its raw materials were extracted, slaves rebelled.[58] Again, this was a global phenomenon happening across industries, on cotton and sugar plantations everywhere from the United States through Martinique to Bahia, Brazil, which saw a Muslim slave uprising in 1835.[59] In other words, at the same time when the industrial proletariat was finding its voice, slaves were finding theirs, linked through the same commodity and sometimes through direct bonds of solidarity among the colonized peoples of the Atlantic: slaves, the Irish, and commoners of all kinds.[60]

Worker unrest in factories and slave rebellions are linked not just because they're expressions of resistance but because they are articulated protests against capitalism's ecology. Every global factory needs a global farm: industrial, service, and technological enterprises rely on the extraction of work and cheap nature, barely accounted for, to thrive. The apps on your iPhone, designed in Cupertino, California, are coded by self-exploiting independent software engineers, depend on chips that are assembled in draconian workplaces in China, and run on minerals extracted in bloody conflict in the Democratic Republic of the Congo. Modern manufacturing relies on layered, simultaneous, and different regimes of work in nature. And with every resistance to it, capitalism has moved the frontiers of work yet again.

CONTROLLING WORK IN NATURE

The technologies of employer power in the workplace are so pervasive that they even made an appearance in a place we might least expect: the Soviet Union, where workers themselves—at least on paper—controlled the conditions of their labor. Although much is still made of how distinct the Soviets were from the capitalist West, the continuities outweigh the contrasts. The Soviet model was trapped by the same relations of work and nature. The logic of twentieth-century state communism was stuck in a sixteenth-century ecology.[61] In fact, the Soviets were rather keen on taking all manner of ideas from their capitalist foes, including those of the American time-and-motion expert Frederick Winslow Taylor, which were embraced—and contested—in Soviet industry. Lenin, who had earlier denounced "man's enslavement by the machine" under Taylorism, insisted in April 1918 that "we must definitely speak of the introduction of the Taylor System.... Without this, it will be impossible to raise productivity, and without that we will not usher in socialism."[62] In agriculture too, industrialization was enthusiastically embraced. Perhaps two thousand American agricultural experts spent time in the Soviet Union between 1927 and 1932, and Soviets visited industrial farms in the States. If Soviet and American approaches varied when it came to the mix of plan and market, they converged in their view of nature.[63] For Stalin (as for the Americans), nature was "an object to be manipulated ... [and] an enemy to be subjugated."[64]

Chinese communism went further in transforming relations of work through collectivism, but it was still infused with a strong Promethean streak. As part of his efforts to free China from famine, Mao declared war on the animals that ate Chinese grain in 1958. A two-day slaughter would, he thought, ensure the perpetual flourishing of China's population. Humans were to kill on sight the four major scourges of fleas, flies, rats, and sparrows. Although the fleas were uncounted, the government catalogued "48,695.49 kilos of flies, 930,486 rats and 1,367,440 individual sparrows."[65] Without sparrows to feed on it, the invertebrate population grew rapidly. Insects ate grain unchecked, contributing to the 1959–61 Great Chinese Famine.

For anxious capitalists, massive Chinese mortality was less of a concern than the threat that peasants might seize title to the land. In general, the threat of workers' power—under various radical banners—caused capitalists to change their strategies. Look, for instance, at the automobile industry. In the 1930s, sit-down strikes in the United States proved overwhelmingly effective in recruiting workers to a cause of militancy and hence forcing management to the negotiating table. In Flint, Michigan, the United Automobile Workers was able to get a contract with General Motors over the course of three months in early 1937. The entry of the United States into the Second World War momentarily stalled union organizing, but strike activity had returned to 1937 levels by 1944 and surged again after peace in 1945.[66] In postwar Japan, automakers tried to avoid the labor unrest characteristic of the American experience. Unable to smash unions entirely, they opted for managerial reorganization: instead of a single, vulnerable factory, they created a cascading series of subcontractors to produce and assemble all the components of a car, through which labor militancy could be defused and concessions more easily squeezed from workers in competition with one another.[67]

When workers' demands couldn't be corralled they were accommodated, even as visions for wider economic and social transformation—particularly those of American communists and socialists—were smashed by McCarthyism in the United States and parallel practices of anti-communism elsewhere.[68] In the global workplace, this accommodation meant the rise of corporatism, what Michael Burawoy has called a shift from "despotic" to "hegemonic" factory regimes.[69] Factory operators learned from one another, but so did workers, with more automotive strikes happening globally. By the 1990s, strikes were able to attract popular support in South Korea by representing not just workers' interests but those of a wider social bloc: citizens outside the factory yearning for more democracy from a state unwilling to concede it.[70] Automobile companies moved production to China, a place that promised freedom from labor unrest, yet worker discontent and protests continue today in China, and around the world.[71]

In summary, the creation of modern work happened in Europe through enclosure, a variegated process that transformed human relationships to the rest of nature and to the way days were spent—even down to the way time was understood. In the colonies, Natures were appropriated and the Indigenous workforce and then African slaves kept firmly in the domain of nature. Capitalism has always experimented with every available kind of labor system simultaneously. Hence the persistence today of slavery—which counts more people at the time of writing than were transported across the Atlantic as slaves[72]—and of wartime work camps in, say, the Democratic Republic of the Congo, alongside new kinds of work in "the sharing economy." In each case, management looks just beyond the horizon of current labor practice to reimagine and reinvent how our working lives might link with one another, and with nature beyond them.

Capitalism, however, could not survive a day without a third moment of work: the appropriation of human reproductive labor, conducted largely outside the cash nexus. The global factory and the global farm each relies on a family, on a community of care. Thus a revolutionary politics of sustainability must recognize—and mobilize through the contradictions of—a tripartite division of work under capitalism: labor power, unpaid care work, and the work of nature as a whole. Worker exploitation is bound together with the appropriation of extrahuman nature and the unpaid work of care. The rise of capitalism, as we have seen, was tightly linked to the expulsion of women from society and into the realm of cheap—and cheapened—natures.[73] It's time now for us to explore the boundaries of what has counted as payable work and as the kind of work offered, by nature, as a "free gift" to the economy.

CHAPTER FOUR

Cheap Care

We don't know enough about Christopher Columbus's wife, Filipa Moniz Perestrelo. We know that her father, Bartolomeo, had been given Porto Santo, off the coast of Madeira, by Portugal's Prince Henry the Navigator.[1] Although her inheritance had already been spent, she brought family nobility to her wedding. She was nineteen when she married Columbus, in 1457 or 1458.[2] He had met her at a Mass in Lisbon, in a church run by nuns associated with the Order of Santiago, a crusading fraternity.[3] Perestrelo had a son in 1479 or 1480 and died in 1484, and little else is certain.[4] We know that Columbus took a mistress (whose cousin he left to die in the New World). As soon as Columbus saw his Indigenous hosts, he noticed that "they go as naked as when their mothers bore them, and so do the women, although I did not see more than one young girl."[5] A month later he kidnapped half a dozen women, thinking that the men he'd already abducted would be more servile with female company.

Figure 1. William Blake, *Europe, Supported by Africa and America*, 1796. Source: Stedman 1796, 394.

On his second voyage, the now Lord Admiral Columbus was accompanied by an Italian aristocrat, Michele de Cuneo, who wrote,

> While I was in the boat I captured a very beautiful Carib woman, whom the said Lord Admiral gave to me, and with whom having taken her into my cabin, she being naked according to their custom, I conceived desire to take pleasure. I wanted to put my desire into execution but she did not want it and treated me with her finger nails in such a manner that I wished I had never begun. But seeing that ... I took a rope and thrashed her well, for which she raised such unheard of screams that you would not have believed your ears. Finally we came to an agreement in such manner that I can tell you that she seemed to have been brought up in a school of harlots.[6]

Even though there's little explicitly about women in Columbus's diaries, they contain a great deal about gender—about how a differentiation by sex mattered in the order of things, about how workers might be managed, about how women might be owned. The language of sex and sexuality cropped up on Columbus's third voyage when he wrote to the Spanish monarchs that the world was not a sphere but more breast shaped, with Paradise on the nipple.[7] Sailing around the world, the resources and people of the "other world" succumbing to him, Columbus conquered virgin lands for his king and queen. There's no necessary reason why the language of sex should also be the language with which silver mines were acquired.[8] Yet as some humans moved across the surface of the planet, bringing it under the reign of property, they compassed it as they would a sexual conquest. The reign of cheap nature and cheap work was, from the beginning, a transformation not just in how and what humans could own but also in who could own and work, how they would be born, and how they would be cared for.

The work of cooking, teaching, nurturing, healing, organizing, and sacralizing predates capitalism. Modern humans' first large-scale ecological transformations were caused by the work of care, particularly through the application of fire.[9] But at capitalism's frontier, care activities underwent dramatic changes, reflecting and amplifying early modern Christian ideas of sex and power. Almost from the beginning, sex mattered in the colonial encounter. The word Columbus used to talk about the Arawak men was *mancebo,* suggesting adolescence and presexuality. Indigenous men were emasculated in Columbus's telling of them, and future colonial wars were characterized by the notion that the defeat of Indigenous warriors by the Spanish involved their sexual as well as military subjugation.[10] Consider, for instance, the 1519 letter to King Charles V of Spain from the council of Veracruz suggesting that he seek the pope's permission to punish Indigenous People because "such punishment [might] serve as a further occasion of warning and dread to those who still rebel, and thus dissuade them from such great evils as those which they work in the service of the devil. For in addition to children and men and women [being] killed and offered in sacrifice, we have learned and have been informed that they are doubtless all sodomites and engage in that abominable sin."[11]

Yucatán Mayan sexuality scandalized Spanish colonialists. This isn't because Mayan society was an egalitarian bacchic love-in. On the contrary, sex was subject to well-defined hierarchies, circumscribed in ways Spanish colonists might have recognized had they not been overwhelmed by unfamiliarity. In place of Adam and Eve's shame at their own nakedness, Mayan gods stabbed their own penises. Instead of putting Communion wafers in their mouths, Mayan noblewomen ran rope through their pierced tongues. In Mayans' belief in the possibility of knowing gods carnally, Spanish colonists saw only the promise of sedition and shame.[12]

Some Yucatán Mayans used colonial prudishness against their colonizers. In his highly original work, Pete Sigal has uncovered stories such as one in which an anonymous local accuses four Catholic priests of having sex in a church:

> Father Díaz, squad corporal, has a woman from Bolonchen called Ántonia Alvarado, whose vagina he repeatedly penetrates before the whole community, and Father Granado bruises Manuela Pacheco's vagina all night.... If a good commoner does that, the priest always punishes him immediately. But look at the priests' excessive fornication, putting their hands on these whores' vaginas, even saying mass like this. God willing, when the English come may they not be fornicators equal to these priests, who only lack carnal acts with men's anuses. God willing that smallpox be rubbed into their penis heads. Amen.[13]

What was normal under Mayan religious codes was retold in imperial cadences as a scandal that demanded swift action by the Spanish. These priests may have been placed elsewhere as a result, but such acts of resistance and subversion weren't able to stop the policing of which bodies did what. In her studies of colonial history, Ann Stoler observes a long line of European colonial fantasies and fears about Indigenous sexualities that sat atop some very rigid ideas about order and power: "Who wedded and bedded whom in the colonies of France, England, Holland and Iberia was never left to chance."[14] Recent archaeology has suggested just how central the policing of sexuality and bodies was to the imperial project. As Barbara Voss notes, the "violent suppression of two-spirits and same-sex sexuality was only part of the program of sexual control implemented by missionaries and military officials. With military support, missionaries also targeted premarital and extramarital sex, polygamy, and the use of birth control. As much as 25 percent of the annual mission budget for the Californias was used to purchase clothes to cover the Native [Californians'] 'indecency.'"[15]

What does this have to do with world-ecology? Everything.[16] Indigenous systems of gender were far more capacious and inclusive than the ones brought from Europe, but they were incompatible with capitalism's ecology.[17] For the order of cheap nature and cheap work to be created, other work needed to happen without being paid at all—most of all, the creation and management of bodies to do that work.[18] This chapter looks at what's called reproductive labor, the work of caring for, nurturing, and raising human communities. Such work is overwhelmingly unpaid because it makes the whole system of wage work possible. Without unpaid work, especially care work, wage work would simply be too expensive.

At the origins of capitalism, strategies used to corral Indigenous Peoples into the pen of Nature were also used to create and manage a category of humans who would perform unpaid care work: women. Human bodies were forced, sometimes medically and always juridically, into one of two inescapable categories: man and woman. The resulting entangled binaries—of Society-Nature, Man-Woman, and paid work–unpaid work—have left us with a way of thinking that has committed humans in capitalism's world-ecology to making spectacular oversights: we continue to think of "real work" solely as wage work and forget the care work that makes it all possible. Note that this is not to make the equation that all women do care work or that care work is done only by women. It's to illuminate the history of how capitalism's world-ecology has tried to make such conflations seem normal. Writing a history of work without care work would be like writing an ecology of fish without mentioning the water. It'd be possible, in a limited fashion, but, once you'd realized the omission, hard to continue. From the beginning, capitalism's ecology has had a keen interest in sex, power, and reproduction—and it's a mark of the importance of that interest that knowledge of it and its history has been so thoroughly suppressed, and too easily forgotten. This history is only just beginning to be rediscovered.[19]

THE GREAT DOMESTICATION

There's no set way for humans to take care of one another.[20] The extraordinary diversity of community forms and population dynamics in human history underscores the point.[21] At every turn, systems of tending to, caring for, and reproducing human life are connected with extrahuman natures. This existential connection not only encompasses the material and biological but extends to our belief systems and modes of thought. Every rite of passage, every springtime fertility ritual, from maypoles to bloodletting, signals the range of ways that human and extrahuman life form through each other. But when we talk of reproductive labor under capitalism, we're referring to a very specific set of arrangements, ones that were rearranged through world-ecology and persist today.[22] Under these arrangements, some humans were confined to new political, social, and ecological units—households—the better to engage in care work in capitalism's ecology. Call this the Great Domestication.

Consider what appear to be entirely independent sets of observations. Between 2010–2014, the Vienna-based World Values Survey received a range of responses to the statement "When jobs are scarce, men should have more right to a job than women." In Iceland, 3.6 percent of people agreed, but in Egypt 99.6 percent did.[23] Why the difference? The easy explanations are culture, religion, tradition, income level. Yet a study in the prestigious *Quarterly Journal of Economics* points the finger at none of these things. Examining data over the past two hundred years, controlling for everything from religion to war to the presence of oil, the authors found that somehow, across a range of countries, a key factor associated with gender inequality is the introduction of a specific agricultural technology: the plough.[24] Individuals who grow up in a society with a tradition of using ploughs aren't just more likely to perpetuate gender inequality at home—it even sticks with them when they migrate. Like good economists, the study's authors haven't a clue why. It's clear that problems of gender, inequality, and discrimination wouldn't disappear if we were now to replace ploughs with some other agricultural technology. The deeper challenge is understanding not just how a particular way of tilling the soil comes to naturalize divisions between men and women but what might be done to move toward equality.

So why might a farming implement ancient enough to be depicted in 2600 BCE Egyptian hieroglyphics be responsible for twenty-first-century chauvinism?[25] At the sixteenth-century frontier in what is now Peru, the chronicler Inca Garcilaso de la Vega reported something that might solve the plough-sexism conundrum.[26] Indigenous People widely viewed the domestication and then harnessing of oxen as bizarre behavior, both for its interruption of the order of nature and for what it said about the domesticators. The Indigenous explanation was that the Spanish were too lazy to till the land themselves and had to train animals to do it for them while they sat around picking food from their teeth. The Spanish were also considered odd because of the land they chose to farm and the way they occupied it. Colonialists preferred the relatively flat plains for their haciendas, while Indigenous People embraced the terracing technologies that can still be seen in and around Cuzco.[27] You can't plough a steep hillside that everyone owns—physics and social convention both exert strong forces against it. It's much easier to plough on large, contiguous, privately owned haciendas. In other words, it wasn't just the plough that was odd—it was the constellation of transformations in work, relations to extrahuman life, and property into which the plough fit. And central to those ideas were newly forming ones around animal and human domestication.

The modern household and its membership have their origins in ecological changes in European capitalism. In *The Working Lives of Women in the Seventeenth Century,* Alice Clark argues that the nuclear household of husband, wife, and children emerged through shifts in the economic geography of care and production on the commons.[28] Recall that women's work on the commons included fuel gathering and gleaning, which made subsistence possible and sometimes provided a marketable surplus. If anything went wrong, social insurance came from networks of support—religious, personal, social—across the community. These arrangements were incompatible with the kinds of agricultural innovation that brought about the widespread use of the plough: larger and larger enclosed landholdings, monocultures, exclusive private property arrangements, and the creation of a workforce motivated by the threats of starvation and imprisonment.

Enclosure made it impossible for peasants to survive on their meager landholdings. Peasants became wageworkers forced to sell their labor to survive. This also set women and men into competition in the labor market. With the commons, dairying had been a way for women to engage in agriculture, sustaining the household through milk and dairy sales. Without a commons, no cattle could be grazed. The market for dairying skills became tight—sheep's wool was far more lucrative than cows' milk, and shearing was gendered as men's work. Women were required only for the paid work of milking and calving cows in the spring. Spring ploughing and autumnal harvesting involved heavier labor and were also often coded as men's work. This division of labor led to different prices for men's and women's employment. It is in the fields that we find the origins of today's global wage gap, a phenomenon in which relations with nature were involved from the beginning.

For modern models of the household to stick, economics wasn't enough. Women and men needed to be schooled and disciplined in their new household responsibilities. Early modern Europeans could agree that the archetype for all human social relations was the relationship between God and man. Kings embodied God's rule over their subjects, and within the family, husbands assumed an analogous role.[29] It is unsurprising that just as papal power declined during the Reformation, fifteenth- and sixteenth-century Europe saw a burst of writing about the church's power and the sovereignty of kings and simultaneously the publication of a number of manuals on the arts of household management. These guides offered instruction to those confused by the new social order fanned by urbanization and industrialization. Among the most influential was William Gouge's *Of Domesticall Duties,* which begins with a quote from Ephesians 5:21: "Submit your selves one to another in the fear of God."[30] It urges submission on women in households by exploring the theme of a wrathful Old Testament God tempered by a New

Testament mercy. In the home, women were to submit to men and servants to their masters, and men were to follow the model of authoritarianism offered by the Heavenly Father.

The hegemony of the modern household wasn't made purely through instruction manuals. It was also made by force. As with cheap work, the bodies of certain kinds of humans needed to be disciplined for the strategy of cheap care to work. Transforming women's bodies into compliant machines of reproduction took force and fear and social policing.[31] The institutions of this policing included the prison, the school, the clinic, the madhouse, and the management of public and private sex and sexuality through violence and shaming.[32] Women heretics were accused of being supernatural, above the order that decreed their place in nature. Witches, those who defied the new order, were subject to dreadful public torture, conducted as pedagogy, lectures in new ways of behavior for those women who were outside the bourgeoisie and unable to read the instruction manuals and who might be tempted to join the resistance.[33] As Silvia Federici notes, the forms of violence that Michel Foucault was interested in—the disciplining of individual bodies to work and reproduce and behave in particular ways—appear on the historical stage only as part of the strategic needs of early capitalism.[34]

To bring this back to the language of world-ecology, the paired discovery of humankind and nature was less anthropocentric than manthropocentric—to borrow Kate Raworth's pointed turn of phrase.[35] The household's violent education was enforced through the law, property law in particular. Although this discussion is best postponed until the examination of cheap lives in chapter 7, it's worth foreshadowing with a little of the urtext of modern capitalist ownership: John Locke's *Second Treatise on Government,* first published in 1689. This document outlines both what can be owned and who can do the owning. It encloses the domains of the new capitalist state from other kinds of human hierarchies. So the *Second Treatise*'s second paragraph states, "The Power of a Magistrate over a Subject, may be distinguished from that of a Father over his Children, a Master over his Servant, a Husband over his Wife, and a Lord over his Slave."[36] This cements a distinction between a public sphere, in which some men might participate as free and equal citizens, and a private sphere, in which slavery, patriarchy, and the legal representation of a wife by her husband can prevail. In other words, the liberal subject was born a man. He was born through violence and the transmission of a particular kind of production system, the global extension of capitalist agricultures, producing new lived realities of what counted as Nature and what as Society.

The social turmoil this propagated is hard to imagine, but in places it looked a lot like the scene shown below. This painting was once viewed as a delightful country landscape. Closer looks by successive critics have shown much more.[37] In his *Mr. and Mrs. Andrews,* now hanging in the National Gallery in London, Thomas Gainsborough painted a tableau of capitalist world-ecology. Let's start on the left, with the most relaxed person: Robert Andrews. He's part of the 1 percent, yet his clothes are as informal as they were ever likely to be when he was in public—Mr. Andrews wears the 1750s equivalent of a "Kiss the Chef" apron. He owned everything you can see here—the Auberies, his family's estate in Sudbury, Essex, as viewed from "a hundred yards to the south-east of the house looking towards Cornard Wood on the Suffolk side of the Stour valley."[38]

This estate was the result of inheritance and investment. Robert Andrews's father, also named Robert Andrews, was an enormously successful silversmith and banker. Of the many in

Figure 2. Thomas Gainsborough, *Mr. and Mrs. Andrews,* circa 1750. The National Gallery, London.

Andrews the elder's debt, the one in the deepest was Frederick, Prince of Wales, for whom Andrews had guaranteed a loan of £30,000 (today that would be $6.4 million).[39] Gainsborough's painting is a trace of the relations of cheap money, of the transformation of cash into war and then back into cash, a portrait of ownership, bought with the spoils of Potosí pulled from the ground a century before. The Auberies was a merger of property from the Andrews family and the family of his wife, Frances Carter. By the time Gainsborough was at his easel to paint this work, his commissions came not only from the nobility but also from a new class of moneyed city dwellers, unrelated to the aristocracy, whose riches had been created by the new cycles of accumulation and plunder begun barely three centuries before.

Many commentators have observed that the painting is unusual in being a study of both the Andrewses and their land. This is a picture of a farm at the frontier of agricultural technology.

Robert Andrews was a published agronomist, appearing in the *Annals of Agriculture* with titles such as "On the Profit of Farming" and "On the Smut in Wheat."[40] The cereal here is in straight lines. It may have been planted using a seed drill,[41] invented by Jethro Tull in 1700 although only becoming popular in the middle of the 1800s. This technology works to solve problems that emerge when agriculture in the countryside looks increasingly like industry in the city: trying to optimize the balance among labor, machinery, inputs, and markets.

Gainsborough offers us another insight, into the relationship between Robert and his wife Frances. While he's the owner of all he surveys, slouching against a tree with his rifle propped against him, she is upright, her hands in her lap over an unfinished part of the painting. Some have suggested that Gainsborough planned to include a pheasant shot by Mr. Andrews and retrieved by his dog.[42] Others have hazarded that this is where a baby Andrews might have been added later.[43] Either way, Frances Andrews is here likened to property, as enclosed as the land her husband owns, as domesticated as the dog by her husband's side.

Gainsborough would have known Robert Andrews the younger, having grown up in the same area and likely attended the same grammar school at the same time. He would have been aware of the elder Andrews's wealth and may even have received patronage from him, knowing that command of such a fortune was forever beyond his own reach.[44] Perhaps that is why some commentators have seen in his representation of Mrs. Andrews a contempt in her look toward the viewer, which says, property though she may be, that we are below her station.[45]

It is these relations of power that accompany the traditions and technologies of cereal-driven capitalist monoculture, hallmarks of the Great Domestication. Gainsborough's painting not only offers a history lesson but is contemporary news: it's a description of social changes being enforced, and contested, around the world today. The Danish economist Ester Boserup, discussing the social relations that then arose, noted an Islamic quote "ascribed to the Prophet himself that a plough never enters into a farm without servitude entering too."[46] Comprehend the destruction of the commons under enclosure, understand the new relations between human production and reproduction, and as a bonus you can solve the mystery of the misogynist plough.[47] It's just that you have to go back not two hundred years but many more to discover how ploughing first became a tradition, fed by the bones of the social systems it destroyed.

FINANCIALIZATION AND WOMEN'S INHERITANCE

New traditions of control put bourgeois women in a bind, particularly in England. The law there enshrined coverture—the status of a married woman, including the placing of her person and property under her husband's authority. Whereas most of Europe recognized three kinds of property in a marriage—his inheritance, her inheritance, and property acquired during the marriage—English law saw only two kinds: her freehold land inheritance and everything else, of which a widow could inherit only one third. Coverture persisted from the Middle Ages into the nineteenth century. So great was its power to rob women of rights and identity, campaigners against it called it "civil death." It is from this institution that a wife's taking of her husband's name originates. True, middle-class wives had power over their domestic staff and other life. (A seventeenth-century slogan found in household manuals: "England is a woman's paradise, a servant's prison, and a horse's hell.")[48] Parents of bourgeois daughters were nonetheless worried. What would happen to the wealth and way of life they'd accustomed their daughters to after their daughters married? What if the husbands were feckless? What if, even if decent, the husbands died young?

The answers to these questions go some way to explaining modern high finance, as a forceful analysis by Amy Louise Erikson suggests.[49] At a time of witch-hunts, open rebellion against coverture was risky. To survive and resist it less overtly, the English developed and accustomed themselves to laws of contract that allowed widows to prepare for their financial security, children under coverture to have an income, and families who'd have to support widows to be assured of a return of their wealth. While these arrangements weren't themselves financial instruments, Erikson argues that they "helped to establish a climate in which the concept of legal security for notional concepts of property became commonplace."[50] This was particularly significant for unmarried bourgeois women—their access to money enabled them to participate in the speculative transactions through which capitalism developed. There's even evidence to suggest that while men were losing their shirts in the South Sea financial bubble, the women who joined this speculative frenzy more often came out ahead.[51] While it's important not to make too much of this—the equities market wasn't terribly big—it's worth observing that the legal and cultural infrastructure of today's financial instruments, of options and derivatives, was laid down to hedge bourgeois women's losses through the household. Unmarried women's participation in finance markets wasn't, of course, the goal of the new nuclear household. We offer it as an example both of the irreducibility of class to gender and, once again, of how the quirks of historical contingency mattered in shaping modern capitalism.[52]

For women who weren't to become part of the investor class, marriage offered other possibilities. As unemployment in the 1600s increased, so did incentives for women to marry to avoid poverty.[53] Yet even as the economic imperatives for women to choose marriage increased, so did the covering philosophy describing this choice as *uncoerced.* This, of course, mirrors the relations of workers under capitalism, who needed to appear free agents at least in theory, even if their freedom boiled down to the choice of working for a pittance, starving to death, or serving in a debtors' prison. A central theorist of this new world was, of course, Adam Smith. He also had thoughts about families and marriage, even if his practical experience was limited. Smith neither fathered children nor married. He lived with his mother, Margaret Douglas, who tended to him through most of his adult life as his dependent. Smith's father had died before his birth, and Douglas had inherited only a third of the property. Smith came into his father's estate aged two. The laws of coverture explain why Douglas was financially dependent on her toddler after her husband died.[54]

In *The Theory of Moral Sentiments,* first published in 1759, Smith drew on his knowledge of North American Indigenous marriage, a contract arranged by elders rather than entered into freely by husband and wife. Why didn't Indigenous People marry freely? Because, Smith reported, echoing Columbus's gendered language, "the weakness of love ... is regarded among savages as the most unpardonable effeminacy."[55] It's an odd logic, but it served to make his point: the best kind of marriage was the kind that happened in Britain, where women and men chose each other as equals in love. It's no surprise that the man most frequently cited as the bedrock of free-market liberty should have celebrated liberty in private love, or that he justified this model by appeal to the inferiority of savage, natural civilizations. But it's still a little ironic that his life's most loving relationship was with his mum.

THE INVENTION OF WOMEN

For the new, capitalist order to flourish, the old order needed extirpation. Kin networks that had supported women, men, and children beyond the nuclear family were destroyed no less than the commons.[56] The extended family and relationships that could sustain families were transformed and professionalized. Rather than perform the work of education in schools, women were corralled to the nursery. Surgeons—always male—replaced midwives.[57] Women's economic activity, insofar as it was permitted, was confined to the domestic sphere, a domain from which politics was correspondingly banished. Women fought back. The French Revolution began with women leading protests for bread, for instance. But the logic of capitalism's ecology demanded that women's history, activism, and resistance be minimized and muted. Men ruled the roost at home, and citizens ruled the public sphere—and to be a citizen you had to be a white male property owner.[58]

To make this system work, the state developed a keen interest in enforcing the categories of man and woman. Humans whose bodies didn't neatly fit were surgically altered to fit one category or the other.[59] Where such categories didn't exist, they had to be invented. Central to the British colonization of Nigeria, for instance, was the transformation of domestic arrangements, the creation of the domestic sphere, and the invention of the juridical category of woman. Although consanguinity is a vital part of Nigerian and many other societies—and comes with its own hierarchies that muddle and sometimes elevate women to a position higher than they would have in a nuclear family—the kinship that matters most in law for liberal citizens is that of conjugality.[60] As Oyèrónkẹ́ Oyěwùmí notes, "There were no women in Yorùbá society until recently. There were, of course, *obìnrin. Obìnrin* are anafemales. Their anatomy, just like that of *ọkùnrin* (anamales), did not privilege them to any social positions and similarly did not jeopardize their access."[61] Oyěwùmí continues:

> The creation of "women" as a category was one of the very first accomplishments of the colonial state.... It is not surprising, therefore, that it was unthinkable for the colonial government to recognize female leaders among the peoples they colonized, such as the Yorùbá.... The transformation of state power to male-gender power was accomplished at one level by the exclusion of women from state structures. This was in sharp contrast to Yorùbá state organization, in which power was not gender-determined.[62]

Just as Spanish colonists had bridled at Mayan sexual adventures, so the British demanded allegiance to their own version of sexual order and power, one that created the legal category of woman and set her in the household, the workshop of reproductive labor.[63] But, of course, to use the term *workshop* is to mischaracterize how housework was viewed. It was considered precisely beyond the domain of wage work, a favor that women did for men, akin to the free gifts that nature offered enterprise.

The cultural foundations for this understanding of women were laid, as Jennifer Morgan and others have documented, in the transatlantic enslavement of African women.[64] Slavers and explorers followed the logic of De Cuneo's reports from Columbus's second voyage, representing Indigenous women as both preternaturally sexual and outside the domains of proper Society—closer to Nature. Central to this idea was a monstrous fecundity. John Atkins, an abolitionist, reported of Guinean women that they engaged in bestiality and had breasts so big that "some could suckle over their shoulder."[65] Other colonists reported women who gave birth without pain. With slavery, fascination was mixed with new imperatives—such as the production of more slaves. Female slaves became financial instruments not only for discharging debt but also for generating interest: some women in Barbados in the 1650s were designated as "increasers," bodies through which more slaves would be produced, thus recompensing the financial burden of sustaining them. Further, this fertility naturally conferred a predisposition to raise other children, a skill that found its way into many an advertisement for slaves sold to white bourgeois families looking for domestic workers.[66]

Always, there was the possibility of resistance. Early in the settler colonist project in North America, Indigenous women straddled the frontiers of the Canadian fur trade—mediating contact, replacing husbands who had paid a bride-price for them with new ones, evading fur-trading companies' attempts at regulation.[67] Their households wouldn't conform to the dyadic, patriarchal model in which men kept women and women kept house. There were, similarly, spaces for women in the United States to engage in entrepreneurial activities—taking in lodgers, for instance—as long as this was for the good of the household, under the ultimate authority of a man somewhere.[68] In Europe, Dutch women from rural areas became domestic workers in cities, formed congresses, and unionized.[69] Yet this resistance always happened in the context of other fights. When emerging nationalists in the Global South fought European empires in the nineteenth and twentieth centuries, they enforced boundaries of sexual politics with increasing vigor. Race, class, and gender were produced simultaneously at these frontiers, in ways that affected both men and women.[70] Like the study of whiteness, investigations of masculinity and its legal cognates are still relatively new, but it's a growth industry, and there's a great deal to learn about the transformations and resistances around kin relationships under hegemonic masculinity.[71]

AFTER THE PLOUGH

What are we to say to those who insist that ploughs aren't destiny? It is possible for a society to recover from the effects of the shift toward capitalism and, under certain conditions, to see a kind of equality flourish. This view was summarized by the IMF in a 2016 report which shows that the lot of women is improving worldwide, based on a range of indicators including health, economic and parliamentary participation, and education.[72] The IMF associates increased gender equality with rises in national income, and the prejudice remains that wealth brings women's lib.

Yet the story is hardly straightforward. Look, for instance, at countries with oil in the Middle East and elsewhere for evidence that income growth inhibits women's rights.[73] Look too at a country like India, a site of gross and persistent inequality despite a 500 percent increase in real per capita income over the past forty years. Certainly, increased access to clean water and health care has helped women,[74] but women and girls continue to work more than men, for less pay and less food.[75] The daily

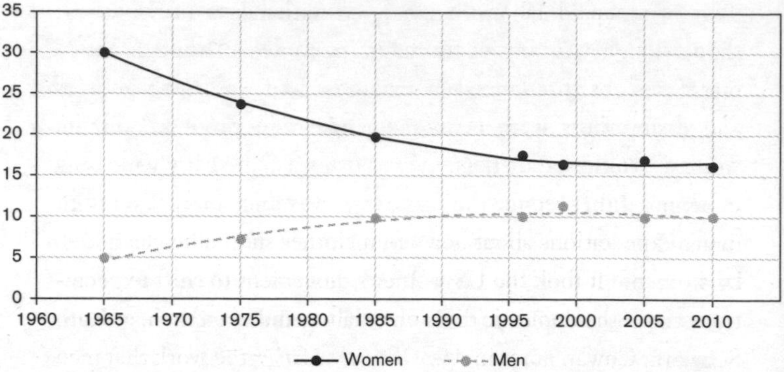

Figure 3. Trends in average weekly housework hours in the United States by gender for individuals aged 25–64. Source: Bianchi et al. 2012, 57–58.

calorie intake of rural Indians has fallen by five hundred over the past forty years, with anemia rates for girls rising over the past ten years.[76] One of the ways to peel this apart is through a time-use survey. Indian time-use surveys show that women and girls are doing far more work in the household than appears in the national system of accounts, with women spending six times more hours collecting food and fuelwood and performing household maintenance than men. While low-income men and women often have multiple, very low-paying jobs, the lowest-paid workers remain women, who also sleep less and have less free time, particularly if they live in rural areas.[77] This isn't just a case of "If only they were richer, they'd be better off." The nation *is* richer, but its poor and working classes are hungrier, and its women are more likely to be overweight or underweight than its men.[78]

In the United States, scholars looking at reproductive labor have noted generally positive trends in the twentieth century, as the figure above suggests. More men have been pitching in with domestic unpaid labor than had been the case previously—though with a ceiling of ten hours per week. Although it was often thought that laborsaving devices like washing machines and dishwashers were technologies to reduce the burden on women, things didn't happen that way. Initially, washing machines didn't reduce the time spent washing. They just raised men's expectations about how often clothes should be cleaned—by women.[79] It took the US women's movement to shift expectations about the domestic division of labor, and even then, as Ruth Schwartz Cowan notes in *More Work for Mother*, the work that men ended up doing was precisely that which was more mechanized. Women's work, meantime, has continued to be more mentally demanding, with multitasking more intense than in men's work in the household, even if over similar durations of time.[80]

In the discussion of cheap work in the previous chapter, we connected rural and urban economics in the link between global farms and global factories. The availability of proletarian labor was possible only because of the transformation of care work into unpaid work, available as one of Nature's "free gifts"—which, as we have seen, are neither free nor gifted. Capitalism not only continues to take care work for granted but also expects the skills developed through this work to be available for sale in the world of commodity production. So it is that gendered ideas lead to women being sought—and cheapened—for their nimble fingers, caring attitudes, and supportive miens (for example) by those looking to hire cheap workers for *maquilas*, call centers, and nursing care industries, those workers having been trained through a lifetime of cheap care and expected to have certain skills *because they are women*.[81]

There are gendered expectations not only of skills transferred from care work but also of flexibility. It might appear that the precariat—workers who lack the job security, pensions, and organizing bodies normally associated with mid-twentieth-century industrial workers in the Global North—is experiencing something new.[82] But mobility, flexibility, and permanent availability have long been hallmarks of care work. Precarious employment has its roots in advances in capitalist workplace logistics as well as in previous regimes of unpaid care. The freelance economy can be read as an extension of the disciplines of care work spread across the entire working world.

The growth in the care economy—estimated to be 70 percent from 2012 to 2022 in the United States, with similar trends globally[83]—keeps care work structurally cheap. Yet it is possible for the US care economy to look the way it does only because of the movements of carers from other parts of the world. America's care economy has a long, global, and racialized ecology, from the sale of imported slaves as wet nurses to more recent migrations of health care professionals from the Global South to the Global North.[84] In some cases that labor is literally reproductive. Advances in fertility technology have produced a boom in the demand for pregnancy surrogates. The world's largest market for wombs is India, where a service that costs $80,000 to $100,000 in the Global North can be had for $35,000 to $40,000 in an industry expected to reap profits in excess of $2 billion in India alone.[85] The frontier of cheap care has deepened and expanded, with vast international networks of care service providers remitting funds across borders to help sustain households elsewhere. The global household has always done the work that makes possible the global factory and the global farm.

One radical response to the fundamental devaluation of care work involves a jujitsu pricing move and the demand that housework be paid. As the 1970s Wages for Housework campaign argued, "Slavery to an assembly line is not a liberation from slavery to a kitchen sink. To deny this is also to deny the slavery of the assembly line itself, proving again that if you don't know how women are exploited, you can never really know how men are."[86] The irony here, of course, is that there's a long history of women who were paid little if at all for their domestic labor: those working under slavery. The United States is not alone in this pattern, with carers from different classes, castes, and indeed nations suffering widespread exploitation in other countries too.[87] And even if payment were a route to recognition, there's much further to go to reach dignity. As Angela Davis put it, "Psychological liberation can hardly be achieved simply by paying the housewife a wage."[88] Yet the insight of Wages for Housework shouldn't be forgotten. To ask for capitalism to pay for care is to call for an end to capitalism.

If introducing money into this ecological relation doesn't guarantee success, perhaps more collective approaches might work. Although states have been there from the creation of the modern household, their role in managing care dramatically increased after the Second World War and the fight for the creation of the welfare state.[89] That welfare state—especially in Western Europe—delivered meaningful gains for working classes in health care, education, and pensions. But state management of care work isn't the same thing as freedom from such work.[90] As Gwendolyn Mink observed, the battles for women's rights have been fought on the terrain of motherhood, and the attendant "victories socialized motherhood rather than citizenship."[91] Karen Orren noticed that labor law in general and care work in particular are domains of "belated feudalism."[92] It was only in 2015, for instance, that US care workers gained recognitions as workers under the 1938 Fair Labor Standards Act, as a result of union and cooperative organizing.[93] In other words, one of the requirements for taking the ecology of the plough out of capitalism's ecology is a commitment to engage in political struggle and not, as the IMF would have it, simply wait for incomes to increase.[94]

The fight to have care work recognized, rewarded, and reduced under neoliberalism becomes yet harder under right-wing economic nationalism. In a number of countries in the Global North—not just in the United States—the difficulties of finding secure work under austerity programs have already led adult children to live with their parents well into their thirties. Austerity also coerces women into caring for not just their adult offspring but, increasingly, their elderly parents. US women now, as Evelyn Nakano Glenn notes, spend more of their lives caring for their elders than for their offspring (eighteen versus seventeen years).[95] The relations of care that they bear have been sharpened by the decline in the real value of pensions, concurrent with the asset stripping of the welfare state. Nationalism, as we'll see in chapter 7, always comes with attending logics of domesticity and homemaking. It is, sadly, entirely conceivable that the gains won by care workers over the past seventy years might be quickly reversed over the next decade.

Yet the struggles of liberation and resistance continue—fought by groups from sex-worker unions to home care collectives—against forms of domination that look strikingly similar to those at the dawn of capitalism's ecology. Studies of trends in international occupational growth in the wake of the latest recession point to a striking rise in gendered work—a move toward a world of soldiering for men and nursing for women.[96] That work is conducted under conditions in which violence continues to be used as a pedagogy of cruelty—as recent surges in brutality against women attest.[97]

If the struggles for the recognition, equal distribution, reduction, and compensation of care work are successful, it will be a hopeful sign of the end of cheap nature—and a shift toward valuations premised on care work, not exploitation. To imagine a world of justice in care work is to imagine a world after capitalism. But while capitalism persists, the cheapness of labor reproduction is based in turn on other cheap things. Just as capitalism's ecology requires cheap care to underwrite cheap work, it also requires fuel for the bodies of workers, to maintain social order. So it is to cheap food that we now turn.

CHAPTER FIVE

Cheap Food

On his first voyage to the New World, Columbus paid far more attention to potential returns from the sale of new plants than to the food he ate. Aboard the *Niña, Pinta,* and *Santa María,* diet followed a protocol so regimented that there's no mention of it in the first two months of the ship's log.[1] When food does crop up, it's two days after first contact, when Columbus writes about an old man who came on board and cried to his friends on the shore to bring the sailors things to eat and drink. Columbus permitted himself the rituals of gastrotourism a month later, on November 5, 1492, when he tried some local food and reported that the Indigenous People had "*mames* which are like carrots and have the flavor of chestnuts; and they have *faxones* and beans of kinds very different from ours." But Columbus wasn't there to taste test. The bulk of his notes look like this: "There are a thousand other kinds of fruits, which it is impossible for me to write about, and all must be profitable."[2]

His daily rations—hardtack (a double-baked wheat biscuit) and a range of cured meats and cheeses—didn't matter enough to make it into his journals. Only on the way home, on January 25, 1493, did he report that the "sailors killed a tunny [dolphin] and a very large shark, which was very welcome as they now had nothing but bread and wine, and some yams from the Indies."[3]

It is such food, the food that sustains working human bodies, that is at the heart of our discussion in this chapter. Madeira's sugar revolution was a central and early part of capitalism's ecology, and Columbus himself introduced the plant to the New World, so that by 1506 it was widely and intensively cultivated on Hispaniola.[4] But the food that matters in that story is not the processed sugar that Columbus and his kind conveyed from Madeira to Genoa but instead the food of sailors and slave families, the sustenance that allows the extraction of cheap work.[5]

Crop varieties matter to soil and human ecology. We cannot talk about food in general but need to recognize its particularities and the way that different crops have formed their own ecologies. Rice, maize, and wheat—Fernand Braudel's "plants of civilization"[6]—have yielded very different forms of power, work, gastronomy, and nature:

> Europe chose wheat, which devours the soil and forces it to rest regularly; this choice implied and permitted the raising of livestock. Now, who can imagine the history of Europe without oxen, horses, plows, and carts? As a result of this choice Europe has always combined agriculture and animal husbandry. It has always been carnivorous. Rice developed out of a form of gardening, an intensive cultivation in which man could allow no room for animals. This explains why meat constitutes such a small part of the diet in rice-growing areas. Planting corn is surely the simplest and most convenient way to obtain one's "daily bread." It grows very rapidly and requires minimal care. The choice of corn as a crop left free time, making possible the forced peasant labor and the

enormous monuments of the Amerindians. Society appropriated a labor force that worked the land only intermittently.[7]

Although capitalism is often associated with coal- and oil-fueled revolutions, transformations in the food system came first. Without food surplus, there's no work outside agriculture. The textbook civilizations—the Sumerians and the Egyptians, the Hans and the Romans, the Mayans and the Incas—grew through revolutions that allowed fewer people to produce more food. The diversity of food relations in the arc of human history from the Neolithic revolution to the dawn of the sixteenth century is breathtaking.[8] But they all shared two common characteristics: a system of agricultural productivity premised on land rather than labor, and a system of controlling food surplus through politics rather than the market.

Capitalist agriculture transformed the planet. Some land became the exclusive domain of specific kinds of crops and crop systems: monocultures designed to bring in flows of cash. Other areas were reserved to house those humans who had been excommunicated from the work of growing on those lands and had gone to live more closely together in places where their labors might be better rewarded—the cities. Cities and fields have long been siblings, bound by another timeless imperative: cheap food for the urban poor. Everyone from Cicero to the imperial Chinese has understood the importance of making sure that city dwellers are sufficiently well fed to prevent urban discontent.[9] What's different about an ecology of cash agriculture is the single-minded focus on profit and the drive for cheap food to feed urban workers and their families not just to prevent riots but also to keep work cheap. As we have seen in the chapters on work and care, maintaining a system of wage work is expensive and becomes more so over time. Cheap food enables that expensive system to yield riches. Those riches flowed through infrastructures of power and production that created a new ecology of the city and the country. Like the relation between employers and workers, it was profoundly unequal. A rural-urban ecology is woven into the fabric of capitalism, one whose patterns formed through Atlantic frontiers, major European cities, the Indian Ocean, and Asia's spice routes.

HOW FOOD MADE THE INDUSTRIAL WORLD

By 1700, most English peasants had been either reduced to cottagers, pushed into agricultural wage work, or forced off the land and into cities—61 percent of England's working population was doing something other than growing food. The *proportion* of city dwellers had doubled over the previous century.[10] The enclosures of the previous two centuries had made agriculture a competitive business, and a cluster of innovations—new ploughs, crop rotations, and drainage systems especially—had made it biologically productive. While historians debate the precise timing of its agricultural revolution, it's clear that by 1700 England was doing the two big things that every great capitalist power must: increasing the agricultural surplus and expelling labor from the farm.[11] It could expel labor from the farm because it was productive in a new sense: labor productivity advanced rapidly, rising nearly 46 percent between 1500 and 1700.[12]

English agriculture was so robust at the dawn of the eighteenth century that it was able to rescue a rapidly proletarianizing Europe from hunger. While we tend to think of industrialization as producing new workers, it's truer to say that the expulsion of labor from agriculture favors new forms of industrialization. Europe's wage-earning population may have grown by as much as sixty million in the two centuries after 1550, and these workers had to be fed cheaply. Every global factory needs a global farm. That global farm in the sixteenth and seventeenth centuries had been Poland, whose wheat and rye filled the bellies of Dutch fishers, sawyers, and peat cutters. By 1700, however, Poland's exports had collapsed—in great measure from soil exhaustion. For the next half century, England was western Europe's granary, its exports growing fivefold. Grain prices held stable in western European cities as a result—but for capitalism, ever hungry for economic growth, stability is never enough.[13] Food prices in England—and across northern Europe—fell.[14]

England's triumph was short lived. Like Poland before it, the island saw its agricultural revolution stall. Farmers progressively "cashed in" their biological reserves.[15] By 1750, a tipping point was reached. Grain exporting ground to a halt. Productivity growth slowed, and food prices rose.[16] Even with sharply rising imports from Ireland, English food prices increased twice as fast as the industrial price index, climbing 66 percent faster than textile prices and 48 percent faster than coal prices between 1770 and 1795.[17]

If this were simply an English phenomenon, it mightn't matter, but productivity slowed, inequality widened, and food became more expensive throughout the Atlantic world. Labor productivity fell or stagnated across western Europe in the half century after 1750.[18] In France the price of bread rose three times faster than wages before 1789's Revolution.[19] In central Mexico too, yields declined, and the price of maize rose 50 percent toward the end of the century.[20] Across Europe between 1730 and 1810, the price of "the chief bread grains" (wheat and rye above all) soared: 250 percent in England and more than 200 percent in northern Italy, Germany, Denmark, Sweden, Austria, and the Netherlands. France experienced lower rates of food price inflation—163 percent in this period—but that was hardly enough to forestall massive social unrest.[21]

By 1760 there were signs of a fundamental change in the English countryside that marked the triumph of agrarian capitalism—as well as its exhaustion. In response to an increasing number of food rebellions across the country and rising grain prices,[22] the scale and tempo of parliamentary enclosure jumped sharply, an attempt to rekindle a flare of productivity by repeating the cause of the agricultural boom. Six times as many Enclosure Acts were passed between 1760 and 1790 as in the three decades prior.[23] In the century after 1750, a quarter of England's cultivated land, previously open fields and commons, was privatized.[24]

This ecology was premised on cheap nature and cheap work, but it also needed cheap food. Cheap food is "cheap" in a specific sense: more calories produced with less average labor time in the commodity system. Certainly, some noncapitalist modes of cultivation have enjoyed very high levels of food production with modest effort. In early nineteenth-century Brazil, swidden agriculture—in which cultivators clear plots of forest for cultivation, then repeat the cycle after several harvests—could yield between 7,000 and 17,600 calories of manioc, maize, and sweet potatoes for every hour of work. By way of contrast, this was somewhere between three and five times greater than England's labor productivity at the same time.[25] But nowhere was rising labor productivity in agriculture sustained for large concentrated populations until the rise of capitalism.

The cheap food model worked like this. Capitalism's agricultural revolutions provided cheap food, which lowered the minimum-wage threshold: workers could be paid less and not starve. This in turn reduced employers' wage bills as the scale of proletarianization increased, allowing the rate of exploitation to rise. Accumulated capital could continue to grow only insofar as a rising food surplus underwrote "cheap" workers.[26] It is a simple model. This system of cheap food didn't emerge on purpose, but understanding its emergence in capitalism's ecology makes it possible to think of and see the world differently—including how the imperatives of providing cheap food have helped to create the modern world.

We quoted Braudel on rice, maize, and wheat—but a central part of Britain's calorie intake in the Industrial Revolution was New World sugar. As Kenneth Pomeranz notes, "Replacing Britain's 1801 consumption of Caribbean sugar with locally grown calories would have required 850,000 to 1.2 million acres of the best wheat land; by 1831—still before the great fall in sugar prices and quintupling of per-capita consumption that followed—the figure is 1.2 to 1.6 million."[27] The story of capitalism is a global one, from the belly out.

Throughout the seventeenth and eighteenth centuries, European governments tried to manage food prices in cities, not always successfully. There were bread riots, led overwhelmingly by women, whose provision of care and dependence on markets put them on the front lines of battles over cheap food.[28] The most famous began the French Revolution. In 1789, as the food-price crisis worsened, Parisian women marched on Versailles to get "the Baker, the Baker's wife, and the Baker's son" (the king and his family).[29] Two years later, a sugarcane colony rose against its French colonizers, with aspirations to the kinds of liberty, equality, and fraternity that were rallying cries in the metropole. Nor were the Haitian and French uprisings alone in an era of worldwide agrarian revolt that stretched from Russia to Peru to North America.[30]

To feed their workers, empires needed food. The Russian revolutionary Vladimir Lenin quoted Cecil Rhodes, the colonialist whose patrician statue has only just been torn down from the steps of the University of Cape Town, as saying in 1895, "I was in the East End of London yesterday and attended a meeting of the unemployed. I listened to the wild speeches, which were just a cry for 'bread', 'bread', 'bread', and on my way home I pondered over the scene and I became more than ever convinced of the importance of imperialism.... The Empire, as I have always said, is a bread and butter question. If you want to avoid civil war, you must become imperialists."[31] Two decades later, in 1917, Lenin found himself at the center of a revolution whose slogan was "Peace, Land, and Bread," building on years of bread riots led, as in the French Revolution 130 years earlier, by women.[32]

Empire provided Europe's industrial workers with cheap food, though at huge cost to people in other parts of the planet. European empire created networks of commodity trade that made the Third World, as Mike Davis argues.[33] One example from an old British colony demonstrates the generalized contempt for peasants held throughout European empires. During the 1845–48 potato famine, poverty and market forces instructed the Irish to work for a living, even if there was no employment to be had and no food they could afford: at the height of the famine, Ireland was exporting around three hundred thousand tons of grain a year to feed the mother country. That the ensuing famine would destroy large parts of the Irish population was, if anything, a bonus. Charles Trevelyan, the British assistant secretary to the Treasury, who controlled funds for famine relief, was quite clear on the matter: "the real evil" was "not the physical evil of the Famine, but the moral evil … of the [Irish] people."[34] Trevelyan received a knighthood for his services to the realm while Ireland starved, and wrote that as a way of curbing unchecked Irish population growth, "the famine is a direct stroke of an all-wise and all-merciful Providence."[35]

Other British colonies were subject to the same forces. Indian customs of feeding the poor were replaced, at gunpoint, by free market relations so that India could export grain.[36] As we saw in chapter 2's discussion of money, military force is never far from financial power, and sometimes the latter can be wielded to pay for the former. Under colonial rule, India was tasked with funding, through taxation, Britain's worldwide imperialism: "Ordinary Indians … paid for such far-flung adventures of the Indian army as the sacking of Beijing (1860), the invasion of Ethiopia (1868), the occupation of Egypt (1882), and the conquest of the Sudan (1896–98)."[37] Colonial exploitation intensified yet further when Germany and the United States—and quickly Japan and the rest of Europe—joined Britain on the gold standard after 1871. The value of India's silver-based rupees collapsed by more than a third between 1873 and 1894—while its payments to Britain were denominated in gold.[38]

Market mechanisms and violence went hand in hand with the flow of cheap food from Asia to Europe. When Britain's warships blockaded China's Pearl River in November 1839, the struggle was over silver and opium—the latter cultivated on plantations across India. The East India Company had monopolized the production and trade of opium at the end of the eighteenth century. A rapidly growing volume of opium found its way—illegally but profitably—to China. The Chinese didn't need to trade with the English, but the English wanted Chinese tea. And for this they needed silver. With the opium trade, Eric

Wolf wryly observes, "the Europeans finally had something to sell to the Chinese."[39] That trade was threatened in 1839 when the Chinese government "refused British smugglers food, water and trade until they promised to stop hauling their shipfuls of opium into China."[40] The first of two Opium Wars was waged over the next few years. At stake was control of the Chinese market. As China was progressively opened to European power and commerce after 1842, among the greatest windfalls for the British was their ability to secure tea plants. By 1851, Robert Fortune had moved some two thousand tea plants and seventeen thousand tea seeds from China—via Hong Kong, then under British control—to the Botanic Garden in Calcutta.[41] By the end of the century, the English were drinking tea grown in India and Ceylon (Sri Lanka), not China.[42]

Britain turned botanical imperialism into something of an art. Rubber seeds were smuggled out of Brazil, nurtured at the Royal Botanical Gardens at Kew in London, and trialed in south and southeast Asia. Sisal, used to manufacture rope and agricultural twine, made a similar migration, from southern Mexico to Asia. For colonial expansion to overcome the malaria endemic to tropical latitudes, cinchona—the source of quinine—was cultivated and spread far from its native home in Brazil.[43]

One of the more significant agricultural innovations emerged, like so many before it, as a result of war and geopolitics: fertilizer. Until the early twentieth century, most inorganic fertilizer was mined. Saltpeter—potassium nitrate (KNO_3)—was an important mineral in agriculture and in gunpowder. In Europe, tensions around managing such food supply inputs helped, as the historian Avner Offer argues, to precipitate the First World War.[44] The Allies oversaw the blockade of Chilean saltpeter mines as a means to cripple German and Austro-Hungarian food supplies, and military campaigns spurred the commercial development of prewar technologies of atmospheric nitrogen fixing, pioneered by the German chemists Fritz Haber and Carl Bosch.[45] Their actions transformed the earth: planetary nitric oxide (NO) and ammonia (NH_3) levels are now five times their pre-1800 levels,[46] and the energy required to manufacture ammonia comes directly from cheap fossil fuel, as we discuss in chapter 6. This is one of the reasons why up to ten calories of oil are now required to produce a single calorie of food.[47]

The twentieth century saw other changes that made these biotechnological interventions seem trivial. The spread of revolutionary communist ideas was the realization of Rhodes's fears and those of his fellow bourgeois. The Russian Revolution was every capitalist's nightmare made real—and governments sought ways to manage and accommodate restive workers rather than run the risk of falling under their hammers and sickles. A former Spanish colony, Mexico, was the site of one such compromise among workers, capitalists, and the state.

The 1910 Mexican Revolution began as an affair of the middle class but soon began to exceed it, with workers and peasants making militant demands. In 1934, Lázaro Cárdenas was elected Mexico's president on a platform to meet those demands: he instituted wide-ranging land reform, redistributing 47 percent of all cultivatable land[48]—and began to nationalize the assets of the oil industry, including the refineries of the Standard Oil Company. Control over cheap energy was a central part of the project of Mexican corporatism.

For the Standard Oil Company's founding family, the Rockefellers, this was nothing short of an outrage. It was also further evidence of the grave threat posed by a growing population and a limited food supply. There was a general fear among the

American ruling class that Malthus's prediction might come true: a collapse of society precipitated when an urban population's hunger outstrips its food supply.

Philanthropists set themselves the task of saving society. "The World Food Problem, Agriculture, and the Rockefeller Foundation," a strategic document issued by the Rockefeller Foundation in 1951, almost a decade after it had begun to work in Mexico, crystallized the themes of insurgency, population, and food: "Whether additional millions … will become Communists will depend partly on whether the Communist world or the free world fulfils its promises. Hungry people are lured by promises, but they may be won by deeds. Communism makes attractive promises to underfed peoples. Democracy must not only promise as much, but must deliver more."[49]

The foundation went to work in Mexico in 1943, recruiting a brilliant young plant breeder, Norman Borlaug, to develop crops to prevent *urban* hunger. That it was urban and not rural hunger that troubled policy makers is vitally important. Food and employment for people in rural areas—where most of the world's hunger was concentrated—was of little concern. Hunger began to matter politically only when the poor came to the cities and translated it into anger, and thence potentially into insurrection and a challenge to the rule of cheap nature. It's here—in the bourgeois concern about that rule and its need for worker quiescence—that we find the origin of what came to be known as the Green Revolution.

The term *Green Revolution* is one to savor. It was coined in 1968 by William Gaud, an administrator of the United States Agency for International Development, who spoke glowingly of a range of interventions: "[Recent] developments in the field of agriculture contain the makings of a new revolution. It is not a violent Red Revolution like that of the Soviets, nor is it a White Revolution like that of the Shah of Iran. I call it the Green Revolution."[50] In other words, the Green Revolution used agriculture, new crop varieties, fertilizers, pesticides, irrigation, landholding mechanisms, marketing approaches, and state power to maintain cheap labor, care, raw materials, and—to acknowledge Iran's impact on international oil markets—energy.

Mexico's Green Revolution program is the embodiment of the regime of cheap food. The orthodox narrative says that Borlaug "realized that Mexico's traditional wheat-growing highland areas could not produce enough wheat to make the country self-sufficient in wheat production."[51] So he set about breeding varieties that would allow cheap wheat to flow freely in urban areas. For this work he was awarded a Nobel Peace Prize in 1970, and such is the allure of this history of the Green Revolution that governments and philanthropists have sought to repeat its success elsewhere, recently through the Alliance for a Green Revolution in Africa. But the official story of the Green Revolution doesn't have it quite right about Mexico. For the majority of Mexican peasants, corn (maize) was a far more important crop than wheat. Nearly ten times more land was planted with corn (4,781,759 hectares, or 11,815,984 acres) than wheat (555,756 hectares, or 1,373,303 acres) in 1950.[52] Wheat tended to be grown by commercial farmers with models and resources more comparable to their US counterparts than those of corn production. Similarly, when the Green Revolution was introduced into India, the crop at the spear tip of research investment was corn, which accounted for less than 3 percent of the country's agricultural output and isn't a staple there at all.[53]

Seed technology wasn't the only mechanism needed for certain crops to jump continents and begin to be cultivated globally. The Green Revolution required agricultural extension services and government field workers to proselytize on behalf of the new crops. It also needed national governments to subsidize farmers, through agricultural marketing boards, to grow more of those crops. Cheap food required the suppression of political dissent. The Green Revolution was, after all, a package of reforms designed to prevent the Red revolutionary political goal of many peasants' and landless workers' movements: comprehensive land and agrarian reform. That's why, in its implementation, the Green Revolution was often an authoritarian program.[54]

It's possible to see the Green Revolution as a success. Globally, grain output more than doubled—and yields, the amount of output per unit area, more than doubled—between 1950 and 1980. In the heartlands of the Green Revolution, yields grew even faster. India's wheat yields shot up 87 percent between 1960 and 1980, close to what American corn farmers experienced in the two decades after 1935.[55] A rising share of all this food was traded on the world market, with global grain exports increasing 179 percent over the 1960s and 1970s.[56] The political commitment to making food cheap through state subsidy and violence worked. Food prices declined 3 percent a year between 1952 and 1972, three times faster than the already steep decline in commodity prices across the twentieth century.[57] Real prices for rice, maize, and wheat declined yet further from 1976 to 2002.[58] Perhaps the greatest success was the effective quieting of peasant demands for land reform and urban demands for political change.

Yet the long Green Revolution's prodigious output achievements did not reduce hunger. If China—where the agricultural revolution was decidedly redder but no less productive for it—is removed from the analysis, the ranks of the hungry swelled by more than 11 percent over the course of the Green Revolution.[59] And while reporters are happy to celebrate the fact that "India's

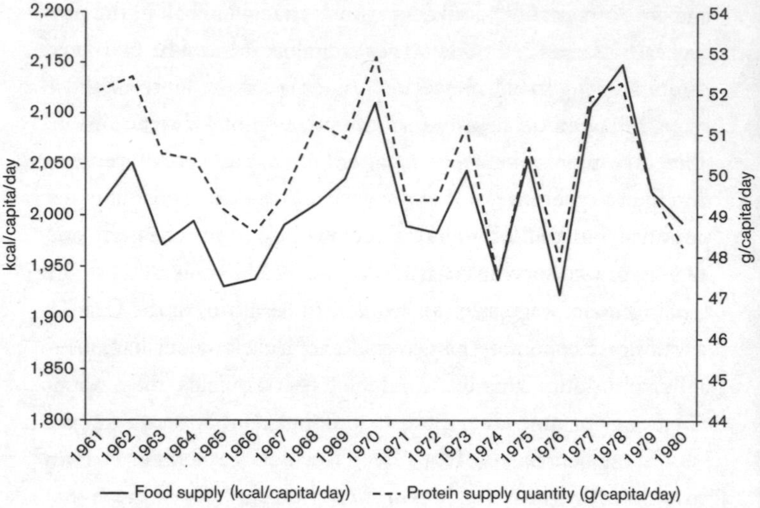

Figure 4. Food and protein supply in India. Source: FAOSTAT, www.fao.org/faostat/en/.

wheat production doubled" from 1965 to 1972[60] and rose steadily throughout the 1970s, the amount that Indians actually ate hardly improved over the same period.

India's pesticide consumption increased seventeenfold from 1955 to 2005, with a large share of that directed at the state of Punjab.[61] Communities where the Green Revolution was practiced most intensively have, more recently, become cancer clusters, with some areas officially declared "cancer stricken villages."[62] But again, the Green Revolution wasn't directed toward Indian villagers—just those workers in the urban cash nexus who might nurse ideas about defecting from capitalism. Through trade agreements, subsidies, and technology, governments have managed food prices, particularly for staples and processed food. Indeed, it is a global phenomenon that from 1990 to 2015, prices of processed food rose far less than those of fresh fruits and vegetables.[63] To get their recommended daily five fresh fruits and vegetables, residents of low-income countries would need to spend at least half of their household income on just these five healthy items, with households in rural areas spending a greater percentage: 70 percent of rural residents in low-income countries can't afford to buy three servings of the cheapest vegetables or two servings of fruit.[64]

Since 1990, wage rates for workers in countries in the Organization for Economic Cooperation and Development have been relatively static. This was a direct consequence, as we noted in chapter 3, of anti-labor policies that scholars aptly call "wage repression." Given consistently low wages in the neoliberal era, it makes sense to look at cheap food as cheap not merely relative to wage costs but directly in terms of price. When we do, it emerges as no accident that a foodstuff whose price has fallen dramatically is chicken in Mexico—a direct consequence of the North American Free Trade Agreement (NAFTA), technology, and the US soybean industry. NAFTA originally excluded agricultural goods, but they were included at the insistence of the Mexican government, which wanted to "modernize" its peasantry by moving them from agriculture into urban circuits of industry.[65] The strategy worked: Mexico's campesino agricultural economy buckled, as evinced by the 2003 El Campo No Aguanta Más (The countryside can't take it anymore) protests throughout the country.[66] Circuits of migration and pools of labor for US agriculture were the result. But at least the chicken was cheap.

Meat has been at the epicenter of the global dietary transformation since the 1970s. As we consider the future of the long Green Revolution, we turn to examine both how we became an increasingly carnivorous planet and how the logic that allows

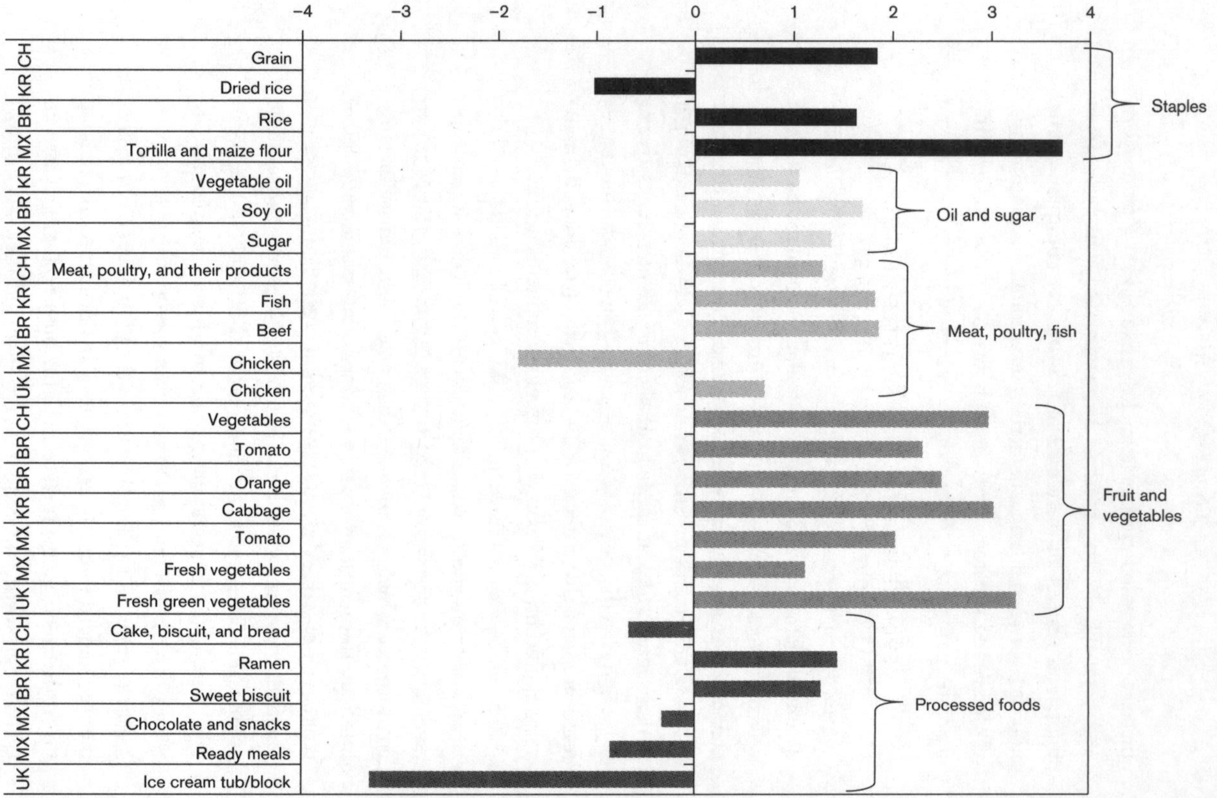

−4
−3
−2
−1
0
1
2
3
4
CH Grain
KR Dried rice
BR Rice
MX Tortilla and maize flour
KR Vegetable oil
BR Soy oil
MX Sugar
CH Meat, poultry, and their products
KR Fish
BR Beef
MX Chicken
UK Chicken
CH Vegetables
BR Tomato
BR Orange
KR Cabbage
MX Tomato
MX Fresh vegetables
UK Fresh green vegetables
CH Cake, biscuit, and bread
KR Ramen
BR Sweet biscuit
MX Chocolate and snacks
MX Ready meals
UK Ice cream tub/block
Staples
Oil and sugar
Meat, poultry, fish
Fruit and vegetables
Processed foods

meat to be manufactured cheaply is twinned with the rise of "nutritionism," a way of treating "hunger not by directly addressing poverty but by prioritizing the delivery of individual molecular components of food to those lacking them."[67] A grim future of cheap food presents itself.

FROM VEGETABLES WITH A LITTLE MEAT TO POVERTY WITH ADDED VITAMINS

The Canadian food scholar Tony Weis has pointed to the scale of recent changes in meat consumption: "In 1961, just over three billion people ate an average of 23 kg [51 pounds] of meat and 5 kg [11 pounds] of eggs a year. By 2011, 7 billion people ate 43 kg [95 pounds] of meat and 10 kg [22 pounds] of eggs a year.... In a mere half-century, from 1961 to 2010, the global population of slaughtered animals leapt from roughly 8 to 64 billion, which will double again to 120 billion by 2050 if current rates of growth continue."[68]

To those with a romantic view of where their food comes from, meat appears to be a raw ingredient rather than a processed one. Yet the industrial labor techniques of simplification, compartmentalization, and specialization first developed in sugar production have found their way into meat production too. Feed and oilseed crops, made possible in the Global South partly by the spread of the Green Revolution, form part of what Weis terms "the industrial grain-oilseed-livestock complex."[69] The creation of markets for uniform grain and meat commodities—such as the Chicago Board of Trade—made it possible for these commodities to become not only cheap food but the backing for financial instruments. These instruments in turn require the uniformity, homogenization, and industrialization of the crops they transform.[70] Such industry demands the invention of new veterinary practices—from intensive breeding to hormonal supplementation to antibiotic use to concentrated animal feeding operations—which have had globally transformative effects on the quality of food, soil, water, and air. Raw meat in the supermarket is, in other words, cooked up by a sophisticated and intensive arm of capitalism's ecology.

One result is a meat-production system that can turn a fertile egg and a nine-pound (four-kilogram) bag of feed into a five-pound (two-kilogram) chicken in five weeks.[71] Turkey production times almost halved between 1970 and 2000, down to twenty weeks from egg to thirty-five-pound (sixteen-kilogram) bird.[72] Other animals have seen similar advances from a combination of breeding, concentrated feeding operations, and global supply chains. Half of the world's pork is eaten in China, and its feed import sources are a planetary affair. As are the consequences: 14.5 percent of all anthropogenic carbon dioxide (CO_2) emissions are from livestock production.[73] One pound (about half a kilogram) of beef requires 1,799 gallons (6,810 liters) of water and seven pounds (three kilograms) of feed to produce.[74]

The environmental consequences of meat production are, of course, external to the profit calculus of the industrial food system. This is one of the reasons why meat is so cheap. Cheap labor is another. The danger is to see "factory farming" as an environmental question and "factory production" as a social question. Given the centrality of cheap labor power in the US neoliberal meat-packing sector, we might also point out the centrality of Latino immigrants. The delivery of this cheap work was made possible by class restructuring on two fronts. One, in the United States, was a strong movement in the 1980s by newly aggressive meat-packing firms—such as Hormel—to destroy union power and replace unionized workers with low-wage immigrant labor.[75] The other was the destabilization of Mexico's agrarian order after 1994 by NAFTA, which resulted in flows of cheap immigrant labor, unemployed workers displaced by capitalism's ecology from one side of the US border to the other.[76]

Despite the considerable environmental and governmental subsidies afforded the meat industry, many people are unable to afford its products. For them the private sector and the international development community have offered an alternative: improved nutrition of industrially produced plant-based food. This is more than a little ironic: industrialization and the Green Revolution bred nutrition *out* of many of the staples in the food system.[77] Those nutrients were casualties of the drive to maximize the yield, shelf life, and consumer acceptability of a standardized commodity. Reintroducing them is a means of increasing the profitability of an ultraprocessed food substance. In a way, the logic of cheap meat production comes full circle, with additives in food designed not to produce profitable animal flesh but to sustain cheap human labor, which, in its turn, will produce more profit further down the line.

You can see this logic at work most acutely in the Global South. The G8's 2013 summit was titled "Nutrition for Growth: Beating Hunger through Business and Science," which points rather clearly to the direction of its—and its partners'—thought. It launched an initiative on hunger, the New Alliance for Food Security and Nutrition, to bring the work of the long Green Revolution to Africa. Recall that the Green Revolution began in the twentieth century as an intervention in class politics, a way to manage the political concerns of hungry and angry urban insurgents. The New Alliance was built on foundations suggested at the World Economic Forum—a group of business interests that the *Financial Times* once called the "masters of the universe"[78]—to address concerns of urban unrest while developing markets for agriculture and food industries.

This helps explain why the New Alliance's largest donor is Yara, the Norwegian fertilizer giant. Yara is keen to address the decades of export-oriented asset stripping of African soils. Deficiencies of nitrogen, potassium, phosphorus, selenium, and other trace elements are a result of their shipment away both under colonial regimes and after independence, in the latter case to repay the World Bank Structural Adjustment Loans taken out by postcolonial countries in the 1980s and 1990s.

It's not just soil that's ripe for amendment—humans are too. The G8 plan requires that foreign corporations be granted increased access to African markets and land and that African bodies be supplemented with fortified processed food to manage some of the diseases associated with poverty and an inability to access food. This is the quintessence of the era of poverty with added vitamins, an agricultural policy that makes it harder for the rural poor to thrive in farming but treats their penury with micronutrients, a policy that combines exploitation with a strategy to prolong and manage that exploitation.[79]

Here we come to an important point about cheap food regimes: they guarantee neither that people are fed nor that they are fed well—as the global persistence of diet-related ill health and malnutrition can attest. Indeed, capitalism's cheap food regimes are, as Farshad Araghi quips, *hunger* regimes.[80]

Meanwhile, capitalism's agricultural frontiers continue to press against the world's peasants, who provide 75 percent of the food in large parts of the Global South.[81] But while the present is bleak, with agricultural frontiers pushing through Amazonia and displacing peasants around the world, a new wrinkle has appeared in the twenty-first century that will fatally undermine capitalism's five-century-long food regime: climate change. The imagery of the frontier lends itself easily to thinking only about land. But the past two centuries have witnessed a very different kind of frontier movement: the enclosure of the atmospheric commons as a dumping ground for greenhouse gas emissions.

In the twenty-first century, agriculture and forestry (which includes land clearance for cash cropping) contribute between a quarter and a third of greenhouse gas emissions.[82] They have to, because they're profoundly energy intensive and have become more so since the 1940s.[83] That's a big problem, because there are no more atmospheric commons to enclose and no obvious way to keep the costs of climate change off capitalism's ledgers. Nowhere is this clearer than in the faltering global farm, whose productivity growth has been slowing, just as it did for English farmers in the middle of the eighteenth century. In American grain agriculture, labor productivity growth has slowed by a third since the 1980s, and Indian wheat yield growth declined by 80 percent between the 1980s and 1990s.[84] Agrobiotechnology's promise of a new agricultural revolution has so far been worse than empty—failing to deliver a new yield boom, creating superweeds and superbugs that can withstand glyphosate and other poisons, and sustaining the cheap food model that is driving the ongoing state shift in the world's climate system.[85]

Frontiers always allowed cash-crop agriculture to boom by treating soil, work, and life as props to advance labor productivity. Climate change represents something much more than a closing frontier—it is something akin to an implosion of the cheap nature model, bringing not the end of easy and cheap natures but a dramatic reversal. As a growing body of research demonstrates, climate change suppresses agricultural productivity. *Climate* refers to extremely diverse phenomena, including drought, extreme rainfall, heat waves, and cold snaps. Braudel's "plants of civilization"—plus soy, the paradigmatic neoliberal crop—have already experienced what agronomists call yield suppression as a result of anthropogenic climate change. How much remains a matter of debate, but many analyses land somewhere in the ballpark of a 3 percent reduction in yields since the 1980s—a value of five billion dollars per year from 1981 to 2002.[86]

Worse, climate change promises absolute declines. Each successive degree Celsius increase in average annual global temperature is accompanied by a greater risk of nonlinear and dramatic effects on global farming. Agricultural yields will decline between 5 and more than 50 percent in the next century, depending on the time frame, crop, location, and extent to which carbon continues to be pumped into the air at today's prodigious rates.[87] World agriculture will absorb two-thirds of all climate change costs by 2050.[88] That means that not just the climate but also capitalism's agricultural model is in the midst of a state shift, one of the abrupt and irreversible moments of change we encountered in the introduction. Bound up with the global factory and global family has been the global farm. With climate change, that food system will break in the coming century.

Through climate change, the end of cheap food threatens a dramatic end for capitalism's ecology, but such food made it possible for cheap workers to survive. Food is not, however, the only requirement for cheap care to be sustained. Historically, after the cost of food, the most important cost facing workers throughout Europe from the sixteenth century on was that of energy. Indeed, it is through the atmospheric consequences of cheap energy that cheap food will end. To understand how, it is to cheap energy that we now turn.

CHAPTER SIX

Cheap Energy

> Here would be a good site for a town or fort, by reason of the good port, good water, good land and an abundance of fuel.
>
> Journal of Christopher Columbus, Tuesday, November 27, 1492

Before Columbus reached the New World, the sugar industry that had schooled him burned Madeira. The trees of Madeira (Portuguese for "wood") were transformed from shipbuilding material to fuel to ashes. This wood became a source of energy not just through some innate property but through specific human relations. Just as the graphite in a pencil might instead become stuff for a hearth or peat transforms from a fertilizer to a combustible for the fireplace or cow dung moves from being a soil amendment to being a cooking fuel, wood was transformed by the relations around it. The configuration of capitalism's ecology has shaped humans' interaction with trees.

Fire has been part of the earth ever since there were things on dry land to burn.[1] Before humans, fire had its rhythms, feeding on several seasons of accumulated kindling and fanned by propitious climate oscillations. Humans have, in their turn, set fire to a wide range of things. It's through cooking that *Homo erectus* became *Homo sapiens*.[2] Grasses were the first fuel, but buffalo dung endures as a rich source of heat. Herodotus observed that fatted animal bones were a fuel in Scythia.[3] Charred mammoth bones suggest the long history of humans' relationship with flames. The Maori colonization of Aotearoa (New Zealand) led to the loss of half its forest.[4] But humans have also recognized the need to stint. *Stint* is usually translated as "forgo"—to perform an act of sacrifice against present consumption—but it's more accurate to understand it as an indelible part of present consumption. You can find such a decision in the Chow dynasty (1122–256 BCE), which engaged in early attempts at forest management, including the establishment of a Police of Forest Foothills.[5] The empire stinted to maintain an energy source.[6]

Capitalism's ecology has a distinctive pyrogeography, one that is part of the fossil record. Indigenous People had thoroughly modified New World landscapes through fire. In eastern North America, they coproduced the "mosaic quality" of forest, savannah, and meadow that Europeans took for pristine nature.[7] Between Columbus's arrival and around 1650, disease and colonial violence reduced Indigenous populations in the Americas by 95 percent. With fewer humans burning and cutting them down, forests recovered so vigorously that the New World became a planetary carbon sink. Forest growth cooled the planet so much that the Indigenous holocaust contributed to the Little Ice Age's severity.[8] By the middle of the seventeenth century, some of the early modern era's worst winters were being recorded across Eurasia and the Americas. Not coincidentally, it was an era of bitter war and political unrest, from Beijing to Paris.[9] To reprise an idea from the introduction, it would be wrong to characterize this episode of genocide and reforestation as anthropogenic. The colonial exterminations of Indigenous Peoples were the work not of all humans, but of conquerors and capitalists. *Capitalogenic* would be more appropriate. And if we are tempted to conflate capitalism with the Industrial Revolution, these transformations ought to serve notice that early capitalism's destruction was so profound that it changed planetary climate four centuries ago.[10]

For many commoners in Europe and beyond, forests and woodlands were—and remain—as essential to survival as food. The destruction of the commons involved more than the creation of hunger. It also removed common rights to gather wood, imposing a poverty of fuel and construction material. In feudal Europe, demographic and settlement expansion in the eleventh and twelfth centuries led to conflict not just over farmland but also over access to forests, which had become lucrative income sources for nobles and kings.[11] When England's King John was forced to sign the Magna Carta in 1215, it's significant that he was also compelled to sign a second document at the same time: the Charter of the Forest. Where the Magna Carta turns on legal and political rights, the Charter of the Forest was about "economic survival": securing for peasants something called estovers, a broad category of subsistence wood products.[12] The Forest Charter was an assurance of English commoners' access to fuel, food, and building materials.

In Germany, as Peter Linebaugh notes, "the first great proletarian revolt of modern history, the Peasants' Revolt of Germany in 1525, demanded the restoration of customary forest rights."[13] These included rights to use "'windfall wood, rootfall trees, and inbowes,' where these latter were defined 'also only to so much thereof as the bees do light on, and the honey that shall be found in the tree, but not to cut any main bough or tree itself by color thereof.'"[14] People have been fighting for centuries over the fuel and construction material that wood can become. It's worth mentioning all this because it's too often forgotten that capitalism's energy revolution began not with coal but with wood—and with the privatization that forest enclosure implies.

This is not to privilege a European and North American history of energy over the histories of deforestation in, say, China. Notwithstanding the moderating effects of the forest police, China's great deforestation one thousand years ago had consequences that persist today: at ten cubic meters (353 cubic feet), the country's per capita forest reserves are an eighth of the world average.[15] But China's world-ecology wasn't committed to global conquest. Europe's was.

The reason to look at energy in Europe lies in the different use of fuel—a kind of cheap nature—as an intrinsic part of capitalism's ecology. Cheap energy is a way of amplifying—and in some cases substituting for—cheap work and care. If cheap food is capitalism's major way of reducing the wage bill, cheap energy is the crucial lever to advance labor productivity. The two can function as a logical sequence, even if the actual history is more complex. First, peasants must be ejected from the commons. These new workers must find wage work in some form. Second, the workshops and factories that employ these workers have to compete with one another. And while there's a long history of bosses' overworking their employees, the competitive struggle between capitalists is ultimately decided by labor productivity. We normally think of labor productivity—that is, the production of more commodities per average hour of work—as something determined by machines. But capitalist machines function because they draw on the work of extrahuman natures, and these have to be cheap, because the demand is limitless. For this reason, the enclosure of terrestrial commons coincided with the enclosure of the subterranean world. At the very moment when peasant life was turned upside down in sixteenth-century England, the country's great coal mines were pumping out coal by the thousands of tons. Here a new layer of cheapness emerges in our picture of the world: capitalism's global factory requires not just a global farm and a global family, but a global *mine* as well.

In this chapter we explore how energy became one of capitalism's cheap things through energy revolutions in Europe and the Americas, and what cheap energy means for the twenty-first century's global ecology. Energy qualifies as a "thing" insofar as it is transformed from part of the web of life into a commodity to be bought and sold. Fossilized life becomes stuff for a fire and an engine's fuel tank only through capitalism's ecology. But capitalism's energy system does several tasks at once. It makes both energy and inputs cheaper: cheap coal makes cheap steel; cheap peat makes for cheap(er) bricks. This reduces the costs of doing business and enhances profitability.[16] Cheap energy also helps keep labor costs down, by controlling one of the largest costs (after food) in a family budget. While enclosure made energy more expensive for most peasants by removing their access to the commons—where, in many parts of the world, collecting resources had fallen to women—it also pulled workers into the cash economy, where they had to pay for their building materials and fuel.[17] Controlling energy costs was another way to manage and sustain cheap work. Energy has always been an indispensable part of life, but to show how it is an indispensable part of capitalism's ecology, we need to begin with a place sitting on top of energy reserves so prodigious that this country scooped itself out of the earth: the Netherlands.[18]

THE DUTCH DISEASE

Let's begin with the words of Peter Voser, who in 2012 was the CEO of Royal Dutch Shell:

> In the United States, for example, the American Petroleum Institute estimates that the industry supports more than nine million jobs directly and indirectly, which is over 5% of the country's total employment. In 2009 the energy industry supported a total value added to the national economy of more than US$ 1 trillion, representing 7.7% of US GDP.
>
> Beyond its direct contributions to the economy, energy is also deeply linked to other sectors in ways that are not immediately obvious. For example, each calorie of food we consume requires an average input of five calories of fossil fuel, and for high-end products like beef this rises to an average of 80 calories. The energy sector is also the biggest industrial user of fresh water, accounting for 40% of all freshwater withdrawals in the United States....
>
> Powerful actors need to make the role of the energy sector and the benefits of our work clear, while demonstrating that we can be trusted to work together across boundaries to face the challenges ahead. In return, society at large will grant a license to operate that is too often missing today.[19]

It was part of Voser's job to engineer the triumph of the fossil fuel industry, over the protests of those such as the Ogoni Ken Saro-Wiwa, who was put to death in 1995, his life rendered cheap by Royal Dutch and Nigeria because he organized against them.[20] As the official history of the company—which was founded to develop oil fields in what is now Indonesia—puts it, "The rise of the Royal Dutch was rendered possible only by the victory in the field of colonial policy of those liberal principles according to which the interests of Asiatic Dominions are best served by the free competition of Western capital and Western labour in the development of the resources of these tropical regions."[21] As the boom, deforestation, and bust of Madeira over seventy years show, capitalism's insatiability for fuel is part of its ecology. Royal Dutch is just the latest player in a long history of cheap energy.

This company was made possible by revenues, and finance, based on a fuel crisis in the fifteenth-century Netherlands, several centuries before its founding. Dutch soil was once filled with black gold: not oil but peat, an energy source still used today for heating and even for generating electricity.[22] It's the youngest of the fossil fuels and offers about two-thirds the energy of coal by weight.[23] Peat is coal's precursor. After enough time and pressure, the former becomes the latter, and peat—and thus coal—was once wetland vegetation. As this vegetation decayed in northern and central Europe, it formed pillow-shaped layers more than a mile (1.6 kilometers) in diameter, which accumulated into raised bogs. By the early Middle Ages, these reached around fifteen feet (4.6 meters) above sea level. Beginning in the eleventh century, however, peasants gathered peat for heating, salt processing, and sale. Mining this topsoil made the Low Countries even lower—and vulnerable to climate change. Indeed, as northern Europe's climate turned colder, wetter, and more turbulent at the end of the thirteenth century, flooding increased across Europe, especially in the North Sea region, where land was sinking. Soggy soils didn't make for fertile land. We know this because taxes on grain cultivation plummeted by 1400 as an agroecological crisis deepened.[24] Surrounding the cities of Amsterdam, Rotterdam, and Utrecht were landscapes that resembled "Swiss cheese, with dozens of water-filled, exhausted peat bogs often separated from each other by nothing more than narrow, vulnerable strips of land on which were scattered the structures of what once had been farms."[25] Climate change and the removal of peatlands coproduced a truly disastrous situation: by 1500, "the North Sea threatened to drown Dutch society."[26] At that point, grain farming had virtually disappeared from the coastal regions.[27]

This had consequences for the Dutch economy. In England, workers were made by the enclosure of land.[28] In the Netherlands, they were made by sinking peat bogs and were dug out by the needs of an expanding dairy and cattle industry.[29] Peat also hooked the country on cheap energy. During the seventeenth century, one and a half million tons of peat were dug out and shipped to the republic's growing cities every year; more than eight thousand boatloads arrived in Amsterdam in 1636 alone.[30] By 1650, the Dutch Republic's per capita energy consumption was higher than India's in 2000.[31]

While the Dutch peasantry was having an increasingly hard time, Dutch capitalism was thriving. Indeed, the latter thrived *because* the former were becoming workers in cities.[32] Central to this process was cheap food. The Dutch began the long sixteenth century with the highest grain prices in western Europe and ended it with some of the lowest.[33] As we mentioned in the previous chapter, this grain came from a frontier in Poland, a country with fertile soils along the Vistula and landlords who were ready to fall into "international debt peonage."[34] Inventive financial arrangements sent Andean silver swiftly out of Amsterdam and Antwerp to Poland in exchange for wheat and rye. The trade deficit formed part of a strategy to keep cheap food flowing to the growing Dutch cities. Just as in Madeira, the Polish rye and wheat boom lasted fifty to seventy-five years. By the 1660s, soil erosion had nearly halved yields, and capitalism's ecology had deepened and expanded beyond Poland's thinned land.[35]

The Dutch owed their superpower status to both an agricultural and an energy revolution. These comprised not just large-scale peat extraction but also the pioneering application—and technological development—of wind power to a wide range of industrial pursuits.[36] From the mid-sixteenth century, windmills of every kind punctuated the Dutch landscape. Along the river Zaan, just to the north of Amsterdam, there were six hundred industrial windmills by the 1730s, one every hundred meters (328 feet).[37]

But the Dutch road to capitalism faced three serious constraints to expansion after 1650. One was that the country had no forests to speak of. This was overcome through the power of ready cash—a resource that it had in abundance. Dutch merchants reached across the North Sea and into the Baltic for cheap timber and a wide range of forest products, necessary not only for shipbuilding but also for bleaching textiles. A second problem was less tractable. Peat was abundant but never particularly cheap. Its cost rose 50 percent faster than the price index in Antwerp between 1480 and 1530.[38] Even with innovations after 1530 that allowed peat extraction below the waterline, prices continued their upward trend, tripling in the northern Netherlands in the century after 1560.[39] Coal was imported, from nearby Liège (now in Belgium) but especially from England, in growing volumes—some sixty-five thousand tons a year by the 1650s.[40] That represented a lot of energy, and the leading energy-intensive industries shifted to coal when possible. Sugar refiners—whose giant five-story buildings were the closest thing to a modern factory you'd see in the seventeenth century—burned so much coal that Amsterdam's city council banned the practice in 1614. But as the city's refineries multiplied—there were a hundred by century's end—so too did demand for cheap, or at least cheaper, energy. Despite the earlier bans that had registered the "insufferably great sorry" that coal burning inflicted on Amsterdam's citizens, year-round coal burning was legalized in 1674.[41] Peat was cleaner but coal cheaper.

These steps could not solve the Netherlands' third problem: the high cost of labor. Dutch success was premised on an agrarian crisis that produced "an elastic supply of labour of proto-proletarians."[42] That elasticity was gone by 1580, and Dutch wages remained the highest in Europe until the middle of the eighteenth century.[43] By 1650—and probably earlier—Dutch capitalists had the highest wage bill in Europe, one that moved still higher after 1680. Between 1590 and 1730, Dutch wages were never less than a third higher than those in the England, and frequently twice that.[44] But, due in no small part to their far more territorial forms of colonialism, the English were soon to catch up.

The transitions to large-scale peat digging in the Netherlands and coal mining in England occurred simultaneously, in the 1530s and 1540s.[45] Our imaginary of the Industrial Revolution tells us that fossil fuels were invented in the eighteenth century—but in fact they, like so much else, were a product of the long sixteenth century. The first great industrialization occurred in the century or so after 1450, unfolding in the great sugar-planting and silver-mining frontiers, as we've seen, but also in shipbuilding, brewing, glassmaking, printing, textiles, and iron and copper smelting.[46] All, in one way or another, consumed prodigious amounts of energy.

In modest amounts, coal had been mined and burned for a very long time; for the Romans, it was the "best stone in Britain."[47] In the century after 1530, England's coal output climbed dramatically, growing eightfold.[48] In Newcastle alone, where coal was king, production grew nearly twentyfold between the 1560s and 1660s, accounting for perhaps a third of all English coal.[49] Coal may have been king in Newcastle, but on a per capita basis, the production of Dutch thermal energy equaled—and mechanical energy exceeded—England's in the seventeenth century.[50] But Dutch energy just wasn't *cheap* enough. England was hardly a low-wage economy at the time, and real wages were also rising fast, despite the success of enclosure and dispossession. Starting at a lower point than those of the Dutch, English wages increased much faster, nearly doubling in the century after 1625.[51] With coal, the English economic advantage was decisive: "The burden of high wages in England, however, was offset by cheap energy."[52]

The high cost of workers and the availability of abundant cheap energy in England drove a series of the eighteenth century's technological breakthroughs: the use of a coal derivative, coke, to make iron, and of the Newcomen steam engine to drain coal mines, whose increasing depths meant constant flooding.[53] Coke had been known since the seventeenth century, but it took a long series of innovations between 1709 and 1755—usually credited to Thomas Darby—to make it profitable for iron production.[54] This liberated England from dependence on charcoal. Coke-fired iron, just 7 percent of English iron output in 1750, accounted for 90 percent in 1784.[55] The cost of producing a ton of iron collapsed, falling 60 percent in the eighteenth century. Cheap energy made cheap iron made cheap tools and machines. So long as abundant energy could be extracted, labor and capital costs were saved, and raw materials became cheaper.[56]

We're not presenting this as a pure English technological miracle. Some explanations would have us think that there would be no real capitalism without English coal. Indeed, coal's significance is easily overstated: the major innovations in textile manufacturing, such as the mechanical loom and the spinning jenny, preceded rather than followed steam's widespread introduction, and as late as 1868, 92 percent of Britain's merchant fleet was powered by wind, not coal.[57] We know enough to realize that capitalism's frontier is nothing if not inventive. It is possible to imagine an English history without coal, with more energy imported and discovered, and to imagine a nineteenth century even more prone to social revolt and revolution than it was. While we suggest that such social turmoil will be the fate of a twenty-first century without frontiers of cheap nature, it's important to understand how cheap energy has intersected with food, care, money, and work in order to see the social order produced through them. We thus present three key twentieth-century moments involving international conflicts around energy.

TWENTIETH-CENTURY FOOD

The first, and arguably the most important, instance in which cheap energy matters today is the Haber-Bosch process, industrialized in the Rhineland-Palatinate laboratories of Badische Anilin- und Soda-Fabrik (BASF) and patented on October 13, 1908. Fritz Haber, a researcher at the University of Karlsruhe, demonstrated a method of using high-temperature and high-pressure industrial chemistry to react hydrogen (H_2) with atmospheric nitrogen (N_2) to produce ammonia (NH_3). Carl Bosch, a BASF engineer, solved substantial mechanical problems involving an operating environment of more than one hundred atmospheres (1,470 pounds per square inch, or 103 kilograms per square centimeter) to commercialize this reaction.[58] There were strategic imperatives behind their research. Guano, an important source of ammonia, had been mined prodigiously and been replaced by Peruvian saltpeter (sodium nitrate, $NaNO_3$) from the Atacama Desert.[59] This "white gold" was vital to the production of gunpowder and to soil fertility, and the British controlled its trade.[60] The Haber-Bosch process delivered a substitute—one so significant that Haber won a Nobel Prize in 1918 and Bosch got his in 1931. As it happens, Alfred Nobel had made his fortune in explosives, and Haber's and Bosch's work provided Germany with key inputs for TNT and gelignite, which Nobel had patented. Their knowledge decoupled the manufacture of gunpowder from the extraction of resources from specific sites and allowed the production of weapons through the use of nothing but energy and air. More than one hundred million deaths in armed conflict can be linked to the widespread availability of ammonia produced by the Haber-Bosch process.[61]

But ammonia is also the stuff of life. Justus von Liebig, who inspired Marx's thinking on metabolism, declared in 1840 that the struggle of agriculture is to reliably produce digestible nitrogen.[62] Normally, the largely inert nitrogen in the air becomes bioavailable through either interaction with lightning or being fixed in soils by microorganisms. It is a prerequisite and, in the right amounts, a stimulant for plant growth. When nitrogen is made bioavailable through the Haber-Bosch process, there's a high energetic cost. The reaction requires hydrogen, which in turn requires cheap fuel. Today the hydrogen for fertilizer production comes primarily from natural gas, although coal and naphtha also work. This makes fertilizer production the largest energy input into US industrial agriculture.[63]

In transmuting air and fossil fuel into a fertilizer, the Haber-Bosch process has reduced the costs of food, work, and care.[64] On arrival, cheap inorganic fertilizer returned higher yields to landowning farmers and lower wages to field workers and sent waves of commodity food and displaced peasants to the cities.[65] This made possible the growth of cereal mountains that found their way into the stomachs of livestock, whose flesh was then devoured by humans in the Global North and soon worldwide. With the end of World War II, ammonia was redirected from ammunition and now blasted into the soil. Two-thirds of the resulting cereal boom in the United States and Europe was used as animal feed. Haber-Bosch allowed the meatification—as Tony Weis puts it—of the global diet.[66] With meat increasingly marketed as an essential component of the modern meal, demand for feed soared. To meet it, farmers in Brazil cleared land to grow soy for livestock, a process that is alone responsible for 2 percent of all capitalogenic greenhouse gases each year.[67] Another example of the fertilizer-food nexus lies in this fact: fertilizer price manipulation contributed to the fall into poverty of forty-four million people during the last food price crisis, in 2007–8.[68] All of this, part of the project to destroy peasant agriculture and Indigenous foodways and replace them with a regime of industrial monocultures, would be unthinkable without energy made into a soil amendment.[69] Or, as Marx put it, "All progress increasing the fertility of the soil for a given time is a progress towards ruining the more long-lasting sources of that fertility. The more a country proceeds from large-scale industry as a background of its development . . . , the more rapid is this process of destruction. Capitalist production, therefore, only develops the techniques and the degree of combination of the social process of production by simultaneously undermining the original sources of all wealth—the soil and the worker."[70]

TWENTIETH-CENTURY COAL AND WORK

Keeping energy cheap requires sustained state intervention. State support is also necessary to keep reproductive labor free and paid labor cheap. When the state fails, we see resistance politics emerge, as in movements as diverse as the twenty-first-century Occupy Nigeria and UK fuel protests.[71] The second twentieth-century connection to cheap fuel links modern protests to the 1525 Peasants' War. Remember that as part of the right to common in the forest, peasants wanted access to wood as fuel and construction material. The politics of resistance in the twentieth century is also linked to both housing and energy.

Workers need roofs over their heads—and roofs are not free. Houses in Colorado at the end of the nineteenth century were made with brick—lumber was far too expensive, while brick could be manufactured with locally available clay and coal. This manufacture made energy vital to housing. Mining technology lowered the price of coal, but labor remained 60–80 percent of its cost. Two ways to keep that cost down were to pay immigrant workers very little and to settle them in company towns, which compelled them to hand back wages for housing and services such as schools, cut-price English lessons, and recreational facilities. With little control over their lives, workers felt the company town akin to refeudalization rather than benign capitalism. When the Rockefeller-owned Colorado Fuel and Iron Company squeezed their wages, coal miners organized.[72] Their strike, from spring 1913 to winter 1914, remains a signal moment in US labor history. On April 20, 1914, around twenty men, women, and children were killed at a striker's camp in Ludlow, Colorado. Subsequent outrage, particularly against the mine owner, John D. Rockefeller Jr., led to congressional investigation and, fueled by further union organization, restrictions on child labor and the introduction of the eight-hour working day.[73]

Timothy Mitchell points out that the labor politics of carbon had a profound impact on the twentieth century. Set aside the discussion of whether a particular country is "cursed" by a resource like fossil fuel or minerals.[74] Look instead at how the extraction of those resources built a working class that was able to resist its exploitation and whose demands for equality could be met through the energy its labor made profitable.[75] All of a sudden, national destinies could be dreamed far bigger than before—precisely because such national dreams were underwritten by cheap energy.

TWENTIETH-CENTURY OIL AND MONEY

The third story of cheap energy in the twentieth century comes from the transformation of energy into money and "the American way of life."[76] The United States was the preeminent oil power of the twentieth century. Although Russia had the pole position as the century opened, with the discovery of oil in Pennsylvania, Texas, and California, the United States quickly took the lead. By 1945, two of every three barrels of oil were produced in the United States.[77] Only in the 1970s did the Soviet Union and then Saudi Arabia displace America as the world's leading oil producer.[78] Global oil production grew prodigiously after World War II, outstripping the era's extraordinary economic growth by almost 60 percent.[79]

When the United States abandoned the gold standard in August 1971,[80] international capital sought refuge from this "Nixon shock" in commodity purchases. At the same time, the Soviet Union—following poor harvests—traded its oil for wheat, driving up the price of bread. Fourteen months later, the Organization of the Petroleum Exporting Countries (OPEC), nominally responding to the Yom Kippur War between Israel and Egypt, announced a 70 percent rise in the oil production tax.[81] World oil prices leaped from three to twelve dollars per barrel. The OPEC countries were responding to the US export of dollar-denominated inflation. As the shah of Iran put it, the United States had "increased the price of wheat you sell us by 300 percent, and the same for sugar and cement."[82] The world paid the higher oil price, and the OPEC countries found themselves sitting on substantial income, reserves of what became known as petrodollars. These reserves needed a return, so they were cycled back to oil-importing countries as low-interest loans. Think of this as money backed not with silver but with oil—a "de facto oil standard."[83] The so-called Volcker shock of 1979 tripled the real interest rates on these petroloans over the next two years.[84] To avoid default, indebted countries, predominantly in the Global South, turned to the only lenders who'd consider them: the International Monetary Fund and the World Bank, institutions that could administer austerity programs, small governments, and free markets through their own shock doctrines.[85] Petrodollars thus made possible the sorry history of neoliberal governance.

The political economy of energy has, however, changed over the past two decades. During the 1980s and 1990s, the costs of bringing a new barrel of oil to the market grew by just under 1 percent a year. That shifted—dramatically—at the end of the century. Between 1999 and 2013, those costs climbed nearly 11 percent every year. In the most expensive oil fields—the top tenth of production, which often predicts future price trends—production costs increased tenfold between 1991 and 2007 and by another two-thirds since.[86] Cheap oil is coming to an end even as climate change is on its way to killing one hundred million people by 2030.[87] And that end is not only about future death; things are already dirtier and more violent than ever, as conflicts stretching from Alberta to Ecuador replay a sixteenth-century battle between Indigenous Peoples and extractivists, once again with planetary implications.

Why is cheap oil so important? It's not that capitalism can't do without fossil fuels. After all, retailers and manufacturers don't care if their electricity comes from ancient fossils, windmills, or solar panels. Cheap oil is so important because today's capitalists don't wish to support the kinds of massive investment that would make a solar transition possible. Clearly, some businesses will cash in on various renewable energy initiatives. It is, however, hard to believe that all of the world's businesses will pitch in the forty-five trillion dollars necessary for a large-scale conversion to renewables by 2050.[88] If a solar transition is to happen under capitalism, it will only be because governments will pay for it.[89] Neoliberal practice has left governments with few policy prescriptions outside tax relief—and in countries like the United States, corporate taxation is already at historic lows, with self-styled "green" tech companies (Apple, Google) the greatest beneficiaries.[90] We will all end up paying to keep their share prices high.

We want to close with a discussion of the *cheap* in *cheap fuel.* The crisis of fuel isn't necessarily a crisis of scarcity or overproduction. The shift away from fossil fuels isn't the end of the regime of cheap energy. Indeed, the climate crisis has afforded an opportunity for finance to present itself as a mechanism of global salvation: it is through carbon credits, offsets, and permits to pollute the atmosphere that the atmosphere will be saved—or so we are told.[91] This is where commoning can finally be ended—through the full financial externalization of collective responsibility, turning what need to be collective decisions on the fate of the commons into a financial product in a global market.

Yet we cannot end a discussion of energy without observing that the International Energy Agency in 2016 announced that the capacity of renewable energy exceeds that of coal.[92] Does this render a discussion of cheap energy moot? Hardly. Look inside the batteries of the solar revolution, and you'll find blood minerals from the Democratic Republic of the Congo and Bolivia.[93] The lithium extraction complex in Bolivia looks like Potosí redux.[94] Damming rivers as a way of tackling climate change has been catastrophic—and part of a strategy to dispossess Indigenous Peoples.[95] Moving away from fossil fuel toward dams still leads to entirely predictable species extinction and may end up increasing greenhouse gas emissions with the decomposing ecology of human-made reservoirs.[96]

Above all, the strategy of cheap fuel doesn't depend on carbon. It has in the past but needn't in the future. Hydroelectric dams, for instance, reveal that the cheap energy strategy always depends on states. It requires the violence meted by public and private sectors, licensed by a world-ecology that stretches back to cheap nature and is possible only because of a collective understanding that cheap energy is part of the *national* bounty. Through collective ideas of communal nationhood, energy is secured in capitalism's ecology, from the subsidized petroleum in India through the oil revenues in Venezuela to the low gas prices in the United States that have substituted for real blue-collar wage growth. For the poor to bear the costs of energy projects, you need a governing set of ideas and institutions that can control and channel ideas of collective destiny in their name. To understand these covering ideas of collective destiny and violence, we move to our final cheap thing: lives.

CHAPTER SEVEN

Cheap Lives

On his third day in the New World, Columbus offered the king and queen of Spain a description of an island that might be fortified,

> though I do not see that it would be necessary, for these people are very simple as regards the use of arms, as your Highnesses will see from the seven that I caused to be taken, to bring home and learn our language and return; unless your Highnesses should order them all to be brought to Castile, or to be kept as captives on the same island; for with fifty men they can all be subjugated and made to do what is required of them.[1]

Columbus learned early that it's one thing to set up a colony and another to maintain it. The *Santa María* foundered on his first expedition, and there wasn't enough room on the other ships to bring its crew home. That Christmas, some of its sailors salvaged what they could from their ship and, under Columbus's command, settled La Navidad on Hispaniola. This complement of around forty colonists included Diego de Araña, a cousin of Columbus's mistress. All were dead when Columbus returned on his second voyage. He learned that his men had been killed for their abuse of Indigenous women. The second voyage was better prepared for native unrest than the first. It was equipped with a colonial mandate, seventeen ships, twelve hundred men, livestock—and their attendant diseases, which scythed through the Indigenous population. Yet while it certainly involved bloody murder, colonialism was never exclusively an act of brute force. Columbus and his descendants had weapons but also an organization and language that legitimated their use of that force. Capitalism may have claimed the New World with guns, germs, and steel,[2] but the New World's order was kept through race, police, and profits. These technologies of hegemony and order are the subject of our final chapter.

In the case of every cheap thing so far, we've seen organized acts of resistance. Women, wageworkers, Indigenous People, and even those members of the ruling class on whose fortunes the sun has set—all have fought, more or less successfully, against the requirement of their subservience. In response, capitalists developed new strategies to forge new frontiers and to deepen existing ones. This cat-and-mouse game of resistance, strategy, and counterstrategy has been the history of capitalism's ecology. Governments, merchants, and financiers scaled new heights of creativity and destruction in the search for profit. But capitalism's ecology has also expanded and consolidated itself through prodigious experimentation in the arts and science of social order. Among the more durable and flexible technologies of social control is one that has become so familiar that it's easy to forget its novelty and peculiarity: the nation-state.

The argument of this chapter is that capitalism's ecology has shaped the modern nation-state and vice versa, through the colonial frontier, through the interactions between early capitalists and "savages," and through the technologies of communication that capitalism fostered at its inception. The ordering and reordering of Society through cheap things has always proceeded by both force and suasion, coercion and consent. To maintain hegemony is, as Antonio Gramsci observed, to recruit and maintain forces from across society in a bloc that is able to continually outmaneuver its rivals.[3] In the pursuit of order and control, the idea of "the nation" became affixed to the state in ways that few could predict and which continue to shape the planet.

Keeping things cheap is expensive. The forces of law and order, domestic and international, are a costly part of the management of capitalism's ecology. We've titled this chapter "Cheap Lives" and not "Expensive State" because we want to focus not on the institutions of government but on their processes and consequences. Technically, lives aren't a cheap thing in the way that the others are—but it would have made for an infelicitous title to admit this earlier. Understand how capitalism has made "cheap lives" a strategy of cheap nature, and you understand not only the forces required to keep money, work, care, food, and energy cheap but also how the most sophisticated and subtle modern institution, the nation-state, still draws on early modern roots and natural science to manage modern life. More important still, as states confront the limits of their ability both to manage the lives in their charge and to provide conducive environments for liberal capitalism, we're reaching the end of an era of cheap lives. We make this argument not with relish for the successor to the liberal nation-state but out of concern for what may follow. We're astute enough students of history to know that what comes next might be far worse.

Like everything else in our tale of cheap things, the components of the modern nation-state and its cheap lives predate capitalism. Classical and early modern physiologists like Henry Cornelius Agrippa, Paracelsus, and Andreas Vesalius produced human typologies, lexicons in which bodies' natural positions in a social hierarchy might be read.[4] Humans who resembled the authors sat at one limit of the hierarchy. At the other end were "monsters." Monstrous physical characteristics could be interpreted, if necessary, as medical manifestations of innate differences in community, providing some of the basis for understanding how different bloodlines could be made and traced.[5] Like *savage,* to which it is kin, the term *monster* ought to trigger alarm for its association with beings that cross the boundary between humans and nonhuman animals. Monstrosity licensed the idea of pure blood—you couldn't have a pure bloodline without the threat of "loathsome copulation" to sully it.[6]

Thoughts on hierarchy and bodies are old. It takes special kinds of institutions to circulate and weaponize them. The nation-state is just such an institution, one that emerged through capitalism and contingency. To understand how, we return to the Black Death. In late medieval Europe, Jewish communities in a range of cities and states had negotiated ways to practice their faith under laws that were not from Rome and interpreted by local bishops but from the Torah and interpreted by rabbis. These truces were always precarious. During the Crusades, Pope Innocent III (r. 1198–1216) issued a *Constitutio Judaeorum* requiring monarchs to respect Jews.[7] At the same time, however, came the requirement that, to receive protection, Jews be distinguishable. They had to wear a badge "made of red felt or saffron yellow cloth"—for their own safety, and to prevent intermarriage with Christians.[8] This policing of blood came to matter a great deal when people with that blood were accused of mass murder.

Enter the Black Death in 1347. Recent DNA analysis from bodies found in plague sites suggests that the bacterium *Yersinia pestis* caused the disease[9] and was brought into Europe by at least two different routes, one through the South of France and another through Norway and the Low Countries. The death toll was higher than it might have been, because of the socioecological turmoil at the end of the Medieval Warm Period that we discussed in the introduction and chapter 1. Medieval Europeans had alternative facts. One influential account, from Louis Sanctus of Beringen in 1348, had the pathogen arrive in a scene familiar to fans of the zombie genre, as ships that had witnessed rains of scorpions in India arrived in Genoa and then, after being sent away, docked in Marseille. Those ashore discovered the crews dead or dying and sent the ships back to sea, but too late to stop the pestilence.[10] Louis Sanctus suggested that the plague was sent as divine retribution for the actions of Queen Joanna of Naples, who'd murdered her husband, Andrew of Hungary.[11]

More important than the fear of Oriental contagion or the particular horror of a woman killing her legal owner were theories that put the blame on the newly conspicuous community of Jews. In response to the pestilence, Jews were tortured and confessed to poisoning cities. Although Pope Clement VI (r. 1342–52) prohibited extrajudicial killing, forced conversion, and desecration of Jewish property in 1348, the slaughter spread throughout Europe as the plague burned through the population. Among many horrors, consider that on January 9, 1349, all of Basel's Jewish children were separated from their parents and forcibly baptized and then the city's six hundred adult Jews burned at the stake "on a sandbank on the Rhine."[12] Thousands were immolated in city-state-sponsored pogroms, and the members of some Jewish communities took their own lives before they could be tortured and killed by their neighbors. These atrocities happened despite repeated mandates from Rome. The Catholic Church's power over Europe's commercial centers was starting to wane, while the precedent that some people might be transformed into things had been set.

SCIENTIFIC RACISM AND COLONIAL POLICY

Blood purity, the state's increasing power relative to Rome, and a body of literature sanctioning the idea of natural orders of humans were all in place. They were used to inform and propel new kinds of governance, and once again the site where new kinds of social-scientific control were practiced was the colonial frontier.

In New Spain, the *sistema de castas* emerged as a way of policing citizens, taxes, and labor requirements, as well as proximity to god. It ranked people according to their blood, with categories emerging like answers to a combinatorial mathematics problem. From the original African slaves, Indigenous People, and Spanish emerged categories like *españoles* (Spaniards), *peninsulares* (Spaniards and other Europeans born in Europe), *criollos* (Spaniards and other Europeans born in the Americas), *indios* (Native Americans), *mestizos* (people of unknown Native American and European heritage), *castizos* (people with 75 percent European and 25 percent Indigenous heritage), *cholos* (people with Native American and some mestizo heritage), *pardos* (people of European, African, and Native American heritage), *mulatos* (people of African and European heritage), *zambos* (people of Native American and African heritage), and *negros* (Africans). In fact, the complexities of gender, sex, and history demanded their own vocabulary and arithmetic:

1. español + negra = mulato
2. mulato + española = testerón or tercerón
3. testerón + española = quarterón
4. quarterón + española = quinterón
5. quinterón + española = blanco or español común
6. negro + mulata = sambo
7. sambo + mulata = sambohigo
8. sambohigo + mulata = tente en el aire
9. tente en el aire + mulata = salta atrás
10. español + india = mestizo real
11. mestizo + india = cholo
12. cholo + india = tente en el aire
13. tente en el aire + india = salta atrás
14. india + negra = chino
15. chino + negra = rechino or criollo
16. criollo + negra = torna atrás[13]

This is a potent mix of grammar, genetics, mathematics, and teleology, with categories suggesting that a child of criollo and African parents would always be "turning back" to Africa or that a mix of *sambohigo* and mulata was "held in the air."[14] Once assigned, these categories were enforced. Which is to say that women's bodies, workers, taxes, religion, and property rights were policed simultaneously. The colonial state produced new categories, new natures, to meet the needs for laborers first for silver specie and then for agricultural production destined for sale and profit in Europe. Each of these governmental categories came with specific duties, privileges, and paperwork, including certifications of purity of blood and tax rates. Some lives were, then, literally cheaper than others.[15]

Natural science contributed to the consolidation of this order. The Swede Carl Linnaeus (1707–78) developed the nomenclature with which humans continue to identify species to this day. In his 1735 *General System of Nature,* he offered a typology that put humans in the class of mammals, the order of primates, the genus of *Homo,* the species of *Homo sapiens.* But he also included observations on different kinds of *Homo sapiens,* noting variations in appearance and character:

Class *mammalia*
Order I. Primates thus genetically
Foreteeth cutting; upper 4, parallel; teats 2 pectoral
HOMO
Sapiens. Diurnal; varying by education and situation
The varieties as follow

1. Four footed, mute, hairy. *Wild man*
2. Copper-coloured, choleric, erect. *American*

   Hair black, straight, thick; *nostrils* wide; *face* harsh; *beard* scanty; *obstinate,* content, free. *Paints* himself with fine red lines. *Regulated* by customs.

3. Fair, sanguine, brawny. *European*

   Hair yellow, brown, flowing; *eyes* blue; *gentle,* acute, inventive. *Covered* with close vestments. *Governed* by laws.

4. Sooty, melancholy, rigid. *Asiatic*

   Hair black; *eyes* dark; *severe,* haughty, covetous. *Covered* with loose garments. *Governed* by opinions.

5. Black, phlegmatic, relaxed. *African*

   Hair black, frizzled; *skin* silky; *nose* flat; *lips* tumid; *crafty,* indolent, negligent. *Anoints* himself with grease. *Governed* by caprice.

Monstrous. Varying by climate or art.
The varieties of this species as follow

1. Small, active, timid. *Mountaineer*
2. Large, indolent. *Patagonian*
3. Less fertile. *Hottentot*
4. Beardless. *American*
5. Head conic. *Chinese*
6. Head flattened. *Canadian*[16]

Some humans, Europeans for instance, were gentle, acute, and inventive, while others were marked by decidedly less benign physiology and character. Science provided the grounding for racial order, and that order in turn legitimized colonialism's civilizing mission. Linnaeus's typology did more than allow some human bodies to be considered property and instruments of debt. It went much further, providing a scientific basis for bodies and lives to be subject to government by a state run by humans who placed themselves at the top of this hierarchy.

To see this synthesized, consider the image on the opposite page. It is an example of a genre popular in the eighteenth century: *casta* painting. These works were often commissioned by colonial bureaucrats keen to portray their activities in New Spain not as the unflattering (and accurate) horror stories of poverty and rapacity that circulated in Europe but as a project of gentility and civilization. In Spain, although most of these pictures were privately held, some were available for public viewing, as at the Gabinete de Historia Natural, the Museum of Natural History's precursor, where visitors might also see mastodon fossils and Chinese gongs.[17] The exhibition of humans in such a venue linked nature, gender, work, society, and civilization plainly and neatly.

This scientific project of national order persists, in the Global North and the Global South. It has survived in no small part

Figure 6. Luis de Mena, *Castas,* circa 1750. Museo de América, Madrid.
Source: Cline 2015, 218.

because it was made normal by its inclusion in national discourses by those masters of colonialism, the English.

NATURE, CIVILIZATION, AND THE BRITISH COLONIAL STATE

Spanish colonial relations were shaped by the demands of the Spanish state and its creditors, particularly the needs for labor and labor control. English capitalists were also concerned with labor, but more especially with land.[18] Cheap labor having been secured through enclosure and the conquest of Celtic peoples, cheap land was the greater priority for English colonialism. The English state developed through the need to secure territory—and to produce ways of governing that secured rights of ownership. The ordering and policing of humans on that land and the securing of title and property were central to the English colonial enterprise. Many of the techniques of social control developed at home were practiced and refined in England's first major colonial outpost, in Ireland. Henry VII's declaration of his title as the king of Ireland in 1542 is a useful moment to explore how the English—and later British—frontier in Ireland functioned as both a far outpost of domestic politics and a local colony.[19] We mentioned in the introduction that the English had staked out a holding around Dublin, with the Irish beyond that Pale. From this area, the English ventured out to begin "plantations," models that aimed to educate the Irish on how agriculture should be done. The late sixteenth century saw various experiments in model farms to show the mechanical and political arrangements for the control of nature.[20] Those farming practices involved large-scale ownership of property by a landlord, with tenants and attendant artisans.[21] Also on the plantations were cattle, sheep, wheat, timber, and specialty crops—woad and madder (sources of blue and red dye, respectively) and hemp.[22]

The early colonists took pains to follow existing international law in acquiring land. England's first plantations were leased from local Irish lords. In other cases, plantations were military plunder, seized from enemies of the state as a legitimate spoil of war. Despite this, things didn't go smoothly. The English commercial, arable farming system clashed with the smaller-scale, pastoral systems of food provision in Ireland, in which bonds were governed less by aristocratic control than by family ties and property was divided among heirs rather than inherited on the basis of primogeniture.[23] The Irish rebelled. They ran their cattle on land enclosed by the English, and the English responded with a military mobilization to protect colonial property.[24] Rebellions throughout the sixteenth century prompted a new strategy in the next century: a more forceful and violently enforced plantation system. The Plantation of Ulster was more directly controlled from London, which organized natural and social experiments that were repeated elsewhere, such as the granting of rights to private corporations to colonize Derry in north central Ireland. Meanwhile, the Indigenous rebellions were repressed with increasing force, the violence being justified by a new rationale for colonization. While the legal parameters of England's presence in Ireland were being debated, and international law being shaped, the reasons that England needed to be in Ireland started to include ideas such as this: "His Majesty is bound in conscience to use all lawful and just courses to reduce his people from barbarism to civility ... for half their land doth now lie waste, by reason whereof that which is habited is not improved to half the value; but when the undertakers [the settlers] are planted among them ..., and that land shall be fully stocked and manured, 500 acres will be of better value than 5000 are now."[25] The argument, sent by a colonial lawyer to the Earl of Salisbury, was that leaving such productive assets in the hands of people unable to use them efficiently amounted to a social crime. The savagery of the Irish confirmed their inefficient use of the land, which confirmed their savagery. Nature, the relentless push of the frontier, and new forms of order and economics made one another. This process found its way from Ireland's frontier into the New World, through the sword of one of England's most venerated heroes, Sir Francis Drake, and the pen of one of liberalism's highest priests, John Locke.[26]

LIBERAL POLICING AT THE ATLANTIC FRONTIER

The British colonial state drew on talent and technologies from both sides of the Atlantic. Francis Drake learned the arts of brutal suppression of Indigenous People in Ireland. Drake helped put to the sword every man, woman, and child on Rathlin Island in 1575 before finding a higher title and greater riches in the New World.[27] More important, though, were the work of statecraft and the building of juridical justifications for states to embark on colonial adventures.[28] In this, John Locke emerged as a poster child of liberal imperialism. His views of private property and personhood drew deeply from his work as a colonial administrator. At the same time that Locke was redrafting the Fundamental Constitutions of Carolina, introduced in 1682, he was writing chapter 5 of the *Second Treatise on Government,* titled "On Property." The Fundamental Constitutions affirm that "every Freeman of Carolina shall have absolute *power and* Authority over his Negro slaves"—Locke oversaw the addition of the part in italics.[29] This is the same Locke who, in the *Second Treatise,* argues that "every man has a property in his own person: this no body has any right to but himself."[30]

A considerable amount of ink has been spilled trying to reconcile these two positions. Some have argued that Locke changed his mind about slavery over the course of his life. But this interpretation runs afoul of his work on the Board of Trade and Plantations toward the end of his life, work in which he seemed more than reconciled to goods made with slave labor. A more compelling recent interpretation reads Locke's proposed treatment of property and the treatment of captives after a just war and observes that they comport well with what his patron, the Earl of Shaftesbury, one of the Lords Proprietors of the Carolinas, wanted to happen in that territory. At the time, a central concern for the Lords Proprietors was the capture, enslavement, and transport of Indigenous People. Locke's theories smoothed the way for the legitimate acquisition and trade of Coosa men who had been captured while fighting off colonists who had encroached on their land in what settlers called the Carolinas. Indigenous slaves, as spoils of war, could be allowed to have no property in themselves—and Locke provided grounds for that in the Fundamental Constitutions. Regarding slaves from Africa, he remained silent.[31] In other words, one of the most enduring contradictions in modern political thought emerged not from some oversight in the system of liberal theory but because one of liberalism's key philosophers was producing work for hire.

This is the context in which the modern liberal subject was made, at a colonial frontier. It shouldn't be surprising that the modern legal person was defined and policed as strictly as the boundaries of the property that this person was allowed to own.[32] Meld these concerns with eighteenth-century scientific racism, and it becomes easier to see how the liberal subject was born not only a man but white too.

The limits of the liberal subject were never more clearly demonstrated than when slaves tried to claim self-ownership. The Declaration of the Rights of Man, promulgated in 1789 during the French Revolution, proclaimed all men free and equal. This signaled to the slaves in the world's largest sugar producer, the French colony of Saint-Domingue, the very real possibility that they might be able to own themselves, that they might be part of "the people,"[33] an idea at the heart of the revolution which was at once capacious and almost instantly restricted. Lasting from 1791 to 1804, the Haitian Revolution built on long histories of slave uprisings and rebellions and established the state that exists today.[34] But the ownership of the island and the lives of those on it was still always in play. The French spent two decades trying to get their colony back and in 1825 settled on a final play—sending three warships to Port-au-Prince to demand compensation for the loss of slaves and other property, to the tune of 150 million francs.[35] The debt was finally repaid in the 1940s.[36]

Haitians underestimated the extent to which their uprising was a threat to liberal Atlantic prosperity and the extent to which they lay beyond the boundary of "the people." They were policed by force, finance, and ideology, reminded that their place lay firmly on the Nature side of the Nature-Society divide. Yet they can hardly be faulted for wanting to master their own destiny—especially at a time when new ideas about the constitutive form of that destiny were emerging wherever printing presses were available to spread them. It was, after all, through the technologies of mass communication that the great ideologies of merit, origin, and futurity were exchanged. Those ideas were literally the flags under which the state could march forth.[37] What Haitians fought for wasn't just a state but a *nation*-state.

THE STATE AND THE NATION

In *Imagined Communities,* the definitive text on nationalism, Benedict Anderson argues that for nationalism to flourish, the authority and access to truth of the clergy and monarchs had to crumble. With these foundations compromised, the bases for community within a state could be reconstructed. Printing presses enabled the replacement of Bibles and edicts as sources of truth with a proliferation of texts, maps, and records that stood for new kinds of authority. From presses flowed not just the daily instrument of community creation—the newspaper—but also vernaculars and reproductions of territory. Geographers and chorographers were in the first ranks of empire, and map making helped to define not only the state—Thomas Hobbes was a keen amateur cartographer—but also the new story of what united the citizens of that state, the story of national blood and soil.[38] In the eighteenth and nineteenth centuries, stories were written in Europe to explain the origins of *das Volk, la patrie,* and good English stock, with variously entertaining folktales used to demarcate the boundaries of national purity. These myths, printed in the spoken languages of the middle class and the poor, were made available—and available for purchase—by new communications technologies. Printing presses changed the way that information and knowledge could flow and how community could be created.

Theocracies and aristocracies ceded to new national bourgeois democracies, with a franchise extended under the Enlightenment's (strictly limited) ideas of equality and self-ownership. With their own vernacular on paper, the bourgeois invited the masses into history, and as Tom Nairn observed, "the invitation card had to be written in a language they understood."[39] Anderson took Nairn's idea further, recognizing that these new texts had their own political economy. Money could be made by circulating visions of popular liberation. Pecuniary concerns and higher literacy rates were the preconditions of a national imaginary. Once the ideas of nationalism were laid in print, they constituted their own matériel, profitably translated, transcribed, mimeographed, pirated, distorted, and republished. For younger readers: nations became A Thing because they were liked, shared, faked, and commented upon.

Race, nation, and print capitalism were tightly linked. Strategies that required cheap care and cheap labor produced and reproduced the racial orders by which bodies were read, categorized, and policed at the boundaries of Society and Nature. Print and narratives that both fixed domestic order and offered future national greatness in reward circulated and confirmed these orders. As Anderson put it,

> nationalism thinks in terms of historical destinies, while racism dreams of eternal contaminations, transmitted from the origins of time through an endless sequence of loathsome copulations: outside history. Niggers are, thanks to the invisible tar-brush, forever niggers; Jews, the seed of Abraham, forever Jews, no matter what passports they carry or what languages they speak and read. (Thus for the Nazi, the Jewish German was always an impostor.) The dreams of racism actually have their origin in ideologies of class, rather than in those of nation: above all in claims to divinity among rulers and to 'blue' or 'white' blood and 'breeding' among aristocracies. No surprise then that … on the whole, racism and antisemitism manifest themselves, not across national boundaries, but within them. In other words, they justify not so much foreign wars as domestic repression and domination.[40]

The securing of domestic order extended everywhere—not just to battlefields but to kitchens and bedrooms too. National myths are concrete, material, and intimate. Sexual habits (confessed all the more frequently because the mass production of literature allowed it)[41] became the proper subject of nationalists. In France, Jacobins prosecuted sex workers as enemies of the revolution, for instance.[42] The physicality of a nation is also manifest in its food, which retains its interest to nationalists. Phrases of the form "as [nation] as [comestible]"—as American as apple pie, as British as roast beef, as Indian as no beef[43]—come about only through sustained work. The first book on obesity, diet, and nation was George Cheyne's 1733 *The English Malady*.[44]

Through the idea of nationalism, states' power to police their citizens extended to everything from productive and reproductive labor through actions in defense of currency and food purity to mental health policy. As the example of Haiti shows, however, it wasn't just European bourgeoisies that adopted and circulated the ideas and technologies of nationalism. Sometimes the idea of a common destiny was turned against colonizers.

Fights for liberation from colonial rule in the Global South invented their own national destinies. The Indian Rebellion of 1857—what the British called the Sepoy Mutiny—was a clash of nationalisms. In a culmination of long-festering resentments over taxation, exploitation, and injustice, the Indian military refused to cooperate with the British. The soldiers were incited by ammunition—specifically by the British issue of a new shell for the 1853 Enfield rifle. The cartridges came wrapped in paper that was pregreased with pork and beef fat. Muslim and Hindu soldiers didn't want to risk damnation by following the manufacturer's instruction to bite off the end of the cartridges before using them. British officers insisted. The ensuing uprising sparked a series of insurrections from India to Jamaica.

The British diagnosed the uprising as stemming not from their colonialism but from their failure to understand that Indians were an indelibly different nation. Rather than continue to try to civilize and Christianize them, the colonist Sir Henry Maine proposed a new strategy.[45] It was subtle and powerful—a technology of governance that persists today: the invention of the category of "the native." Through it, the government supervised the judicial creation and management of different religious communities and sects within them, deepening the state's control of its subjects' lives. This strategy was born of anticolonial resistance—in response to which, Mahmood Mamdani argues, in "claiming to protect authenticity against the threat of progress, the settler defined and pinned the native."[46] This is the strategy of cheap lives in three words: "define and rule."[47] It is a regime whose legacy can be seen in any number of postcolonial states, from South Africa to India, from Canada to Peru. But the political technology of "native" wasn't enough to prevent the end of the British East India Company's rule over India, in which the uprising proved a signal moment.[48] The battle for national independence was won across the Global South in the nineteenth and twentieth centuries. But these new nation-states continued to exist within capitalism's ecology, with consequences that are increasingly clear in the twenty-first century.

ALTERNATIVE NATIONALISMS

Consider the country in which a vocal group who identified as the heartland of the nation found their destiny frustrated by the liberal, internationalist ambitions of a ruling party and voted instead for a man who offered in his own personage the firm authority of technocratic rule. A man who promised to get things done for the nation in defiance of Islamic and other terrorist attempts to frustrate national destiny. In this country, ideas of nation, religion, a perceived history of misrule by internationalists, and a betrayal of national greatness propelled a leader to popular preeminence, a man transparent to all on social media yet opaque in his backroom deals. His rule enriched an already wealthy class, but the transfer of wealth happened at the same time that a war on terror and national dissent was prosecuted with noisy, attention-grabbing bravado.[49] We have Narendra Modi's India in mind, but his rise is one among many upsets to a particular hegemonic order of liberal internationalism.

Hegemony, the idea with which we began this chapter, is never secure or guaranteed. It must always be maintained, by force and suasion. The role of workers in the nation-state, of whatever nation, has been as subservient partners in a hegemonic bloc of forces. The nation is a fiction in permanent flux, written and rewritten to interpret and order its destiny—and thus the present. But the ideas of the nation and its economic destiny aren't the exclusive domain of a particular hegemonic bloc. Indeed, this is why we see in moments of capitalist crisis—like the one we're living through today—the rise of alternate interpretations of national destiny. The logic of capitalism's ecology, its regime of cheap things, has run afoul of nationalism's language of *shared* destiny. With capitalism's riches so glaringly concentrated—sixty-two people own as much as the planet's poorest three and a half billion—should it be surprising that the hegemony of a liberal bloc has started to crumble?[50] It's a development long in the making, a phenomenon that we've called "global fascism."[51]

The angst of collective identity presents itself in a moment of uncertainty just as much in the twenty-first century as in the sixteenth, fueled by concerns around trade and economic insecurity. Quite where nation-states move from here is an open question, with possibilities along a spectrum running from a far more horrific politics than we have yet seen this century to a more emancipated world.

Yet the idea of nationhood, of community and a vision for the future circulated, debated, and lived by a large number of people, isn't automatically toxic or authoritarian. Particularly if it exists in opposition to capitalism's ecology, as many nations still do.[52] Recall that the United States is a country of more than 500 nations: the Bureau of Indian Affairs recognizes 566. Australia records a similar number of Aboriginal nations, Canada has more than 600, and India has 255 Indigenous nations, whose members total 7 percent of its population. Through recent scholarship and activism, Indigenous groups have explored what a nonpatriarchal Indigenous nationhood might look like. Centrally, it would involve renegotiating relationships around care, nature, and work and managing territory under governance arrangements that strip the state out of the nation-state dyad. Quite where these relations might end up is unclear.

The Kino-nda-niimi Collective of activists involved in the Idle No More movement in Canada presents a series of visions of what it might be to live in nations outside capitalism's ecology.[53] Glen Sean Coulthard in his *Red Skin, White Masks* presents another, with lessons on the dangers of engaging with the state in this new national enterprise.[54] He's right. In the Plurinational State of Bolivia, as it's now called, Indigenous leadership has paid for an expanded welfare system with mining receipts. It's not clear that this new nation-state is a break from capitalism's ecology, if to save Pachamama—the revered Andean earth goddess—the government licenses her destruction.[55] We are not optimistic that the electoral success of Indigenous and other nations holding alternative views of the web of life can guarantee transformative change. But with increasing militancy in other settler colonies—particularly those in North America around extractive industries—and ongoing calls for more radical transformation in Bolivia, it is a source of hope for us that such experiments thrive and that lives might be revalued under these alternative nationalisms.

As we approach our conclusion, it's worth rehearsing once more why a chapter on lives fits into a book about cheap things. In the introduction, our discussion of things nodded to the process through which Nature was cleaved to Society as a strategy within capitalism's ecology. This chapter has shown how the idea of human lives—recognized and ordered by the state—developed within a racialized and patriarchal hierarchy. The state manages those lives within that hierarchy, one that presents itself to us and through which we live as a nation. To imagine that white supremacy might be ended by a redefined nation is to misunderstand the series of power operations that have led to the modern form of the nation within capitalism's ecology and to underestimate the historical inertia of the nation-state. Revolutionary politics requires an expansive, postcapitalist vision of governance and reckoning, and it is to the horizon of such a politics that our analysis drives us in our conclusion.

Conclusion

Our cheap things didn't magically make themselves. They emerged through a violent alchemy of ideas, conquest, and commerce in the modern world. At its heart has been a series of binaries that entwined with each other from the beginning: Society and Nature, colonizer and colonized, man and woman, the West and the Rest, white and not-white, capitalist and worker. Each of these dualisms has not merely worked to describe and categorize the world but *served practically* to dominate and cheapen the lives of nearly all humans and the rest of nature. Understanding capitalism as a world-ecology of power, capital, and nature helps us see how deeply each half of these is embedded in the other, how mightily the powerful have worked to police the sharp boundaries between them, and how forcefully those boundaries have been contested.

Slaves, Indigenous People, women, and workers—not exclusive categories, as we've seen—have experienced *and resisted* those always connected binaries from the beginning. Even at capitalism's dawn there was trouble at the frontier, as free and slave workers fraternized and resisted in Madeira. Their lives were cheapened, they lived the contempt of their masters and employers, and they fought back. The refusal of many Indigenous People and workers—then and now—to fold into capitalism's ecology prompted responses from governments and a search by investors for new terrains to seed and new models of order, profit, and extraction.

Humans' experiences of and responses to capitalist strategies don't come with transcendent instructions for success—for there are none. We make our politics from the ideas of our times. We are creatures of capitalism's ecology and thus, as we argued in the introduction, we're ill prepared to deal with the state shift that this ecology has produced through us. Take, for instance, contemporary attempts to address the problem of cheap nature. If you want to see a modern meld of Cartesian and capitalist thinking, here's an exercise: jump online, find an ecological footprint calculator, and answer its questions. You'll be told how many planets would be required if everyone lived the same way you do. (The average of our footprints is four planets: we're not proud.) Progressive environmentalists use the ecological footprint to highlight the human overshoot[1] of the planet's carrying capacity, because since the 1960s they have measured *overpopulation* by "not population density but the numbers of people in an area relative to its resources and the capacity of the environment to sustain human activities."[2] Overpopulation is, in other words, defined by a calculation of carrying capacity. To take these carrying capacities for granted is to blame future environmental destruction on the poor and working classes in the Global North and Global South as they struggle for some sort of parity with those who program the footprint calculator. Such Malthusian thinking makes despair inevitable, and inevitably racist.

The limits of production, consumption, and reproduction are fixed only by the system in which we find ourselves. Such limits are neither outside nor inside but both, knitted together by capitalism's ecology of power, production, and nature. The individual footprint teaches us to think of consumption as determined by "lifestyle choices"[3] rather than socially enforced logics. If you have been gentrified out of your old neighborhood and need to commute an hour to your job, your ecological footprint isn't a lifestyle choice. It's a choice in the same way that English peasants, once kicked off the land, were "free" to find wage work—or starve. Worse yet, footprint thinking teaches us to consider the drivers of planetary crisis as grounded in the aggregations of "people" and "consumption" rather than in systemic dynamics of capitalism and empire. Recall that in the thirteenth century, on the eve of famine, epidemic disease, and feudal crisis, French peasants in Normandy might have produced substantially more food if their feudal seigneurs had granted them autonomy. Today's peasants make similar claims and have good evidence to suggest that agroecological farming can yield more, and sequester more carbon, than industrial agriculture.[4] Any number of women's movements have fought for women's autonomy over their own bodies (with lower fertility rates one of many consequences). Yet neither peasant autonomy nor feminism features as an option in the individuating operations of carbon calculation. The ecological footprint, like so many environmentalist concepts these days, performs the very separation—of Nature from Society—that accompanied the rise of capitalism. Remember our exhibit A: the Anthropocene.

In defense of the footprint calculator, we might ask: does it not acknowledge the reality of our times, of planetary crisis, epochal climate shifts, mass extinction? Yes, but these modes of thought explain our present, disastrous state of affairs by consistently and significantly underestimating how the present is the product of a long past, of a bloody history of power, capital, and class, entwined in the web of life. At stake is *how* we understand population, nature, and limits. As the Berkeley geographer Nathan Sayre explains,

> That the concept of carrying capacity has limits does not mean that the limits it purports to specify are nonexistent or meaningless—far from it. The point, rather, is that such limits are rarely static or quantifiable, let alone predictable and controllable. One can liken the world to a ship, but that does not make the world *like* a ship. To conceive of environmental limits in abstraction from time and history—as somehow intrinsic to an idealized nature—is to mistake the model of reality for reality itself.... It is unclear whether the concept of carrying capacity has any content at all without the idealism, stasis, and numerical expression that have clung to it throughout its history. What is clear is that it is a very dull tool for understanding.[5]

Fortunately, there are movements that have sharper tools for understanding how our relations in the web of life might be different, movements that are well placed to develop a postcapitalist counterhegemony.[6]

For instance, the international peasant movement La Via Campesina knows the importance of climate change and a transformative respect for nature and human life.[7] Many of its members understand the practices of agroecology and "an end to all forms of violence against women"[8] but also the need for stability—access to credit, grain storage, energy, and extension services, ways of bridging the gap between the city and the country.

In the settler colony of the United States, the Movement for Black Lives has policy briefs on everything from fossil fuel to community finance to militarization to—vitally—reparations.[9] The disability rights movement has offered a critique not just of built public space but of race, gender, and class.[10] Indigenous women in the Americas, whose bodies have been on the front line of capitalism's ecology for the better part of six centuries, are calling attention to and making visible that violence.[11] Idle No More protests in Canada and the protests at Standing Rock in North Dakota are committed to decolonization and confronting the coloniality of power. The Argentine socialist feminist movement Pan y Rosas (Bread and roses) is organizing against femicide. And proposals for a climate change exit strategy are proving points of organization and convergence across a range of thinkers and activists who are considering the dramatic redistribution of resources that a movement beyond capitalism will require.[12]

At capitalism's frontiers, communities not only experience the multiple fronts of accumulation but are both resisting and developing complex and systemic responses.[13] John Jordan, an activist and cofounder of the United Kingdom's Reclaim the Streets movement, argues that resistance and alternatives are "the twin strands of the DNA of social change."[14] That change will need resources and space to develop. There is no road map for a class struggle that simultaneously reinvents humans' relations with and within the web of life. If we are made by capitalism's ecology, then we can be remade only as we in turn practice new ways of producing and caring for one another together, a praxis of redoing, rethinking, reliving our most basic relations.

To contribute to that effort, we submit some ideas to supplement the vital organizing currently under way, ideas that can help to sense both the past and the present differently—at a scale, with an acknowledgment of life, and over time spans that cannot fit the Capitalocene. While we might despair of ever seeing systemic change, the history of revolutions is the history of the unexpected, and the impossible, happening. The great promise is that humans—and what humans become—can thrive with the rest of the planet after the Capitalocene. Let's call it *reparation ecology*. It's an idea that doesn't translate well—French, for instance, has *réparation du préjudice écologique*, which refers to a restoration of the environment after humans have damaged it. But that's a flawed path, because the idea of a nature that can be restored is both backward looking and rests on a vision of pristine nature that developed through genocide and conquest.

We're thinking bigger and differently here, using reparation as a way of remembering how capitalism's ecology has made the world—and our capacity to think and act—and of learning to interact with the web of life differently. Emphatically, we do not think of reparation exclusively in monetary terms. This is not a search for damages nor a quest for the person in the world who most suffers as a result of capitalism's ecology. But knowing that there is someone whose only fault is to be born now, likely a woman, Indigenous, harmed by climate change and pollution, and whose life will be rendered demonstrably worse by the cumulative actions of everyone able to read this sentence, how might we live differently?

The outlines of such a program must include recognition, reparation, redistribution, reimagination, and recreation.

RECOGNITION

To understand world-ecology is to face history and the future. It is to recognize that the way we live and the very categories of thought that separate humans and the natural world are historical—not eternal—realities. Capitalism's binary code works, moreover, not just as description but as a normative program for ordering—and cheapening—humans and the rest of nature. The recognition we call for is not individual-therapeutic but institutional and systemic. Recognizing the relationship between humans and what humans have wrought, at the level of social institutions—from government to business to social change organizations—is both necessary and dangerous. Those institutions have often been studied as if, to borrow a metaphor from chapter 4, they were fish out of the water; the fundamental link to environments and environment making has too often been dropped from the frame. States have, in the process of recognition, betrayed the very groups they purported to recognize. One need only look to contemporary relations between states and Indigenous People, everywhere, to see this in play. Glen Sean Coulthart's lessons, drawn from aboriginal struggles in Canada, suggest that engagements with the state must be limited if attempts to live beyond it are to succeed.[15] Yet seeing capitalism's ecology is not enough. It needs to be changed. Hence reparation.

REPARATION

There's no easy calculus for the computation of suffering and repayment. To search for one is to suppose that the Book of the Dead is a subgenre of accountancy, kept with a double entry—one for the loss and one for the restitution. Reparation is neither so easy nor ever final. Consider the case of Guatemala. Diane Nelson's helpfully titled *Reckoning* charts the attempt to compass and account for the long war sparked by the United Fruit Company's reign over cheap bananas in Guatemala and the company's response to a crisis of land reform that precipitated a CIA coup. Nelson follows the long-fought demands for accountability and reparations, which finally resulted in the payment of a debt for war crimes that became, in part, a fund for planting trees. Of one of her informants, she reports, "In Joyabaj, Doña Miguela's husband has received some money but hasn't planted anything. She's incensed because he spent it on another woman instead of helping their youngest son get to the United States."[16] In other hands, this might be evidence of the futility of reparations, of the hopelessness of changing one thing when everything must change. Nelson instead offers it as a demonstration of a victorious political effort, one that the state spent decades trying to smash. That the reparation was spent in ways contrary to its purpose is a much better problem to have than not to have any funds at all.

It's also important to remember that states are not the only bodies culpable for damage and subsequent reparation. Corporations owe debts too. Consider Dow Chemical—now the owner of Union Carbide, responsible for the Bhopal disaster—or the corporations whose coffers have been filled with, in the words of the Movement for Black Lives, "wealth extracted from our communities through environmental racism, slavery, food apartheid, housing discrimination and racialized capitalism."[17] Yet the balance of reckoning will never level. Not because an equation for lives and suffering is incalculable, but because the process of reparation involves active historical debate. There's no "year zero" that can serve as an accounting stand-in for the casualties of slavery, conquest, and class war. Finally, understanding the full range of damage caused by capitalism's ecology, on whom and what that damage was inflicted, will require not just money but the imagining of nonmonetary redistribution.

We recognize that reparation ecology comes at a cost. There is trouble ahead. Suggesting an alternative to capitalism is as welcome now as it was when the unnamed Tlaxcalan witch in chapter 1 was killed more than four centuries ago. When communists in the United States did it in the 1950s, they were persecuted; when environmentalists do it today, they too become a focus of the security state.[18] The practice of decolonization is more dangerous than simple solidarity because it's more likely to work.[19] Ultimately, it asks "What do you have?," "How do you get it?," and perhaps most seditiously, "What do you want?" Answers will involve the distribution of resources that have little to do with market capitalism. Of course, markets allot resources, but what we have in mind is a rather different form of redistribution.

REDISTRIBUTION

A look at the gendered fate of Nelson's Guatemalan reparation points to how a cash payout for crimes is unlikely to bring justice by itself. Reparation ecology, by contrast, asks not "Who gets what?" but "Who got what, and who should pay for *that?*" In the case of patriarchy, the redistribution of domestic work is a central part of what we imagine reparation ecology to involve. Similarly, we hope that such redistribution would include energy to warm and cool homes and food in a diet cleaved from its capitalist imperatives, with both governed by regimes of commoning. To do that, you need land, places where humans can connect with extrahuman life, zones of engagement where humans can daily renew their relationships with the web of life. This calls for permanent reimagination.

REIMAGINATION

Decentering humans and undoing the real abstractions of Nature and Society can only be done concretely. Defensive actions against systems that enforce these abstractions—such as the Standing Rock campaign—can yield victories but are always part of a longer struggle.[20] To decolonize "one name at a time," one map at a time, as Biidewe'anikwetok suggests, is both a physical and a psychological task.[21] There's a danger of this becoming the sort of enterprise that demands far too much time on the therapist's couch. This is not to disparage the important psychoanalytical work that emerges from climate change[22] but to recognize that it belongs not in oak-paneled rooms but on shop floors and in fields, offices, and classrooms. This reimagination is a collective act of liberation. Never under capitalism have the majority been asked about the world we'd like to live in. To dream, and dream seditiously, is something that many humans need to practice, for we have been prevented from doing it for centuries. And the shop floors and community centers and classrooms and kitchen tables where these dreams will be shared are themselves subject to reimagination. Rather than seeing work as drudgery, restoration ecology offers joy, looking for working and living spaces to be filled with equitable chances for recreation.

RECREATION

There is currently a small boom in manifestos for the end of work, premised on the idea of robots managing the tasks that involve drudgery, thus freeing humans to have almost unlimited leisure.[23] While there's a danger in such analyses of forgetting the intimate and violent relations of capitalist machinery and cheap nature, we are grateful that they raise the hope that humans might find meaning and dignity outside the Protestant work ethic, itself a painful colonial legacy.[24] This is not to argue against hard work. It is, however, to demand meaningful, pleasurable work—and a liberatory dissolution of the work-life-play relationship, emerging through workers' struggle. Here we find the idea of contributive justice useful. Restorative justice has had some currency in the US criminal justice system as an alternative to incarceration.[25] The logic is that restorative justice returns affairs to the status quo. But what if the status quo isn't good enough or is downright horrible? In writing about backbreaking agroecological work, Cristian Timmermann and Georges Félix find that the application of deep knowledge to land, self-determination, and connection to the web of life offers a chance not only to engage in paid labor but to contribute to a better state of justice, to make oneself, ones' community, and the world better.[26] The joys of both idleness[27] and good work are ones that we celebrate under the rubric of "reparation ecology."

These ideas, we suggest, offer a way to think beyond a world of cheap things to imagine how we might live without the real abstractions of Nature and Society and the strategies that capitalism's ecology has spawned. If this sounds revolutionary, so much the better.

Notes

INTRODUCTION

Epigraph. Nietzsche 2001, §125, 120.

1. Roberts 1989; Hansen and Sato 2012.

2. Carrington 2016; Working Group on the 'Anthropocene' 2016. Here we refer to the Anthropocene as a field of geological inquiry: the Geological Anthropocene. It is distinct from its widely circulated sibling, the Popular Anthropocene, which encompasses a broad discussion of the origins of ecological crisis. See Moore 2016, 2017a, 2017b.

3. Barnosky et al. 2012, 52.

4. See, e.g., the excellent N. Klein 2014.

5. Barnosky et al. 2004.

6. Louys, Curnoe, and Tong 2007.

7. Humans in Africa, it is hypothesized, managed to force megafauna to adapt—hence almost no evidence for extinction there. See, e.g., the simulations of Channell and Lomolino 2000.

8. Ruddiman et al. 2016.

9. Ceballos et al. 2015.

10. Moore 2016, 78–115; 2017a; 2017b.

11. Bunge 2015.

12. Liu et al. 2006.

13. Evans 2014.

14. Bunge 2015.

15. Oxfam America 2015.

16. Seabury et al. 2014.

17. Dunkley 2014.

18. McMichael 1998; Kaimowitz and Smith 2001; Gale, Lohmar, and Tuan 2005.

19. We capitalize here because Indigenous Peoples' movements themselves choose to do so.

20. Jowett 1914, 383–85. See also Glacken's (1967) read on the long history of human questions about nature: Was it made for humans? Has its physical geography changed humans? And have humans changed it from its original state?

21. Chew 2001.

22. Mielants 2002, 2008.

23. Lamb 2002; Fagan 2008; Büntgen et al. 2011.

24. Fagan 2008, 12, 20–21.

25. Hoffmann 2014, 116.

26. B. Campbell 2010; Mayhew 2013.

27. M. Williams 2003, 93. See also Wickham 1994.

28. Nairn et al. 2004; Dribe, Olsson, and Svensson 2015.

29. Ruiz 1994.

30. Jordan 1997; Fagan 2008; B. Campbell 2010.

31. Hilton 1951.

32. Bois 1984, 264. This echoes twentieth and twentieth-first-century calls for agroecological farming from, e.g., Altieri 1999; Rosset and Martínez-Torres 2012.

33. Ziegler 2013, 40. The literature on the Black Death is large. See, e.g., McNeill 1976; Cantor 2002; Ruddiman 2005; DeWitte 2015.

34. L. White 1962, 75; Moore 2003b.

35. DeWitte 2015.

36. McNeill 1976.

37. Calculated from Broadberry, Campbell, and van Leeuwen 2011. See also Lappé et al. 2013; on declining arable productivity, Broadberry et al. 2010, 36.

38. Levine 2001, 325–400; Hilton 2003, esp. 95–133; Cohn 2007b.

39. Elvin 2004.

40. Cohn 2006, ch. 2.

41. China's fifteenth-century fleet was larger and more powerful than that of the Portuguese. The Chinese navy wasn't, however, tasked with urgently supplementing returns to the crown; Portugal's was. It needn't have been this way. The history of the modern world is rife with contingency, with strategies to fix crises tried and failed, and with paths not taken.

42. Moore 2009.

43. Cadamosto (1455) 1937, 9.

44. Verlinden 1970, 216–17.

45. Cats distinguish themselves by not giving a damn about sweetness (Li et al. 2005), but they've always been an odd lot.

46. Van Dillewijn 1952.

47. Schwartz 2004.

48. Mintz 1985, 82.

49. W. Phillips 2004, 29.

50. Ibid., 33.

51. Mintz 1985.

52. Moore 2007.

53. Moore 2010e.

54. Ramsey 1920.

55. Afonso de Albuquerque, quoted in Vieira 2004, 45.

56. Madeira crashed in the 1520s and was overtaken by São Tomé in the 1550s, which crashed and was overtaken by Pernambuco in the 1590s, which crashed and was overtaken by Bahia in the 1630s, which crashed and was overtaken by Barbados in the 1680s, which crashed and was overtaken by Jamaica and Haiti in the 1720s–1750s.

57. Bulbeck et al. 1998.

58. Thomas 1997.

59. Dann and Seaton 2001; Spínola et al. 2002.

60. The seminal work on how sugar has transformed the planet is Mintz 1985.

61. Dann and Seaton 2001.

62. This is the unspoken assumption behind Schumpeter's (1976) description of capitalism's creative destruction.

63. LaDuke 1994.

64. Le Grange 2012.

65. Barnhill 2005; L. Williams 2012, 95.

66. Levins and Lewontin 1985; Moore 2015.

67. Bull and Maron 2016.

68. Pigou 1920; J.E. Meade 1952.

69. E.g., Martinez-Alier 2014.

70. Goodfriend, Cameron, and Cook 1994.

71. Capitalism has often viewed the work of nature as a "free gift"—a term that appears in Engels's editing of Marx (1967a, 745). The reality is that the work of nature—including human nature—is neither "free" nor "gifted" to capital.

72. J. Jackson 1997.

73. Worm et al. 2006; World Economic Forum 2016.

74. Moore 2014.

75. Abulafia 2008.

76. Wallerstein 1974, 347; Abu-Lughod 1989; McMichael 2000.

77. Wallerstein 1974, 44. See also Moore 2003a.

78. See, e.g., Fine (2001) skewer the nonsense of "social capital" theory.

79. Marx 1973b, 33.

80. Marx 1976, 376.

81. Arrighi and Moore 2001.

82. Arrighi 1994.

83. Piketty 2014; using payroll instead of tax records, Galbraith and Hale 2014; with a different technique but allied findings, Veblen (1899) 1973.

84. Arrighi and Moore 2001.

85. Vieira 1996.

86. Moore 2003a. The simultaneous exploitation of labor and nature and the alienation of nature integral to capitalism's ecology is known in the literature as "the metabolic rift." See Foster 1999; Wittman 2009; Schneider and McMichael 2010; Moore 2011.

87. Vieira 1996.

88. This, incidentally, is why *The Communist Manifesto* says that all history is the history of class struggle—because of the back-and-forth, the dialectic, between worker resistance and bourgeois compulsion.

89. Disney 2009, 114.

90. Bales, Trodd, and Williamson 2009.

91. Belser 2005.

92. O. Patterson 1982.

93. After the initial journeys of first contact, captains on colonial ships traveled with their wives, families, and retinue (Boxer 1975). The written record is almost completely silent about these women, save the occasional surviving will in which wealthier women's wishes about what to do with their property—slaves, furniture, clothes—are recorded. It is clear, however, that women's reproductive work was policed. Slaves who slept with white free women were executed (Vieira 1996).

94. H. Klein 2004, 225.

95. Federici 2004, 77.

96. For a discussion of women's work in early modern and modern Europe, see Honeyman and Goodman 1991; Frader 2004; Wiesner-Hanks 2008. See also the broader and excellent discussions in Meade and Wiesner 2004; Delle, Mrozowski, and Paynter 2000.

97. As Federici (2004) notes, the witch and Caliban—who represent, respectively, the women and people of color who did not know their place in the new order—are simultaneous capitalist phenomena.

98. Ibid., 92.

99. UNDP 1995.

100. City of London 2016; Payne 2016.

101. Safri and Graham 2010, 111.

102. Schwartz 1985.

103. Carney 2001.

104. Patel 2013; Patel and McMichael 2009.

105. Holt-Giménez and Patel 2009; Aldrete 2013. See generally De Ste. Croix 1981.

106. De Vries 1993; Brown and Hopkins 1956.

107. USDA 2017a, "Percent of Consumer Expenditures Spent on Food, Alcoholic Beverages, and Tobacco That Were Consumed at Home, by Selected Countries, 2015."

108. USDA 2017b, tables 51–53.

109. Ervin and Ogden 2013; Sheiham and James 2014. See also the work of the World Public Health Nutrition Association more generally.

110. Verlinden 1970.

111. This wood is thus an example of one of the earliest "flex crops" (Borras et al. 2014).

112. Boyle 2008, 57.

113. Vieira 1996.

114. Dussel 2008.

115. Parise 2008.

116. Dussel 2008, 12.

117. Buzan, Wæver, and Wilde 1998.

118. Moore 2015. See also Moore 2016; Moore et al. 2017; C. Campbell and Niblett 2016. A growing literature on world-ecology can be found at www.academia.edu/Documents/in/World-Ecology.

119. Edwards 2009.

120. Timmermann and Félix 2015.

121. Livingston 2016.

122. Patel et al. 2014.

123. See the General Social Survey conducted by NORC, at http://gss.norc.org/.

124. N. Klein 2014.

125. Garrett and Jackson 2015, 288, quoting Walker in *Alice Walker: Beauty in Truth* (directed by Pratibha Parmar, 2013).

126. Drawing, with gratitude, on Watts 1983; Peet and Watts 2004.

1. CHEAP NATURE

1. Behar 1987, 127.

2. *The Oxford English Dictionary* (Simpson and Weiner 1989) uses, for example, this instance: "c1330 *Arthour & Merlin* (Auch.) (1973) l. 8270 Þe v was Dedinet þe saueage."

3. A later example given in Simpson and Weiner 1989 to demonstrate this use comes from John Locke's 1690 *Essay on Human Understanding:* "The more than Brutality of some savage and barbarous Nations."

4. R. Williams 1976, 292.

5. Foucault 2003.

6. Braudel 1953; Wallerstein 1974; Moore 2016.

7. Pomeranz 2000.

8. Gunaratne 2001.

9. Lo 1955.

10. Broadberry and Gupta 2006.

11. Elvin 2004.

12. Sohn-Rethel 1978; Jameson 1998; Toscano 2008; Schneider and McMichael 2010; La Berge 2014; Toscano 2016.

13. Wang, Surge, and Walker 2013.

14. Crumley 1994; Lieberman 2009.

15. Bois 1984.

16. Merchant 1980; Moore 2015.

17. Wallerstein 1974; Moore 2003b.

18. Mumford 1934; Kicza 1992; Sued-Badillo 1992; Abulafia 2008; Bleichmar 2009.

19. Modest 2012, 86. Though, to be fair, it wasn't Columbus who first laid eyes on the New World. He had offered a silk doublet to the man who first saw land, together with the ten thousand maravedis a year promised by the king and queen of Spain for the first sighting of the Indies. A sailor named Rodrigo de Triana spotted the land at 2 AM on October 12, 1492 (Columbus 2003). But Columbus kept the reward, which was delivered to him until his death and funded by a tax on the butchers of Seville.

20. Columbus 2003, 123.

21. Elliott 1963, 68–69.

22. Elliott 1984, 312.

23. Werlhof 1988; Rai 1993.

24. Stavig 2000. This use of the Spanish word *natural,* like the English *nature* and *society,* transformed in this era too, from meaning "a native of a particular city" to signifying something more akin to "part of nature."

25. D. Arnold 1996.

26. Dussel 2008.

27. Descartes 1985, 142–43.

28. De Vries and Van der Woude 1997; Moore 2010a, 2010b.

29. Amrine 2010.

30. Bacon 1861, 296. For feminist critiques see Merchant 1980; Harding 1991. Bacon's defenders are legion—see, e.g., Soble 1995; Vickers 2008—but his indictment, most recently pressed in Merchant 2013, is to our minds far more persuasive.

31. Daly 1990.

32. Dussel 2014, 44. See also Grosfoguel and Mielants 2006.

33. Cobarrubias and Pickles 2009.

34. Mumford 1934, 20.

35. Ingold 1993; Brotton 1997; Wintle 1999.

36. Chaudhuri 1985; Pearson 1987.

37. Ingold 1993; Taylor 2004.

38. Brotton 1997, 166.

39. Descartes 1985, 142–43.

40. Proletarianization is nearly always partial: a more accurate term might be "semiproletarianization." See Wallerstein 1983.

41. Brenner 1976, 61–62.

42. Ibid., 44.

43. Whittle 1998, 56.

44. Brenner 1976, 2001, 1993.

45. J.C. Scott 1985; Kain and Baigent 1992.

46. Wood 2007.

47. Wallerstein 1974, 255.

48. R. Allen 2000, 8.

49. Montaño 2011, 157.

50. As capitalism's center of gravity shifts toward Asia, it's striking to see the revalorization of certain kinds of traditional knowledge. The Nobel Prize in Physiology or Medicine given in 2015 for work prompted by Chinese medicine would have been unthinkable at the award's founding.

51. Earl of Northampton, an adviser to Henry VIII, quoted in Lustick 1985, 23. See also Ohlmeyer 2016. One response by the Irish to enclosure was the rundale, a communal form of agricultural ownership and collective management that offered an alternative to English rule but in the end—especially given constraints on land expansion—also pooled labor into groups that traveled to Scotland to find work. Yager 2002; Gannon 2015.

52. Moore 2017a.
53. U. Phillips 1929.
54. Naylor 2016.
55. *Al Jazeera* 2016.
56. Sherwood and Huber 2010; Pal and Eltahir 2016.
57. Inani 2015.
58. Bromwich 2016. There is a tight connection over the long run between the frequency and intensity of flooding and relatively small changes in climate (Knox 1993).

2. CHEAP MONEY

Epigraphs. Francisco de Quevedo y Villegas, quoted in Felloni and Laura 2014, 12 (authors' translation); Felipe Guamán Poma de Ayala, quoted in Dussel 2014, 43.

1. Harrisse 1888. Columbus also married into wealth, which his obsession with transatlantic crossing had turned into debt by 1484 (Mohawk 1992, 26).
2. The Centurione family also had stakes in the mining of alum, a key ingredient in wool processing.
3. Catz 1993, 22–23.
4. Boyle 2008, 54–55.
5. Kicza 1992.
6. Nader 2002, 402.
7. Thomas 2013, 48.
8. McCarthy 1915; Sued-Badillo 1992.
9. Majid 2009, 31; Kaplan 2010; Thomas 2013, 48.
10. McCarthy 1915.
11. Ch. 1 of Neal 2015 summarizes the prehistory of money well.
12. Ibid., 16.
13. Braudel 1977, 64–65.
14. See, Hills, Thomas, and Dimsdale 2010 for more on long-run trends in interest rates and war.
15. Moore 2015.
16. Arrighi 1994; Arrighi and Silver 1999.

17. Headrick 1988; Stone 1999.
18. Shaikh 2011, 45.
19. Day 1978, 12.
20. Wei, Fang, and Su 2014.
21. Atwell 2002, 97.
22. McNally 2014.
23. Atwell 2002, 97.
24. Weatherford 2009, 126.
25. Wallerstein 1974.
26. Patterson 1972, 230. For England, see M. Allen 2001.
27. Ehrenberg 1985; Häberlein 2012; Steinmetz 2016.
28. Nef 1941.
29. Vilar and White 1976.
30. Day 1978, 47; Ruggiero 2015. Indeed, the sharp uptick in the velocity of exchange in northwest Europe figured prominently in the reorientation of silver flows toward Antwerp and away from Venice and Danzig (now Gdańsk)—see Munro 2003, 11. With an expanding bullion supply and rising velocity of exchange, the price of money declined correspondingly. The interest rate in Antwerp may have fallen by as much as half between 1480 and 1520; Italy's fell too, but by much less, something on the order of 20 percent (Homer and Sylla 1996, 142; see also Koenigsberger and Mosse 1968, 50).
31. Blanchard 2001, 110–11.
32. Holborn 1982, 72.
33. Agricola (1556) 1950, 8.
34. Westoby 1989, 56. See also Birrell 1987.
35. Blickle 1981.
36. Ibid., 198–99.
37. Münzer 1524, quoted in Marx 2000, 68.
38. Braudel 1972, 339, 388–89.
39. Epstein 1996.
40. Lopez 1964.
41. Braudel 1972, 339.
42. Coles 1957, 18.
43. Heers 1961; Dotson and Agosto 1998, 11.

44. Coles 1957, 19.

45. To keep track of public finances, double-entry bookkeeping was necessary. The earliest Casa ledgers, dating from 1340, are in this format. Although this system was developed independently in Korea (O. Miller 2007) and drew on ideas that were established in the Middle East (Zaid 2004), it's not insignificant that it was a technology that features in modern finance. It is not an accident either that accountants are the ultimate executioners of financial necessity (economists are their overpaid dramaturges).

46. Felloni and Laura 2014, 65.

47. Spence 1870.

48. Epstein 1996, 281.

49. Epstein 2001, xi.

50. See, e.g., Gleeson-White 2012. Boland 2009 explains the absence from Ferguson 2009 in more prosaic terms.

51. Neal 2015, 50–51.

52. Lopez 1964; Abu-Lughod 1989; Epstein 1996, 273.

53. Lopez 1964.

54. Thomas 2013, 48.

55. Elliott 1963, ch. 3.

56. Bagnall 1999.

57. Parker 1996; Eltis 1998.

58. Tilly 1992, 79.

59. Parker 1976.

60. 't Hart, Brandon, and Goossens 2008; Tallett 2010, 169–73.

61. Tallett 2010, 170.

62. Black 1991, 30; Tallett 2010, 169.

63. Dauverd 2014, 60.

64. Ibid., 61.

65. Barrera-Osorio 2010.

66. Suárez de Figueroa (1617) 1914, 20, quoted in Elliott 1992, 96.

67. Lynch 1964, 61–62.

68. Tallett 2010, 175.

69. Palmer 1974, 561. Nor was this exceptional: France's spending on war and debt service reached 75 percent in 1788, on the eve

of revolution (Michael Duffy 1980, 7). See also P. Anderson 1975, 32–33.

70. Elliott 1963, 90.

71. P. Anderson 1975, 70. Revenues tripled in nominal terms; estimate deflated for price inflation.

72. Franklin 1950, 69.

73. P. Anderson 1975, 33.

74. Langley 2002.

75. Fernow 1911; Westermann 1996; Moore 2007, ch. 2.

76. Von der Heydt-Coca 2005.

77. Ibid., 286.

78. Studnicki-Gizbert and Schecter 2010, 96. See also Moore 2010d.

79. Bakewell 1987, 242; Moore 2007.

80. Moore 2007; Studnicki-Gizbert and Schecter 2010, 96.

81. Moore 2010d.

82. Flynn and Giraldez 1995, 2002.

83. Flynn and Giráldez 2002.

84. Flynn and Giráldez 1995, 205. See also Flynn 1984.

85. Gotzek et al. 2015.

86. Schumpeter 1961, 138.

87. Braudel 1984, 604.

88. Arrighi and Moore 2001, 61.

89. Ruth Hall et al. 2015.

90. Bennett, Govan, and Satterfield 2015.

91. Cahan, Marboe, and Roedel 2016.

92. Hildyard 2016. The rise of "microfinance" has extended the base from which capital is extracted—particularly, in the Global South, to women (Keating, Rasmussen, and Rishi 2010; Roy 2010).

93. Varoufakis 2016.

94. Harvey 2005.

95. IMF 2015.

96. IMF 2014.

97. Apostolopoulou and Adams 2015.

98. EU 2017.

3. CHEAP WORK

1. Columbus, quoted in Koning 1976, 82.
2. Epstein (2001) was troubled by this too.
3. W. Phillips 2013.
4. Stevens-Arroyo 1993.
5. Maxwell 1975, 53 (emphasis added).
6. Note that this might be considered the origin of the policing of knowledge in capitalism's ecology, long before the biopolitics of knowledge appeared on Foucault's radar, as we discuss in ch. 4.
7. Zorrilla 2006, 253–54. Authors' translation.
8. Reséndez 2016.
9. Roper and Brockington 1984.
10. Quirk 1954; Roper and Brockington 1984; Parise 2008.
11. Mies 1986, 77. See also Moore 2015.
12. M. Davis 2004, 13.
13. Seabrook 2003.
14. De Ste. Croix 1981; O. Patterson 1982.
15. Applebaum 1992; Boissonnade and Power 2011.
16. Cicero (45 BCE) 1933; D. Arnold 1996.
17. Moore 2003b.
18. This, incidentally, is the genealogy of the modern food bank.
19. Mumford (1934) 2010.
20. Wickham 2008, 10.
21. Dohrn-van Rossum 1996, 283.
22. Thompson 1967, 63.
23. Price 1992, 64, 60.
24. Nguyen 1992.
25. Kinsbruner 2005, 142.
26. Spinden 1920.
27. G. Jones 1989.
28. Thompson 1967, 90–91.
29. Alatas 1977; Schwartz 1978; Tinker 1993.
30. F. R. Godfrey, quoted in Select Committee of the Legislative Council on the Aborigines 1859, 71, in Nanni 2011, 12.

31. Dredge 1839–43, quoted in Nanni 2011, 23.

32. See also, for nineteenth-century California, Hurtado 1988, ch 2.

33. Sahlins 1972, 24; Harris 1978. See also Minge-Klevana et al. 1980; Fischer-Kowalski et al. 2010. The disciplines of time management are never fully effective. Foot-dragging and time theft remain ways that wageworkers resist their employers. See J. C. Scott 1985.

34. Pew Research Center 2010.

35. Reséndez 2016.

36. Moore 2010d.

37. Paul-Majumder and Begum 2000.

38. Mintz 1985, 47.

39. Linebaugh and Rediker 2000; Hart 1991; J. C. Scott 1985.

40. Stein 1984; Renda 2001; Macdonald 2010; Santiago-Valles 2005.

41. Marx 1967b, 133.

42. Marx 1976, 638.

43. Marx 1973a, 13 (emphasis added).

44. The tragedy of this false conflict once again surfaced in September 2016 around the projected completion of the Dakota Access Pipeline—a nearly twelve-hundred-mile (nineteen-hundred-kilometer) pipeline to carry North Dakota crude oil to southern Illinois. The AFL-CIO, the United States' major labor federation, called on the federal government to ensure the pipeline's completion, even as the Standing Rock Sioux and their allies organized significant opposition to the federal government's incursion on their land and threat to their water supply. But the Sioux also found support in the labor movement, not least from the union National Nurses United, which declared the project a "continual threat to public health" (Registered Nurse Response Network 2016). This convergence of labor, ecological, and First Nation social movement politics suggests a development glimpsed by James O'Connor three decades ago (1988). As capitalism extends the cash nexus into key domains of socioecological reproduction, it not only threatens the well-being of human and extrahuman natures but also establishes new conditions of anticapitalist struggle.

45. USBC 1909, 132 (available at www2.census.gov/prod2/decennial/documents/00165897ch14.pdf).

46. Johnson 2013.

47. Solar 2012.
48. Calculated from Atkin 1992, 17–18.
49. Page and Walker 1991, 294.
50. Friedmann 1978, 546.
51. Wolf 1982.
52. Page and Walker 1991, 308.
53. Sinclair 1906, 412–13.
54. The struggle around different visions of what the world might be is an international one, and Silver 2003 helpfully charts the global rhythm of worker uprisings.
55. Robert Hall 1989.
56. Hornborg 2006.
57. Beckert 2014, 192.
58. Aptheker 1943.
59. Genovese 1992; Tomich 1990; Wish 1937; Reis 1993.
60. Linebaugh and Rediker 2000.
61. Although it would be foolish to underestimate the extraordinary intellectual creativity of Russians—communist and otherwise—in the 1920s.
62. Lenin 1965, 152. See also Bailes 1977.
63. Fitzgerald 2003, 157–83. Kagarlitsky 2008 effectively contests the notion that the Soviet project unfolded within the ideological and geographical envelope of "communism," apart from the flux and flow of capitalism. Soviet industrialization and agroindustrialization depended heavily on imports—and credit—from leading capitalist states (Nove 1992).
64. Josephson 2013, 74. Josephson (along with others) is at pains to emphasize just how different were Soviet and capitalist views of nature—a conclusion at some variance with our own.
65. Dunn 2017, 57.
66. Lichtenstein 2002, 234.
67. Silver 2003, 68–69.
68. M. Davis 1986.
69. Burawoy 1983.
70. Sonn 1997, discussed in Silver 2003, 64.
71. Butollo and ten Brink 2012.

72. ILO 2014.

73. Mies 1986; Werlhof 1988; Federici 2004; Moore 2015; Habermann 2016.

4. CHEAP CARE

1. O'Connell 2004.

2. Catz 1993, 33.

3. Despite her inheritance, Columbus wasn't able to fund his journey across the Atlantic. He had to wait for his Genoan connections to bankroll that voyage.

4. Barreto 1992, O'Connell 2004, and others offer as yet unresolved debate about Columbus and Perestrelo.

5. Columbus 2003, 111.

6. Michele de Cuneo, in Morison 1963, 212, quoted in Keller 1994, 59.

7. Ibid.

8. Although see the discussion in ch. 2 about nature and science.

9. Berna et al. 2012; Bowman et al. 2009. See also Balée 2006. The field of historical ecology is one to which we're keen to contribute an analysis of gender.

10. Zamora 1990. For an extended discussion, see Trexler 1995.

11. Trexler 1995, 1.

12. Sigal 2000, ch. 4.

13. Ibid., 65.

14. Stoler 2010, 47. See also Lugones 2007.

15. Voss 2008, 196.

16. Mies 1986; Dunaway 2015.

17. McClintock 1995 provides the outline here.

18. Federici 2004, 8.

19. J. W. Scott 1999.

20. We take the title of this section from Bayly 2004, 49, and develop the idea further here.

21. Seccombe 1992; Coontz and Henderson 2016.

22. To be clear, we aren't interested in rehearsing a Whig history of patriarchy. Martha Howell's (2010) work reminds us that while many

of the foundations of capitalism were laid between 1300 and 1600, reading them as directly and intentionally leading toward our modern world is to shrink both our and our predecessors' worlds.

23. See WorldValuesSurvey.org for full data.

24. Alesina, Giuliano, and Nunn 2013.

25. Breasted 1919, 424.

26. La Vega 1688, 378.

27. Donkin and Wenner-Gren Foundation for Anthropological Research 1979, 5.

28. A. Clark 1919.

29. Amussen 1988, ch. 1.

30. Gouge 1622, 1.

31. Federici 2004; Mies 1986. See also Ariel Salleh's important work (e.g., Salleh 1997).

32. Foucault 1973, 1979, 1980, 2008.

33. Segato 2014.

34. Federici 2004, 15–16.

35. Raworth 2014. See also Merchant 1980; Federici 2004.

36. Locke 2003, 101.

37. Gold 1984; Prince 1988; Rose 1993; Berger 2008.

38. Belsey 2013.

39. Corri 1983.

40. Belsey 2013.

41. Belsey (2013) disagrees, though it's certainly the case that Andrews was a diligent and successful farmer.

42. Postle 2002, 16.

43. Rose 1993.

44. Corri 1983.

45. Stoneman 2015.

46. Boserup 1970, 34.

47. McKeon 1995. See also Snell 1987, whose data, McKeon notes, come exclusively from southern England.

48. Platter 1937, 181–82, quoted in Amussen 1988, 48.

49. Erickson 2005.

50. Ibid., 5.

51. Carlos, Maguire, and Neal 2006.

52. Eisenstein 1979.

53. Hill 1989.

54. Rae 1895; Marçal 2015.

55. A. Smith (1759) 1976, 240–41.

56. D. Smith 1993.

57. Bloch 1978.

58. Connell 1990, 511, notes how this idea of a nominally unsexed citizen persists in liberal theory.

59. See, e.g., Barbin 1980; Herdt 1994.

60. Sudarkasa 1986; Mamdani 1996.

61. Oyěwùmí 1997, 78.

62. Ibid., 124–25.

63. Also note that having created the category of woman, white settler states gave them the vote sometimes decades before metropolitan ones did (Connell 1990, 521).

64. Morgan 1997. See also K. Hall 1996a.

65. Atkins (1735) 1970, 50, quoted in Morgan 1997, 188.

66. Morgan 2004.

67. Van Kirk 1983.

68. Ulrich 1991; Folbre 2006.

69. Lutz 2002.

70. Stoler 1989.

71. Connell 1995 offers an overview; Strasser and Tinsman 2010 has a fine literature summary for Latin American studies.

72. Stotsky et al. 2016, 39.

73. Inglehart and Norris 2003.

74. Bhattacharya 2006.

75. Safri and Graham 2010.

76. National Nutrition Monitoring Bureau 2012; Planning Commission 2012.

77. Hirway and Jose 2011.

78. F. Arnold et al. 2009.

79. Cowan 1983; Bittman, Rice, and Wajcman 2004. Kenyon (2010) points to the limits of time-use surveys in capturing this additional

deepening of the demands on women's time—yet another sign of the impact of capitalism's ecology on the great domestication.

80. S. Offer and Schneider 2011.

81. Tsing 2015, 66; Wright 2006.

82. Standing 2016.

83. Yeates 2005; ILO 2015; Maybud 2015.

84. Glenn 1992.

85. Rudrappa 2015.

86. Dalla Costa and James 1973, 40.

87. Yeates 2009.

88. A. Davis 1983, 373.

89. Piven 1990.

90. Wakeman 1868, 29.

91. Mink 1990, 93.

92. Orren 1991.

93. Rolf 2016.

94. Rosen 2000; Fraser 2012; Goldberg 2014. See Schlozman, Burns, and Verba 1999 for the importance of unions in particular.

95. Glenn 2010.

96. Falquet 2006.

97. Segato 2014. These attacks can be systematized under the guise of a cultural intervention, as with the persistence of witch-hunts in Africa. Federici 2008.

5. CHEAP FOOD

1. Mariana-Costantini and Ligabue 1992.

2. Columbus 2003, 139.

3. Ibid., 232–33.

4. Ratekin 1954.

5. Solow 1987, 718.

6. Braudel 1981, 256.

7. Braudel 1977, 11–12.

8. To be sure, the gamut of human food systems extends well beyond the "plants of civilizations," to pastoralism, swidden agriculture, fisher communities, and nomadism.

9. Patel and McMichael 2009; Bruins and Bu 2006.

10. Maddison 2007, 43.

11. Excellent surveys of the English agricultural revolution include Thirsk 1987 and Overton 1996.

12. Calculated from G. Clark 2002. England wasn't home to the first modern agricultural revolution—the Dutch were first, and the English learned capitalist agriculture from them. But England's more expansive demography and size, coupled with sharply rising coal use, make its agricultural revolution a useful point of discussion.

13. Ormrod 2003, 213–18; calculations based on R. Davis 1954, 302.

14. Ormrod 2003, 214.

15. Overton 1996, 197.

16. R. Davis 1954. See also Moore 2010c; Broadberry, Campbell, and van Leeuwen 2011.

17. G. Clark, Huberman, and Lindert 1995.

18. R. Allen 2000, 20.

19. Hufton 1983, 304.

20. Lipsett-Rivera 1990; Arroyo Abad, Davies, and van Zanden 2012.

21. Abel 1980, 197–98.

22. Charlesworth 1983.

23. Mantoux 1961, 141–42; Slicher van Bath and Ordish 1963, 319; R. Jackson 1985.

24. Hobsbawm and Rude 1969, 27.

25. G. Clark 2007, 67–68.

26. Moore 2010c.

27. Pomeranz 2002, 442.

28. Hufton 1971.

29. Colwill 1989, 67.

30. Slaughter 1986; Wallerstein 1989; Bayly 2004.

31. Lenin 1987, 229.

32. Engel 1997.

33. M. Davis 2001. See also Bohstedt 2016.

34. Charles Trevelyan, quoted in Ranelagh 1999, 117.

35. Trevelyan, quoted in Handy 2009, 332.

36. M. Davis 2001.
37. Ibid., 302.
38. Ibid., 303.
39. Wolf 1982, 258.
40. Lovell 2012, 20.
41. Fortune 1852, 357.
42. Brockway 1979a, 26–29.
43. Brockway 1979b.
44. A. Offer 1991.
45. Erisman et al. 2008.
46. Galloway et al. 2004.
47. Manning 2004.
48. Alcantara 1973, 25.
49. Advisory Committee for Agricultural Activities 1951, 4, cited in Brinkmann 2009, 5.
50. Gaud 1968.
51. Dubin and Brennan 2009, 21.
52. Dirección General de Estadística 1955, 13–16.
53. Patel 2013.
54. Ibid.
55. Calculated from Cochrane 1979, 128; EPI 2012, 2013, 2014.
56. Moore 2010c.
57. Calculated from Fuglie and Wang, 2012, 2; Grantham 2011.
58. See FAOSTAT database at www.fao.org/faostat/en/#home.
59. Rosset 2000.
60. Specter 2014.
61. Tiwana et al. 2009.
62. Kumar and Kumar 2016, 3.
63. Wiggins and Keats 2015.
64. V. Miller et al. 2016.
65. Patel 2007, ch 3.
66. McMichael 2009.
67. Patel et al. 2014, 22.
68. Weis 2013, 1–2.
69. Ibid., 126.

70. Cronon 1991.

71. PennState Extension 2015.

72. EPA 2012.

73. Gerber et al. 2013.

74. Olson-Sawyer 2013.

75. Burbach and Flynn 1980; Moody 1988; Rachleff 1993.

76. Bello 2009, 39–53.

77. Robinson 2013.

78. Giles 2017.

79. Patel et al. 2014.

80. Araghi 2013.

81. Herrero et al. 2017.

82. IPCC 2007, 36; 2014.

83. Moore 2015, 252.

84. Fuglie, MacDonald, and Ball 2007; Matuschke, Mishra, and Qaim 2007.

85. Gurian-Sherman 2009.

86. Lobell and Field 2007.

87. Peng et al. 2004; Cerri et al. 2007; Kucharik and Serbin 2008; Lobell, Schlenker, and Costa-Roberts 2011; National Research Council 2011; Challinor et al. 2014; Shindell 2016.

88. Braconier, Nicoletti, and Westmore 2014.

6. CHEAP ENERGY

Epigraph. Columbus 2003, 161.

1. Bowman et al. 2009.

2. Berna et al. 2012.

3. Herodotus 1945, 311, referenced in Heizer 1963, 188.

4. Mcglone and Wilmshurst 1999.

5. Teng 1927.

6. Humans continue to manage the sustainable use of forest resources. When human communities have enough autonomy and access to a base that allows them to recover from occasional catastrophic

losses, they are able to common—to collectively manage their resources—together successfully (Thirsk 1964). Twenty-first-century forest commoners, for instance, are better caretakers of trees than either corporations or central governments (Chhatre and Agrawal 2009).

7. Cronon 1983, 51.
8. Dull et al. 2010.
9. Parker 2014.
10. S. Lewis and Maslin 2015.
11. Birrell 1987.
12. Linebaugh 2008, 6, 306.
13. Ibid., 55.
14. P. Lewis 1811, 186, quoted in ibid., 8.
15. Elvin 2004, 20.
16. The argument has been made for more than a century. See Luxemburg (1913) 2003; Wallerstein 1974; Bunker 1985.
17. Leach 1987, 64; Nathan and Kelkar 1997; Gylfason and Zoega 2002.
18. Huber 2009; Abramsky 2010.
19. World Economic Forum 2012, 3.
20. Westra 1998.
21. Gerretson 1953, 1.
22. Andriesse 1988.
23. Smil 2010, 83; R. Allen 2013; Oram 2013. Wrigley (1990, 59) is less optimistic about peat's energy density, thinking it only half that of coal by weight.
24. Van Dam 2001.
25. De Vries and van der Woude 1997, 38.
26. Van Dam 2001.
27. Davids 2008.
28. Brenner 1976.
29. Brenner 2001.
30. Zeeuw 1978; De Vries and van der Woude 1997, 182.
31. Smil 2010, 83.
32. De Vries and van der Woude 1997; van Dam 2001.

33. De Vries and van der Woude 1997, 199–200.
34. Wallerstein 1974, 121–22.
35. Topolski 1962; Moore 2010b.
36. Davids 2008, 239, 408–9.
37. Van der Woude 2003.
38. De Vries and van der Woude 1997, 37.
39. Van der Woude 2003.
40. Unger 1984, 245–46.
41. Van der Woude 2003, 75.
42. Van Zanden 1993, 172, cited in Davids 2008, 18.
43. De Vries and van der Woude 1997, ch. 12.
44. Ibid., 631.
45. Nef 1934; De Vries and van der Woude 1997, 37–40.
46. Nef 1964 is the classic account of this early industrialization. See also Moore 2016, 78–115; 2017a.
47. Solinus, *Collectanea rerum memorabilium* (*Polyhistor*) 22, quoted in Freese 2003, 15.
48. Malanima 2009, 61.
49. Braudel 1981, 369.
50. Wrigley 1990, 59.
51. De Vries and van der Woude 1997, 631.
52. R. Allen 2009, 105.
53. Ibid., especially 156–81.
54. Ibid., 217–37.
55. Fremdling 2005.
56. Von Tunzelmann 1981.
57. Bonneuil and Fressoz 2016, 108–9.
58. Smil 1999.
59. Foster and Clark 2009.
60. A. Offer 1991.
61. Erisman et al. 2008.
62. Foster 1999; Finlay 2002, 120.
63. Beckman, Borchers, and Jones 2013, 14.
64. Erisman et al. 2008, 637.
65. Wills 1972; Patel 2013.
66. Weis 2013, 72.

67. Woods et al. 2010.

68. Gnutzmann and Śpiewanowski 2016.

69. Friedmann 1993.

70. Marx 1976, 638.

71. Chiluwa 2015; Doherty et al. 2003.

72. Andrews 2008.

73. Zinn 2003.

74. Watts 2004.

75. Mitchell 2009.

76. Painter 2014.

77. Huber 2013.

78. Kander, Malanima, and Warde, 2013, 260–64; Painter 2014.

79. World oil output increased 7.79 percent between 1950 and 1973, against 4.9 percent GDP growth (calculated from Maddison 2007, 380; EPI 2010, 2).

80. Prashad 2012 tells the story compellingly.

81. Mitchell 2011, 184.

82. Shah of Iran, quoted in D. Smith 1973, in Prashad 2012, 57.

83. K. Phillips 2009, 15.

84. Panitch and Gindin 2012.

85. N. Klein 2007.

86. Baffes et al. 2008, 60; IMF 2008, 95; Bina 1990; FTI Consulting 2016; Chapman 2014.

87. DARA and the Climate Vulnerable Forum 2012.

88. IEA 2008, 3.

89. Parenti 2016.

90. Srnicek and 2017.

91. Larry Lohmann's work on the subject is indispensable. A good introduction is Lohmann 2008.

92. IEA 2016.

93. In Virunga National Park, DRC, the main battle in the protection of mountain gorillas is being fought against the charcoal industry. The industry's strategy is to slaughter the gorillas to remove the need for a national park, so as ultimately to gain access to its trees (Emmanuel DeMerode, personal communication).

94. Revette 2016.

95. International Rivers Network 2011.

96. Benchimol and Peres 2015.

7. CHEAP LIVES

1. Columbus 2003, 114.

2. See Diamond 2005.

3. Gramsci 1978. See also S. Hall 1996.

4. Hannaford 1996.

5. Grosfoguel and Mielants 2006.

6. B. Anderson 2006, 149.

7. Anonymous 1893, 128.

8. Graetz (1894) 1967, 612. See also Hannaford 1996, 113–15.

9. Haensch et al. 2010. Note that this conflicts with Cohn's (2002) and Cantor's (2002) hypothesis that a range of different pathogens, including anthrax, produced the Black Death.

10. Aberth 2005, 21–22.

11. Goldstone 2011, 2.

12. Cohn 2007a, 20.

13. Cahill 1994, 339.

14. Katzew 2004, 190–92.

15. Martínez 2011.

16. Linné 1806, 375–76.

17. Deans-Smith 2005.

18. Montaño 2011, 23.

19. Cavanagh 2013.

20. The use of gardens as an expression of taming savagery isn't an exclusively European phenomenon (Drayton 2000). The Chinese used similar imagery to justify the conquest of Uighurs (W. Jones 1971). Such improvement became intertwined with nationhood (Helgerson 1992).

21. Canny 2001, 120.

22. Ibid., 148–51.

23. Wily 2012.

24. Montaño 2011, 2.

25. Sir John Davies, to the Earl of Salisbury, 1610, quoted in E. Wood 2003, 81–82.

26. The idea of a frontier helps to resolve the debate about whether Ireland was colony or kingdom, part of Britain or of the Atlantic. To read Ireland as a frontier is to understand it as a place in flux—not transition but flux—between these categories.

27. In a 1993 article titled "Columbus in Ireland," Milan Rai describes the various ways the occupying forces tried to subjugate Irish rebels, from setting fire to the harvest, a tactic used by the Earl of Essex against the O'Connors in 1599—"so that," as a contemporary put it, "all the county was on fire at once" (quoted in Falls 1950, 240)—to the destruction of forest commons, a maneuver that appeared in the US Indian Wars almost three centuries later. The use of fire as a weapon to prevent workers' survival through any means but selling their labor to capitalists is, note again, an idea that emerges through experiments at colonial frontiers and is then brought elsewhere. The English government rewarded scalping in Ireland, paying generously for the heads of troublesome rebels. Many of the veterans of campaigns against the Irish found sinecures in the Americas. Some brought back home the lessons they learned there, along with crops. The Irish apparently turned to the potato, first mentioned in Ireland in 1606, as a dietary staple because, on Oliver Cromwell's orders, the Commonwealth Army deliberately destroyed Irish agriculture—but the potato lies hidden underground. Colonel George Cooke, then the governor of Wexford, reported on sorties in March 1652: "In searching all the woods and bogs we found great store of corn, which we burnt, also all the houses and cabins we could find; in all of which we found plenty of corn: we continued burning and destroying for four days, in which time we wanted no provision for horse or man to lie in, though we burnt our quarters every morning and continued burning all day. He was an idle soldier that had not a fat lamb, veal, pig, poultry or all of them, every night for his supper. The enemy in these parts chiefly depended upon this country for provision. I believe we have destroyed as much as would have served some thousands of them until the next harvest" (quoted in Ellis 1988, 37). Cooke had

earlier emigrated to New England and served as the speaker of the Massachusetts Assembly in 1646. The New World from which he had returned was itself a frontier and, in this process of transatlantic travel, the destinies of Europe's and America's colonized people shaped one another.

28. Scarth 2010; Moloney 2011; Neocleous 2014.

29. Armitage 2004, 609.

30. Locke, *Second Treatise,* §27, quoted in ibid., 609.

31. Pitts 2010; Hinshelwood 2013.

32. Foucault 2008.

33. Resnick 1992.

34. Santiago-Valles's (2005) global survey of eighteenth- and nineteenth-century slave revolts is particularly helpful here.

35. Stein 1984.

36. Renda 2001.

37. One-third of national flags contain some kind of religious iconography (Theodorou 2014).

38. See, e.g., B. Anderson 2006; Montaño 2011.

39. Nairn 1977, 340.

40. B. Anderson 2006, 149–50.

41. Foucault 1980, especially 15–50.

42. Mosse 1988, 8–12.

43. Appadurai 1988.

44. See Patel 2007, ch. 4, for more on Cheyne.

45. Mantena 2010.

46. Mamdani 2012, 30.

47. Mamdani 2012.

48. David 2002.

49. Halperin 2013; McMichael 2017.

50. Hardoon, Ayele, and Fuentes-Nieva 2016.

51. Patel and McMichael 2004.

52. M. Davis 2015.

53. Kino-nda-niimi Collective 2014.

54. Coulthard 2014.

55. Webber 2017.

CONCLUSION

1. Wackernagel and Rees 1996; Wackernagel and Silverstein 2000; Wackernagel et al. 2002.

2. Ehrlich and Ehrlich 1990, 38.

3. Wackernagel and Rees 1996, 113.

4. De Schutter 2010.

5. Sayre 2008, 132. See also Moore 2015.

6. Gramsci 1978.

7. Even so, some La Via Campesina members have betrayed these principles, like the Bharatiya Kisan Union in its anti-Muslim actions—hinted at by Brass 1995 and confirmed in 2013 by riots in Muzaffarnagar.

8. La Via Campesina 2009.

9. There were more than thirty briefs at https://policy.m4bl.org/downloads/ at the time of writing.

10. McRuer 2006; L. Davis 2016.

11. Lucashenko 1996; Quijano 2000; Barker 2006; Grey and Patel 2014.

12. Foster 2013.

13. Barkin and Lemus 2016.

14. N. Klein 2014, 405.

15. Coulthard 2014.

16. Nelson 2009, 300.

17. Movement for Black Lives, n.d.

18. Potter 2013.

19. Walia 2014.

20. Kino-nda-niimi Collective 2014.

21. Biidewe'anikwetok 2014.

22. Dodds 2011.

23. E.g., Srnicek and Williams 2015.

24. Hudson and Coukos 2005.

25. Latimer, Dowden, and Muise 2005.

26. Timmermann and Félix 2015.

27. See, e.g., Hörning, Gerhard, and Michailow 1995 for new notions of time.

References

Abel, Wilhelm. 1980. *Agricultural Fluctuations in Europe: From the Thirteenth to the Twentieth Centuries*. London: Methuen.

Aberth, John. 2005. *The Black Death, 1348–1350: The Great Mortality of 1348–1350; a Brief History with Documents*. New York: Palgrave Macmillan.

Abramsky, Kolya. 2010. *Sparking a Worldwide Energy Revolution: Social Struggles in the Transition to a Post-petrol World*. Edinburgh: AK Press.

Abulafia, David. 2008. *The Discovery of Mankind: Atlantic Encounters in the Age of Columbus*. New Haven, CT: Yale University Press.

Abu-Lughod, Janet L. 1989. *Before European Hegemony: The World System A.D. 1250–1350*. New York: Oxford University Press.

Advisory Committee for Agricultural Activities. 1951. "The World Food Problem, Agriculture, and the Rockefeller Foundation." June 21. Rockefeller Foundation Records, Administration, Program and Policy, RG 3.1, series 908, box 14, folder 144. Rockefeller Archive Center, New York. Available at http://rockefeller100.org/items/show/3780.

Agricola, Georgius. (1556) 1950. *De re metallica*. Translated by Herbert Hoover and Lou Henry Hoover. New York: Dover.

Alatas, Syed Hussein. 1977. *The Myth of the Lazy Native: A Study of the Image of the Malays, Filipinos and Javanese from the 16th to the 20th Century and Its Function in the Ideology of Colonial Capitalism*. Abingdon, Oxford: Frank Cass.

Alcantara, Cynthia Hewitt de. 1973. "The 'Green Revolution' as History: The Mexican Experience." *Development and Change* 4, no. 2: 25–44.

Aldrete, Gregory S. 2013. "Riots." In *The Cambridge Companion to Ancient Rome*, edited by Paul Erdkamp, 425–40. Cambridge: Cambridge University Press.

Alesina, Alberto, Paola Giuliano, and Nathan Nunn. 2013. "On the Origins of Gender Roles: Women and the Plough." *Quarterly Journal of Economics* 128, no. 2: 469–530.

Al Jazeera. 2016. "Heatwave Continues to Bake Parts of the Middle East." August 28. www.aljazeera.com/news/2016/08/heatwave-continues-bake-parts-middle-east-160828091709175.html.

Allen, Martin. 2001. "The Volume of the English Currency, 1158–470." *Economic History Review* 54, no. 4: 595–611.

Allen, Robert C. 2000. "Economic Structure and Agricultural Productivity in Europe, 1300–1800." *European Review of Economic History* 4, no. 1: 1–25.

———. 2009. *The British Industrial Revolution in Global Perspective*. Cambridge: Cambridge University Press.

———. 2013. "Anthropocenic Poetics: Ethics and Aesthetics in a New Geological Age." In "Energy Transitions in History: Global Cases of Continuity and Change," edited by Richard W. Unger. Special issue of *Rachel Carson Center Perspectives* 2013, no. 2: 11–15.

Altieri, Miguel. 1999. "Applying Agroecology to Enhance the Productivity of Peasant Farming Systems in Latin America." *Environment, Development and Sustainability* 1: 197–217.

Altvater, Elmar. 2007. "The Social and Natural Environment of Fossil Capitalism." *Socialist Register* 2007: 37.

Amrine, Frederick. 2010. "The Unconscious of Nature: Analyzing Disenchantment in *Faust I*." *Goethe Yearbook* 17, no. 1: 117–32.

Amussen, Susan Dwyer. 1988. *An Ordered Society: Gender and Class in Early Modern England*. Oxford: Basil Blackwell.

Anderson, Benedict. 2006. *Imagined Communities: Reflections on the Origin and Spread of Nationalism*. Rev. ed. London: Verso.

Anderson, Perry. 1975. *Lineages of the Absolutist State*. London: New Left Books.

Andrews, Thomas G. 2008. *Killing for Coal: America's Deadliest Labor War*. Cambridge, MA: Harvard University Press.

Andriesse, J.P. 1988. *Nature and Management of Tropical Peat Soils*. Rome: Food and Agricultural Organization of the United Nations.

Anonymous. 1893. "Israel." *Quarterly Review*, vol. 176, 106–39. London: John Murray.

Apostolopoulou, Evangelia, and William M. Adams. 2015. "Neoliberal Capitalism and Conservation in the Post-crisis Era: The Dialectics of 'Green' and 'Un-green' Grabbing in Greece and the UK." *Antipode* 47, no. 1: 15–35.

Appadurai, Arjun. 1988. "How to Make a National Cuisine: Cookbooks in Contemporary India." *Comparative Studies in Society and History* 30, no. 1: 3–24.

Applebaum, Herbert A. 1992. *The Concept of Work: Ancient, Medieval, and Modern*. Albany: State University of New York Press.

Aptheker, Herbert. 1943. *American Negro Slave Revolts*. New York: Columbia University Press.

Araghi, Farshad. 2013. "The End of Cheap Ecology and the Future of 'Cheap Capital.'" Paper presented at the Annual Meeting of the Political Economy of World-Systems Section of the American Sociological Association, University of California, Riverside, April 11–13.

Armitage, David. 2004. "John Locke, Carolina, and the *Two Treatises of Government*." *Political Theory* 32, no. 5: 602–27.

Arnold, David. 1996. *The Problem of Nature: Environment, Culture and European Expansion*. Oxford: Blackwell.

Arnold, Fred, Sulabha Parasuraman, P. Arokiasamy, and Monica Kothari. 2009. *Nutrition in India*. National Family Health Survey (NFHS-3), India, 2005–6. Mumbai: International Institute for Population Sciences. http://rchiips.org/nfhs/nutrition_report_for_website_18sep09.pdf.

Arrighi, Giovanni. 1994. *The Long Twentieth Century: Money, Power and the Origins of Our Times*. London: Verso.

Arrighi, Giovanni, and Jason W. Moore. 2001. "Capitalist Development in World Historical Perspective." In *Phases of Capitalist Development: Booms, Crises and Globalizations*, edited by Robert Albritton, Makoto Itoh, Richard Westra, and Alan Zuege, 56–75. London: Palgrave Macmillan.

Arrighi, Giovanni, and Beverly J. Silver. 1999. *Chaos and Governance in the Modern World System*. Minneapolis: University of Minnesota Press.

Arroyo Abad, Leticia, Elwyn Davies, and Jan Luiten van Zanden. 2012. "Between Conquest and Independence: Real Wages and Demographic Change in Spanish America, 1530–1820." *Explorations in Economic History* 49, no. 2: 149–66.

Atkin, M. 1992. *The International Grain Trade*. Cambridge: Woodhead.

Atkins, John. (1735) 1970. *A Voyage to Guinea, Brazil, and the West Indies in His Majesty's Ships, the Swallow and Weymouth*. London: Cass.

Atwell, William S. 2002. "Time, Money, and the Weather: Ming China and the 'Great Depression' of the Mid-Fifteenth Century." *Journal of Asian Studies* 61, no. 1: 83–113.

Bacon, Francis. 1861. *The Philosophical Works of Francis Bacon*. Edited by James Spedding, Robert Leslie Ellis, and Douglas Denon Heath. Vol. 4. London: Longman.

Baffes, John, Donald Mitchell, Elliot Riordan, Shane Streifel, Hans Timmer, and William Shaw. 2008. *Global Economic Prospects 2009: Commodities at the Crossroads*. Global Economic Prospects and the Developing Countries. Washington DC: World Bank. http://documents.worldbank.org/curated/en/586421468176682557/Global-economic-prospects-2009-commodities-at-the-crossroads.

Bagnall, Nigel. 1999. *The Punic Wars: Rome, Carthage, and the Struggle for the Mediterranean*. London: Pimlico.

Bailes, Kendall E. 1977. "Alexei Gastev and the Soviet Controversy over Taylorism, 1918–24." *Soviet Studies* 29, no. 3: 373–94.

Bakewell, Peter J. 1987. "Mining." In *Colonial Spanish America*, edited by Leslie Bethell, 203–49. Cambridge: Cambridge University Press.

Balée, William. 2006. "The Research Program of Historical Ecology." *Annual Review of Anthropology* 35, no. 1: 75–98.

Bales, Kevin, Zoe Trodd, and Alex Kent Williamson. 2009. *Modern Slavery: The Secret World of 27 Million People*. Oxford: Oneworld.

Barbin, Herculine. 1980. *Herculine Barbin: Being the Recently Discovered Memoirs of a Nineteenth-Century French Hermaphrodite*. Translated by Richard McDougall. New York: Pantheon.

Barker, Joanne. 2006. "Gender, Sovereignty, and the Discourse of Rights in Native Women's Activism." *Meridians: Feminism, Race, Transnationalism* 7, no. 1: 127–61.

Barkin, David, and Blanca Lemus. 2016. "Third World Alternatives for Building Post-capitalist Worlds." *Review of Radical Political Economics* 48, no. 4: 569–76.

Barnhill, David Landis. 2005. "Buddhism." In *The Encyclopedia of Religion and Nature*, edited by Bron Raymond Taylor, 236–39. London: Thoemmes Continuum.

Barnosky, Anthony D., Elizabeth A. Hadly, Jordi Bascompte, Eric L. Berlow, James H. Brown, Mikael Fortelius, Wayne M. Getz, et al. 2012. "Approaching a State Shift in Earth's Biosphere." *Nature* 486, no. 7401: 52–58.

Barnosky, A. D., P. L. Koch, R. S. Feranec, S. L. Wing, and A. B. Shabel. 2004. "Assessing the Causes of Late Pleistocene Extinctions on the Continents." *Science* 306, no. 5693: 70–75.

Barrera-Osorio, Antonio. 2010. *Experiencing Nature: The Spanish American Empire and the Early Scientific Revolution.* Austin: University of Texas Press.

Barreto, Mascarenhas. 1992. *The Portuguese Columbus, Secret Agent of King John II.* New York: St. Martin's.

Bayly, C. A. 2004. *The Birth of the Modern World, 1780–1914: Global Connections and Comparisons.* Malden, MA: Blackwell.

Beckert, Sven. 2014. *Empire of Cotton: A Global History.* New York: Knopf.

Beckman, Jayson, Allison Borchers, and Carol A. Jones. 2013. *Agriculture's Supply and Demand for Energy and Energy Products.* Washington DC: United States Department of Agriculture Economic Research Service.

Behar, Ruth. 1987. "The Visions of a Guachichil Witch in 1599: A Window on the Subjugation of Mexico's Hunter-Gatherers." *Ethnohistory* 34, no. 2: 115–38.

Bello, Walden F. 2009. *The Food Wars.* London: Verso.

Belser, Patrick. 2005. *Forced Labour and Human Trafficking: Estimating the Profits.* Geneva: International Labor Organization. http://digitalcommons.ilr.cornell.edu/forcedlabor/17/.

Belsey, Hugh. 2013. "Andrews, Robert (1725–1806)." In *Oxford Dictionary of National Biography,* edited by Lawrence Goldman. Oxford: Oxford University Press. www.oxforddnb.com/view/article/95074.

Benchimol, Maíra, and Carlos A. Peres. 2015. "Predicting Local Extinctions of Amazonian Vertebrates in Forest Islands Created by a Mega Dam." *Biological Conservation* 187: 61–72.

Bennett, Nathan James, Hugh Govan, and Terre Satterfield. 2015. "Ocean Grabbing." *Marine Policy* 57: 61–68.

Berger, John. 2008. *Ways of Seeing.* London: Penguin.

Berna, Francesco, Paul Goldberg, Liora Kolska Horwitz, James Brink, Sharon Holt, Marion Bamford, and Michael Chazan. 2012. "Microstratigraphic Evidence of In Situ Fire in the Acheulean Strata of Wonderwerk

Cave, Northern Cape Province, South Africa." *Proceedings of the National Academy of Sciences* 109, no. 20: E1215–E1220.

Bhattacharya, Prabir C. 2006. "Economic Development, Gender Inequality, and Demographic Outcomes: Evidence from India." *Population and Development Review* 32, no. 2: 263–92.

Bianchi, Suzanne M., Liana C. Sayer, Melissa A. Milkie, and John P. Robinson. 2012. "Housework: Who Did, Does or Will Do It, and How Much Does It Matter?" *Social Forces* 91, no. 1: 55–63.

Biidewe'anikwetok. 2014. "Reclaiming Ourselves One Name at a Time." In *The Winter We Danced: Voices from the Past, the Future, and the Idle No More Movement,* edited by the Kino-nda-niimi Collective, 163–66. Winnipeg: ARP.

Billig, Michael. 1995. *Banal Nationalism.* London: Sage.

Bina, Cyrus. 1990. "Limits of OPEC Pricing: OPEC Profits and the Nature of Global Oil Accumulation." *OPEC Review* 14, no. 1: 55–73.

Biro, Andrew. 2005. *Denaturalizing Ecological Politics: Alienation from Nature from Rousseau to the Frankfurt School and Beyond.* Toronto: University of Toronto Press.

Birrell, Jean. 1987. "Common Rights in the Medieval Forest: Disputes and Conflicts in the Thirteenth Century." *Past and Present* 117: 22–49.

Bittman, Michael, James Mahmud Rice, and Judy Wajcman. 2004. "Appliances and Their Impact: The Ownership of Domestic Technology and Time Spent on Household Work." *British Journal of Sociology* 55, no. 3: 401–23.

Black, Jeremy. 1991. *A Military Revolution? Military Change and European Society, 1550–1800.* London: Macmillan.

Blanchard, Ian. 2001. "International Capital Markets and Their Users, 1450–1750." In *Early Modern Capitalism: Economic and Social Change in Europe, 1400–1800,* edited by Maarten Prak, 107–24. London: Routledge.

Bleichmar, Daniela. 2009. "A Visible and Useful Empire: Visual Culture and Colonial Natural History in the Eighteenth-Century Spanish World." In *Science in the Spanish and Portuguese Empires, 1500–1800,* edited by Bleichmar, Paula De Vos, Kristin Huffine, and Kevin Sheehan, 290–310. Stanford, CA: Stanford University Press.

Blickle, Peter. 1981. *The Revolution of 1525: The German Peasants' War from a New Perspective.* Translated by Thomas A. Brady and H.C. Erik Midelfort. Baltimore: Johns Hopkins University Press.

Bloch, Ruth H. 1978. "Untangling the Roots of Modern Sex Roles: A Survey of Four Centuries of Change." *Signs* 4, no. 2: 237–52.

Bohstedt, John. 2016. "Food Riots and the Politics of Provisions from Early Modern Europe and China to the Food Crisis of 2008." *Journal of Peasant Studies* 43, no. 5: 1035–67.

Bois, Guy. 1984. *The Crisis of Feudalism: Economy and Society in Eastern Normandy, c. 1300–1550.* Cambridge: Cambridge University Press.

Boissonnade, Prosper, and Eileen Power. 2011. *Life and Work in Medieval Europe.* Abingdon, Oxford: Routledge.

Boland, Vincent. 2009. "The World's First Modern, Public Bank." *Financial Times,* April 17. www.ft.com/content/6851f286–288d-11de-8dbf-00144feabdc0.

Bonneuil, Christophe, and Jean-Baptiste Fressoz. 2016. *The Shock of the Anthropocene: The Earth, History and Us.* London: Verso.

Borras, Saturnino M., Jr., Jennifer C. Franco, Ryan Isakson, Les Levidow, and Pietje Vervest. 2014. "Towards Understanding the Politics of Flex Crops and Commodities: Implications for Research and Policy Advocacy." Amsterdam: Transnational Institute.

Boserup, Ester. 1970. *Woman's Role in Economic Development.* London: Allen and Unwin.

Bowman, D.M., J.K. Balch, P. Artaxo, W.J. Bond, J.M. Carlson, M.A. Cochrane, C.M. D'Antonio, et al. 2009. "Fire in the Earth System." *Science* 324, no. 5926: 481–84.

Boxer, C.R. 1975. *Women in Iberian Expansion Overseas, 1415–1815: Some Facts, Fancies and Personalities.* New York: Oxford University Press.

Boyle, David. 2008. *Toward the Setting Sun: Columbus, Cabot, Vespucci, and the Race for America.* New York: Walker.

Braconier, Henrik, Giuseppe Nicoletti, and Ben Westmore. 2014. "Policy Challenges for the Next 50 Years." OECD Economic Policy Paper No. 9, Organization for Economic Cooperation and Development, Paris. www.oecd-ilibrary.org/economics/policy-challenges-for-the-next-50-years_5jz18gs5fckf-en.

Brass, Tom. 1995. *New Farmers' Movements in India.* Ilford, London: Frank Cass.

Braudel, Fernand. 1953. "Qu'est-ce que le XVIe siècle?" *Annales: Économies, Sociétés, Civilisations* 8, no. 1: 69–73.

———. 1972. *The Mediterranean and the Mediterranean World in the Age of Philip II.* Translated by Siân Reynolds. Vol. 1. London: Collins.

———. 1977. *Afterthoughts on Material Civilization and Capitalism.* Translated by Patricia Ranum. Baltimore: Johns Hopkins University Press.

———. 1981. *The Structures of Everyday Life: The Limits of the Possible.* Translated and revised by Siân Reynolds. London: Collins.

———. 1984. *The Perspective of the World.* Translated by by Siân Reynolds. Vol. 3 of *Civilization and Capitalism, 15th–18th Century.* New York: Harper and Row.

Breasted, James Henry. 1919. "The Origins of Civilization." *Scientific Monthly,* October, 289–578.

Brenner, Robert. 1976. "Agrarian Class Structure and Economic Development in Pre-industrial Europe." *Past and Present* 70: 30–75.

———. 1993. *Merchants and Revolution: Commercial Change, Political Conflict, and London's Overseas Traders, 1550–1653.* Princeton, NJ: Princeton University Press.

———. 2001. "The Low Countries in the Transition to Capitalism." *Journal of Agrarian Change* 1, no. 2: 169–241.

Brinkmann, Mankel. 2009. "Fighting World Hunger on a Global Scale: The Rockefeller Foundation and the Green Revolution in Mexico." www.rockarch.org/publications/resrep/brinkmann.pdf.

Broadberry, S.N., B.M.S. Campbell, Alexander Klein, Mark Overton, and Bas van Leeuwen. 2010. "English Economic Growth, 1270–1700." CAGE Online Working Paper Series 2010, no. 21, Department of Economics, University of Warwick, Coventry, UK.

Broadberry, Stephen, Bruce Campbell, and Bas van Leeuwen. 2011. "English Medieval Population: Reconciling Time Series and Cross Sectional Evidence." www.basvanleeuwen.net/bestanden/medievalpopulation7.pdf.

Broadberry, Stephen, and Bishnupriya Gupta. 2006. "The Early Modern Great Divergence: Wages, Prices and Economic Development in Europe and Asia, 1500–1800." *Economic History Review* 59, no. 1: 2–31.

Brockway, Lucile H. 1979a. *Science and Colonial Expansion: The Role of the British Royal Botanic Gardens.* New York: Academic.

———. 1979b. "Science and Colonial Expansion: The Role of the British Royal Botanic Gardens." *American Ethnologist* 6, no. 3: 449–65.

Bromwich, Jonah Engel. 2016. "Flooding in the South Looks a Lot like Climate Change." *New York Times,* August 16. www.nytimes.com/2016/08/17/us/climate-change-louisiana.html.

Brotton, Jerry. 1997. *Trading Territories: Mapping the Early Modern World.* Ithaca, NY: Cornell University Press.

Brown, E.H. Phelps, and Sheila V. Hopkins. 1956. "Seven Centuries of the Prices of Consumables, Compared with Builders' Wage-Rates." *Economica* 23, no. 92: 296–314.

Bruins, Hendrik J., and Fengxian Bu. 2006. "Food Security in China and Contingency Planning: The Significance of Grain Reserves." *Journal of Contingencies and Crisis Management* 14, no. 3: 114–24.

Bulbeck, David, Anthony Reid, Tan Lay Cheng, and Wu Yiqi. 1998. *Southeast Asian Exports since the 14th Century: Cloves, Pepper, Coffee, and Sugar.* Singapore: Institute of Southeast Asian Studies.

Bull, J.W., and M. Maron. 2016. "How Humans Drive Speciation as Well as Extinction." *Proceedings of the Royal Society B: Biological Sciences* 283, no. 1833.

Bunge, Jacob. 2015. "How to Satisfy the World's Surging Appetite for Meat." *Wall Street Journal,* December 4. www.wsj.com/articles/how-to-satisfy-the-worlds-surging-appetite-for-meat-1449238059.

Bunker, Stephen G. 1985. *Underdeveloping the Amazon: Extraction, Unequal Exchange, and the Failure of the Modern State.* Chicago: University of Chicago Press.

Büntgen, Ulf, Willy Tegel, Kurt Nicolussi, Michael McCormick, David Frank, Valerie Trouet, Jed O. Kaplan, et al. 2011. "2500 Years of European Climate Variability and Human Susceptibility." *Science* 331, no. 6017: 578–82.

Burawoy, Michael. 1983. "Between the Labor Process and the State: The Changing Face of Factory Regimes under Advanced Capitalism." *American Sociological Review* 48, no. 5: 587–605.

Burbach, Roger, and Patricia Flynn. 1980. *Agribusiness in the Americas.* New York: Monthly Review Press.

Burkett, Paul, and John Bellamy Foster. 2006. "Metabolism, Energy, and Entropy in Marx's Critique of Political Economy: Beyond the Podolinsky Myth." *Theory and Society* 35, no. 1: 109–56.

Butollo, Florian, and Tobias ten Brink. 2012. "Challenging the Atomization of Discontent." *Critical Asian Studies* 44, no. 3: 419–40.

Buzan, Barry, Ole Wæver, and Jaap de Wilde. 1998. *Security: A New Framework for Analysis*. Boulder, CO: Lynne Rienner.

Cadamosto [Alvise da Ca' da Mosto]. (1455) 1937. *The Voyages of Cadamosto and Other Documents on Western Africa in the Second Half of the Fifteenth Century*. Translated and edited by G.R. Crone. London: Hakluyt Society.

Cahan, Bruce B., Irmgard Marboe, and Henning Roedel. 2016. "Outer Frontiers of Banking: Financing Space Explorers and Safeguarding Terrestrial Finance." *New Space* 4, no. 4: 253–68.

Cahill, David. 1994. "Colour by Numbers: Racial and Ethnic Categories in the Viceroyalty of Peru, 1532–1824." *Journal of Latin American Studies* 26, no. 2: 325–46.

Campbell, Bruce. 2010. "Nature as Historical Protagonist: Environment and Society in Pre-industrial England." *Economic History Review* 63, no. 2: 281–314.

Campbell, Chris, and Michael Niblett, eds. 2016. *The Caribbean: Aesthetics, World-Ecology, Politics*. Liverpool: Liverpool University Press.

Canny, Nicholas P. 2001. *Making Ireland British, 1580–1650*. Oxford: Oxford University Press.

Cantor, Norman F. 2002. *In the Wake of the Plague: The Black Death and the World It Made*. New York: HarperCollins.

Carlos, Ann M., Karen Maguire, and Larry Neal. 2006. "Financial Acumen, Women Speculators, and the Royal African Company during the South Sea Bubble." *Accounting, Business and Financial History* 16, no. 2: 219–43.

Carney, Judith Ann. 2001. *Black Rice: The African Origins of Rice Cultivation in the Americas*. Cambridge, MA: Harvard University Press.

Carrington, Damian. 2016. "The Anthropocene Epoch: Scientists Declare Dawn of Human-Influenced Age." *Guardian*, August 29. www.theguardian.com/environment/2016/aug/29/declare-anthropocene-epoch-experts-urge-geological-congress-human-impact-earth.

Catz, Rebecca. 1993. *Christopher Columbus and the Portuguese, 1476–1498*. Westport, CT: Greenwood.

Cavanagh, Edward. 2013. "Kingdom or Colony? English or British? Early Modern Ireland and the Colonialism Question." *Journal of Colonialism and Colonial History* 14, no. 2.

Ceballos, Gerardo, Paul R. Ehrlich, Anthony D. Barnosky, Andrés García, Robert M. Pringle, and Todd M. Palmer. 2015. "Accelerated Modern Human-Induced Species Losses: Entering the Sixth Mass Extinction." *Science Advances* 1, no. 5.

Cerri, Carlos Eduardo P., Gerd Sparovek, Martial Bernoux, William E. Easterling, Jerry M. Melillo, and Carlos Clemente Cerri. 2007. "Tropical Agriculture and Global Warming: Impacts and Mitigation Options." *Scientia Agricola* 64: 83–99.

Challinor, A.J., J. Watson, D.B. Lobell, S.M. Howden, D.R. Smith, and N. Chhetri. 2014. "A Meta-analysis of Crop Yield under Climate Change and Adaptation." *Nature Climate Change* 4, no. 4: 287–91.

Channell, Rob, and Mark V. Lomolino. 2000. "Trajectories to Extinction: Spatial Dynamics of the Contraction of Geographical Ranges." *Journal of Biogeography* 27, no. 1: 169–79.

Chapman, Ian. 2014. "The End of Peak Oil? Why This Topic Is Still Relevant despite Recent Denials." *Energy Policy* 64: 93–101.

Charlesworth, Andrew. 1983. *An Atlas of Rural Protest in Britain, 1548–1900*. London: Croom Helm.

Chaudhuri, K.N. 1985. *Trade and Civilisation in the Indian Ocean: An Economic History from the Rise of Islam to 1750*. Cambridge: Cambridge University Press.

Chew, Sing C. 2001. *World Ecological Degradation: Accumulation, Urbanization, and Deforestation, 3000 B.C.–A.D. 2000*. Walnut Creek, CA: AltaMira.

Cheyne, George. 1733. *The English Malady; or, A Treatise of Nervous Diseases of All Kinds....* London: G. Strahan.

Chhatre, Ashwini, and Arun Agrawal. 2009. "Trade-Offs and Synergies between Carbon Storage and Livelihood Benefits from Forest Commons." *Proceedings of the National Academy of Sciences* 106, no. 42: 17667–70.

Chiluwa, Innocent. 2015. "'Occupy Nigeria 2012': A Critical Analysis of Facebook Posts in the Fuel Subsidy Removal Protests." *Clina* 1, no. 1: 47–69.

Cicero, Marcus Tullius. (45 BCE) 1933. *De natura deorum; Academica*. Translated by H. Rackham. Vol. 19 of *Cicero in Twenty-Eight Volumes*. London: William Heinemann.

City of London. 2016. *Total Tax Contribution of UK Financial Services*. 9th ed. London: City of London Corporation.

Clark, Alice Shaw. 1919. *Working Life of Women in the Seventeenth Century*. London: G. Routledge and Sons.

Clark, Gregory. 2002. "The Agricultural Revolution and the Industrial Revolution: England, 1500–1912." Unpublished manuscript. Department of Economics, University of California, Davis. http://faculty.econ.ucdavis.edu/faculty/gclark/papers/prod2002.pdf.

———. 2007. *A Farewell to Alms: A Brief Economic History of the World*. Princeton, NJ: Princeton University Press.

Clark, Gregory, Michael Huberman, and Peter H. Lindert. 1995. "A British Food Puzzle, 1770–1850." *Economic History Review* 48, no. 2: 215–37.

Cline, Sarah. 2015. "Guadalupe and the Castas: : The Power of a Singular Colonial Mexican Painting." *Mexican Studies / Estudios Mexicanos* 31, no. 2: 218–47.

Cobarrubias, Sebastián, and John Pickles. 2009. "Spacing Movements: The Turn to Cartographies and Mapping Practices in Contemporary Social Movements." In *The Spatial Turn: Interdisciplinary Perspectives*, edited by Barney Warf and Santa Arias, 36–58. London: Routledge.

Cochrane, Willard W. 1979. *The Development of American Agriculture: A Historical Analysis*. Minneapolis: University of Minnesota Press.

Cohn, Samuel K., Jr. 2002. "The Black Death: End of a Paradigm." *American Historical Review* 107, no. 3: 703–38.

———. 2006. *Lust for Liberty: The Politics of Social Revolt in Medieval Europe, 1200–1425—Italy, France, and Flanders*. Cambridge, MA: Harvard University Press.

———. 2007a. "The Black Death and the Burning of Jews." *Past and Present* 196: 3–36.

———. 2007b. "Popular Insurrection and the Black Death: A Comparative View." *Past and Present* 195, suppl. 2: 188–204.

Coles, Paul. 1957. "The Crisis of Renaissance Society Genoa, 1488–1507." *Past and Present* 11: 17–47.

Columbus, Christopher. 2003. "Journal of the First Voyage of Columbus." In *The Northmen, Columbus and Cabot, 985–1503*, edited by Julius E. Olson and Edward Gaylord Bourne, 85–258. Original Narratives of Early American History. New York: Charles Scribner's Sons, 1906. Available at www.gutenberg.org/files/18571/18571-h/18571-h.htm.

Colwill, Elizabeth. 1989. "Just Another *Citoyenne?* Marie-Antoinette on Trial, 1790–1793." *History Workshop* 28, no. 1: 63–87.

Connell, R. W. 1990. "The State, Gender, and Sexual Politics." *Theory and Society* 19, no. 5: 507–44.

———. 1995. *Masculinities.* Berkeley: University of California Press.

Coontz, Stephanie, and Peta Henderson, eds. 2016. *Women's Work, Men's Property: The Origins of Gender and Class.* London: Verso.

Corri, Adrienne. 1983. "Gainsborough's Early Career: New Documents and Two Portraits." *Burlington Magazine* 125, no. 961: 210–16.

Coulthard, Glen Sean. 2014. *Red Skin, White Masks: Rejecting the Colonial Politics of Recognition.* Minneapolis: Minnesota University Press.

Cowan, Ruth Schwartz. 1983. *More Work for Mother: The Ironies of Household Technology from the Open Hearth to the Microwave.* New York: Basic.

Cronon, William. 1983. *Changes in the Land: Indians, Colonists, and the Ecology of New England.* New York: W. W. Norton.

———. 1991. *Nature's Metropolis: Chicago and the Great West.* New York: W. W. Norton.

———. 1995. *Uncommon Ground: Toward Reinventing Nature.* New York: W. W. Norton.

Crumley, Carole. 1994. "The Ecology of Conquest." In *Historical Ecology: Cultural Knowledge and Changing Landscape,* edited by Crumley, 183–201. Santa Fe: School of American Research Press.

Dalla Costa, Mariarosa, and Selma James. 1973. *Power of Women and the Subversion of the Community.* 2nd ed. Bristol: Falling Wall.

Daly, Mary. 1990. *Gyn/ecology: The Metaethics of Radical Feminism.* Boston: Beacon.

Dann, Graham M. S., and A. V. Seaton. 2001. "Slavery, Contested Heritage and Thanatourism." *International Journal of Hospitality and Tourism Administration* 2, nos. 3–4: 1–29.

DARA and the Climate Vulnerable Forum. 2012. *Climate Vulnerability Monitor: A Guide to the Cold Calculus of a Hot Planet.* 2nd ed. Madrid: Estudios Gráficos Europeos.

Dauverd, Céline. 2014. *Imperial Ambition in the Early Modern Mediterranean: Genoese Merchants and the Spanish Crown.* Cambridge: Cambridge University Press.

David, Saul. 2002. *The Indian Mutiny: 1857.* London: Viking.

Davids, Karel. 2008. *The Rise and Decline of Dutch Technological Leadership: Technology, Economy and Culture in the Netherlands, 1350–1800.* Vol. 1. Leiden: Brill.

Davis, Angela Y. 1983. *Women, Race and Class.* New York: Vintage.

Davis, Lennard J. 2016. *The Disability Studies Reader.* 5th ed. New York: Routledge.

Davis, Mike. 1986. *Prisoners of the American Dream: Politics and Economy in the History of the US Working Class.* London: Verso.

———. 2001. *Late Victorian Holocausts: El Niño Famines and the Making of the Third World.* London: Verso.

———. 2004. "The Urbanization of Empire: Megacities and the Laws of Chaos." *Social Text* 22, no. 4: 9–15.

———. 2015. "Marx's Lost Theory: The Politics of Nationalism in 1848." *New Left Review* 93: 45–66.

Davis, Ralph. 1954. "English Foreign Trade, 1660–1700." *Economic History Review* 7, no. 2: 150–66.

Day, John. 1978. "The Great Bullion Famine of the Fifteenth Century." *Past and Present* 79: 3–54.

Deans-Smith, Susan. 2005. "Creating the Colonial Subject: Casta Paintings, Collectors, and Critics in Eighteenth-Century Mexico and Spain." *Colonial Latin American Review* 14, no. 2: 169–204.

Decker, Ethan H., Scott Elliott, Felisa A. Smith, Donald R. Blake, and F. Sherwood Rowland. 2000. "Energy and Material Flow through the Urban Ecosystem." *Annual Review of Energy and the Environment* 25, no. 1: 685–740.

Delle, James A., Stephen A. Mrozowski, and Robert Paynter. 2000. *Lines That Divide: Historical Archaeologies of Race, Class, and Gender.* Knoxville: University of Tennessee Press.

Descartes, René. 1985. *Philosophical Writings of Descartes.* Translated by John Cottingham, Robert Stroothoff, and Dugald Murdoch. Vol. 1. Cambridge: Cambridge University Press.

De Schutter, Olivier. 2010. "Agro-ecology and the Right to Food: Report Submitted by the Special Rapporteur on the Right to Food, Olivier De Schutter, to the Sixteenth Session of the Human Rights Council." Edited by the General Assembly. New York: United Nations. http://www2.ohchr.org/english/issues/food/docs/A-HRC-16-49.pdf.

De Ste. Croix, G.E.M. 1981. *The Class Struggle in the Ancient Greek World: From the Archaic Age to the Arab Conquests.* London: Duckworth.

De Vries, Jan. 1993. "Between Purchasing Power and the World of Goods: Understanding the Household Economy in Early Modern Europe." In

Consumption and the World of Goods, edited by John Brewer and Roy Porter, 85–132. London: Routledge.

De Vries, Jan, and Ad van der Woude. 1997. *The First Modern Economy: Success, Failure, and Perseverance of the Dutch Economy, 1500–1815.* Cambridge: Cambridge University Press.

DeWitte, Sharon N. 2015. "Setting the Stage for Medieval Plague: Pre–Black Death Trends in Survival and Mortality." *American Journal of Physical Anthropology* 158, no. 3: 441–51.

Diamond, Jared M. 2005. *Guns, Germs, and Steel: The Fates of Human Societies.* New York: W. W. Norton.

Dirección General de Estadística, ed. 1955. *Tercer censo agrícola ganadero y ejidal, 1950.* Mexico City: Dirección General de Estadística.

Disney, Anthony R. 2009. *A History of Portugal and the Portuguese Empire.* Vol 2. Cambridge: Cambridge University Press.

Dodds, Joseph. 2011. *Psychoanalysis and Ecology at the Edge of Chaos: Complexity Theory, Deleuze|Guattari and Psychoanalysis for a Climate in Crisis.* London: Routledge.

Doherty, Brian, Matthew Paterson, Alexandra Plows, and Derek Wall. 2003. "Explaining the Fuel Protests." *British Journal of Politics and International Relations* 5, no. 1: 1–23.

Dohrn-van Rossum, Gerhard. 1996. *History of the Hour: Clocks and Modern Temporal Orders.* Chicago: University of Chicago Press.

Donkin, R. A., and Wenner-Gren Foundation for Anthropological Research. 1979. *Agricultural Terracing in the Aboriginal New World.* Tucson: University of Arizona Press.

Dotson, John, and Aldo Agosto. 1998. Introduction to *Christopher Columbus and His Family: The Genoese and Ligurian Documents,* edited by Dotson and Agosto, translated by Dotson, 5–26. Los Angeles: UCLA Center for Medieval and Renaissance Studies / Repertorium Columbianum.

Drayton, Richard Harry. 2000. *Nature's Government: Science, Imperial Britain, and the "Improvement" of the World.* New Haven, CT: Yale University Press.

Dredge, James. 1839–43. "Diary: 1 Sept. 1839–8 Oct. 1843." State Library of Victoria, Australia.

Dribe, Martin, Mats Olsson, and Patrick Svensson. 2015. "Famines in the Nordic Countries, AD 536–1875." Lund Papers in Economic History: General Issues 138. Department of Economic History, Lund University.

Dubin, H.J., and John P. Brennan. 2009. "Fighting a 'Shifty Enemy': The International Collaboration to Contain Wheat Rusts." In *Millions Fed: Proven Successes in Agricultural Development,* edited by David J. Spielman and Rajul Pandya-Lorch, 19–24. Washington DC: International Food Policy Research Institute.

Duffy, Michael. 1980. *The Military Revolution and the State, 1500–1800.* Exeter: University of Exeter Press.

Duffy, Mignon. 2005. "Reproducing Labor Inequalities: Challenges for Feminists Conceptualizing Care at the Intersections of Gender, Race, and Class." *Gender and Society* 19, no. 1: 66–82.

Dull, Robert A., Richard J. Nevle, William I. Woods, Dennis K. Bird, Shiri Avnery, and William M. Denevan. 2010. "The Columbian Encounter and the Little Ice Age: Abrupt Land Use Change, Fire, and Greenhouse Forcing." *Annals of the Association of American Geographers* 100, no. 4: 755–71.

Dunbar-Ortiz, Roxanne. 2014. *An Indigenous Peoples' History of the United States, ReVisioning American History.* Boston: Beacon Press.

Dunaway, Wilma A. 2015. "The Double Register of History: Situating the Forgotten Woman and Her Household in Capitalist Commodity Chains." *Journal of World-Systems Research* 7, no. 1: 2–29.

Dunkley, Claudia S. 2014. *Global Warming: How Does It Relate to Poultry?* Athens: University of Georgia Extension Service. http://extension.uga.edu/publications/detail.cfm?number=B1382.

Dunn, Rob. 2017. *Never Out of Season.* New York: Little, Brown.

Dussel, Enrique. 2014. "Anti-Cartesian Meditations: On the Origin of the Philosophical Anti-discourse of Modernity." *Journal for Cultural and Religious Theory* 13, no. 1: 11–53. www.jcrt.org/archives/13.1/dussel.pdf. Translation by George Ciccariello-Maher of "Meditaciones anti-cartesianas: Sobre el origen del anti-discurso filosófico de la Modernidad." *Tabula Rasa* 9 (2008): 153–98. www.revistatabularasa.org/numero-9/09dussel.pdf.

Dwyer, Rachel E. 2013. "The Care Economy? Gender, Economic Restructuring, and Job Polarization in the U.S. Labor Market." *American Sociological Review* 78, no. 3: 390–416.

Edwards, Mark A. 2009. "Nationalization, De-nationalization, Re-nationalization: Some Historical and Comparative Perspective." *Pace Law Review* 30: 124–53.

Ehrenberg, Richard. 1985. *Capital and Finance in the Age of the Renaissance: A Study of the Fuggers and Their Connections*. Fairfield, NJ: A.M. Kelley.

Ehrlich, Paul R., and Anne H. Ehrlich. 1990. *The Population Explosion*. New York: Simon and Schuster.

Eisenstein, Zillah R. 1979. *Capitalist Patriarchy and the Case for Socialist Feminism*. New York: Monthly Review Press.

Elliott, John Huxtable. 1963. *Imperial Spain, 1469–1716*. New York: St. Martin's.

———. 1984. "Spain and America in the Sixteenth and Seventeenth Centuries." In *Colonial Latin America*, 287–340. Vol. 1 of *The Cambridge History of Latin America*, edited by Leslie Bethell. Cambridge: Cambridge University Press.

———. 1992. *The Old World and the New: 1492–1650*. Cambridge: Cambridge University Press.

Ellis, Peter Berresford. 1988. *Hell or Connaught! The Cromwellian Colonisation of Ireland, 1652–1660*. Belfast: Blackstaff.

Eltis, David. 1998. *The Military Revolution in Sixteenth-Century Europe*. Vol. 3. London: I.B. Tauris.

Elvin, Mark. 2004. *The Retreat of the Elephants: An Environmental History of China*. New Haven, CT: Yale University Press.

Engel, Barbara Alpern. 1997. "Not by Bread Alone: Subsistence Riots in Russia during World War I." *Journal of Modern History* 69, no. 4: 696–721.

EPA (United States Environmental Protection Agency). 2012. "Poultry Production Phases." http://infohouse.p2ric.org/ref/02/01244/www.epa.gov/agriculture/ag101/poultryphases.html.

EPI (Earth Policy Institute). 2010. "World on the Edge—Energy Data—Oil." www.earth-policy.org/datacenter/pdf/book_wote_energy_oil.pdf.

———. 2012. "Wheat Production, Area, and Yield in India, 1960–2011." September 27. Excel file. Available at www.earth-policy.org/data_center/C24.

———. 2013. "World Average Corn, Wheat, and Rice Yields, 1960–2012." January 17. Excel file. Available at www.earth-policy.org/data_center/C24.

———. 2014. "Fertilizer Consumption and Grain Production for the World, 1950–2013." January 8. Excel file. Available at www.earth-policy.org/data_center/C24.

Epstein, Steven. 1996. *Genoa and the Genoese, 958–1528*. Chapel Hill: University of North Carolina Press.

———. 2001. *Speaking of Slavery: Color, Ethnicity, and Human Bondage in Italy*. Ithaca, NY: Cornell University Press.

Erdkamp, Paul, ed. 2013. *The Cambridge Companion to Ancient Rome*. Cambridge: Cambridge University Press.

Erickson, Amy Louise. 2005. "Coverture and Capitalism." *History Workshop Journal* 59, no. 1: 1–16.

Erisman, Jan Willem, Mark A. Sutton, James Galloway, Zbigniew Klimont, and Wilfried Winiwarter. 2008. "How a Century of Ammonia Synthesis Changed the World." *Nature Geoscience* 1, no. 10: 636–39.

Ervin, R. Bethene, and Cynthia L. Ogden. 2013. *Consumption of Added Sugars among U.S. Adults, 2005–2010*. NCHS Data Brief 122. Hyattsville, MD: National Center for Health Statistics.

EU (European Union). 2017. *Labour Market and Labour Force Survey (LFS) Statistics*. Brussels: European Union.

Evans, Terry. 2014. "Global Poultry Trends 2014: Poultry Set to Become No. 1 Meat in Asia." *Poultry Site*, last modified September 2. www.thepoultrysite.com/articles/3230/global-poultry-trends-2014-poultry-set-to-become-no1-meat-in-asia/.

Fagan, Brian. 2008. *The Great Warming: Climate Change and the Rise and Fall of Civilizations*. New York: Bloomsbury.

Falls, Cyril. 1950. *Elizabeth's Irish Wars*. London: n.p.

Falquet, Jules. 2006. "Hommes en armes et femmes 'de service': Tendences néolibérales dans l'évolution de la division sexuelle et internationale du travail." *Cahiers du genre* 40: 15–37.

Fanon, Frantz. 2016. "The Fact of Blackness." In *Postcolonial Studies: An Anthology*, edited by Pramod K. Nayar, 15–32. Malden, MA: John Wiley and Sons.

Fantone, Laura. 2007. "Precarious Changes: Gender and Generational Politics in Contemporary Italy." *Feminist Review* 87: 5–20.

Federici, Silvia. 2004. *Caliban and the Witch*. New York: Autonomedia.

———. 2008. " Witch-Hunting, Globalization, and Feminist Solidarity in Africa Today." *Journal of International Women's Studies* 10, no. 1: 21–35.

Felloni, Giuseppe, and Guido Laura. 2014. *Genova e la storia della finanza: Dodici primati? / Genoa and the History of Finance: Twelve Firsts?* Translated by Marina Felloni and Authumn Wiltshire. www.giuseppefelloni.it/rassegnastampa/GenovaFinanza12primati.pdf.

Ferguson, Niall. 2009. *The Ascent of Money: A Financial History of the World*. London: Penguin.

Fernández-Armesto, Felipe. 1982. *The Canary Islands after the Conquest: The Making of a Colonial Society in the Early Sixteenth Century*. Oxford: Oxford University Press.

Fernow, Brian E. 1911. *A Brief History of Forestry in Europe, the United States and Other Countries: A Course of Lectures Delivered before the Yale Forest School*. 3rd ed. Toronto: University of Toronto Press.

Fine, Ben. 2001. *Social Capital versus Social Theory: Political Economy and Social Science at the Turn of the Millennium*. London: Routledge.

Finlay, Mark R. 2002. Review of *Enriching the Earth: Fritz Haber, Carl Bosch, and the Transformation of World Food Production*, by Vaclav Smil. *British Journal for the History of Science* 35, no. 1: 97–123.

Fischer-Kowalski, Marina, Simron J. Singh, Lisa Ringhofer, Clemens M. Grünbühel, Christian Lauk, and Alexander Remesch. 2010. "Sociometabolic Regimes in Indigenous Communities and the Crucial Role of Working Time: A Comparison of Case Studies." Social Ecology Working Paper 121, Institute of Social Ecology, IFF—Faculty for Interdisciplinary Studies, Klagenfurt University, Vienna. https://is.muni.cz/el/1423/jaro2013/HEN633/um/Fischer-Kowalski_et_al_Sociometabolic_regimes.pdf.

Fitzgerald, Deborah Kay. 2003. *Every Farm a Factory: The Industrial Ideal in American Agriculture*. New Haven, CT: Yale University Press.

Flynn, Dennis O. 1984. "Use and Misuse of the Quantity Theory of Money in Early Modern Historiography." In *Münzprägung, Geldumlauf und Wechselkurse / Minting, Monetary Circulation and Exchange Rates: Akten der C7-Section des 8th International Economic History Congress Budapest 1982*, edited by Eddy van Cauwenberghe and Franz Irsigler, 383–419. Trier: Trierer Historische Forchungen.

Flynn, Dennis O., and Arturo Giráldez. 1995. "Born with a 'Silver Spoon': The Origin of World Trade in 1571." *Journal of World History* 6, no. 2: 201–21.

———. 2002. "Cycles of Silver: Global Economic Unity through the Mid-Eighteenth Century." *Journal of World History* 13, no. 2: 391–427.

Folbre, Nancy. 2006. "Measuring Care: Gender, Empowerment, and the Care Economy." *Journal of Human Development* 7, no. 2: 183–99.

Fortune, Robert. 1852. *A Journey to the Tea Countries of China*. London: John Murray.

Foster, John Bellamy. 1999. "Marx's Theory of Metabolic Rift: Classical Foundations for Environmental Sociology." *American Journal of Sociology* 105, no. 2: 366–405.

———. 2013. "James Hansen and the Climate-Change Exit Strategy." *Monthly Review* 64, no. 9: 1–19.

Foucault, Michel. 1973. *The Order of Things: An Archaeology of the Human Sciences.* New York: Vintage.

———. 1979. *Discipline and Punish: The Birth of the Prison.* Translated by Alan Sheridan. New York: Vintage.

———. 1980. *The History of Sexuality.* Translated by Robert Hurley. Vol. 1, *An Introduction.* New York: Vintage.

———. 2003. *Society Must Be Defended: Lectures at the Collège de France, 1975–1976.* Edited by Mauro Bertani and Alessandro Fontana. Translated by David Macey. London: Macmillan.

———. 2008. *The Birth of Biopolitics: Lectures at the Collège de France, 1978–1979.* Edited by Michel Senellart. Translated by Graham Burchell. Basingstoke: Palgrave Macmillan.

Frader, Laura Levine. 2004. "Gender and Labor in World History." In *A Companion to Gender History,* edited by Teresa A. Meade and Merry E. Wiesner, 26–50. Malden, MA: Wiley-Blackwell.

Franklin, Benjamin. 1950. Letter to Jean-Baptiste Leroy, November 13, 1789. In *The Writings of Benjamin Franklin.* Edited by Albert Henry Smyth. Vol. 10, *1789–1790.* New York: Macmillan.

Fraser, Nancy. 2012. "Feminism, Capitalism, and the Cunning of History: An Introduction." Working paper FMSHWP-2012-17. Paris: Fondation Maison des sciences de l'homme. https://halshs.archives-ouvertes.fr/halshs-00725055/document.

Freese, Barbara. 2003. *Coal: A Human History.* New York: Basic.

Fremdling, Rainer. 2005. "Industrialization and Scientific and Technological Progress." In *History of Humanity: Scientific and Cultural Development.* Vol. 4, *The Nineteenth Century,* edited by Peter Mathias and Nikolaï Todorov, 80–94. London: UNESCO/Routledge.

Friedmann, Harriet. 1978. "World Market, State, and Family Farm: Social Bases of Household Production in the Era of Wage Labor." *Comparative Studies in Society and History* 20, no. 4: 545–86.

———. 1993. "The Political Economy of Food: A Global Crisis." *New Left Review* I/197: 29–57.

Fry, Matthew. 2013. "Cement, Carbon Dioxide, and the 'Necessity' Narrative: A Case Study of Mexico." *Geoforum* 49: 127–38.

FTI Consulting. 2016. *Oil Price Drivers: Bottom of the Barrel?* www.fticonsulting.com/~/media/Files/emea--files/insights/reports/fti-oil-price-drivers-report.pdf.

Fuglie, Keith O., James M. MacDonald, and Eldon Ball. 2007. "Productivity Growth in US Agriculture." Washington DC: US Department of Agriculture. www.ers.usda.gov/webdocs/publications/42924/11854_eb9_1_.pdf.

Fuglie, K.O., and S.L. Wang. 2012. "New Evidence Points to Robust but Uneven Productivity Growth in Global Agriculture." *Amber Waves* 10, no. 3: 1–6.

Galbraith, James K., and J. Travis Hale. 2014. "The Evolution of Economic Inequality in the United States, 1969–2012: Evidence from Data on Inter-industrial Earnings and Inter-regional Incomes." *World Economic Review* 3: 1–19.

Gale, Fred, Bryan Lohmar, and Francis Tuan. 2005. *China's New Farm Subsidies.* United States Department of Agriculture WRS-05-01. www.ers.usda.gov/webdocs/publications/wrs0501/30113_wrs0501_002.pdf.

Galloway, J.N., F.J. Dentener, D.G. Capone, E.W. Boyer, R.W. Howarth, S.P. Seitzinger, G.P. Asner, et al. 2004. "Nitrogen Cycles: Past, Present, and Future." *Biogeochemistry* 70, no. 2: 153–226.

Gannon, Clodagh O'Malley. 2015. "Exploring the Links between Communality, the Metabolic Relationship, and Ecological Sustainability: A Case Study of a North-west of Ireland Community (c. 1930s–50s)." PhD thesis, Department of Sociology, National University of Ireland Maynooth. http://eprints.maynoothuniversity.ie/6324/.

Garrett, Rebecca, and Liza Kim Jackson. 2015. "Art, Labour and Precarity in the Age of Veneer Politics." *Alternate Routes: A Journal of Critical Social Research* 27: 279.

Gaud, W.S. 1968. "The Green Revolution: Accomplishments and Apprehensions." Address to the Society of International Development, Washington DC, March 8. www.agbioworld.org/biotech-info/topics/borlaug/borlaug-green.html.

Genovese, Eugene D. 1992. *From Rebellion to Revolution: Afro-American Slave Revolts in the Making of the Modern World.* Baton Rouge: Louisiana State University Press.

Gerber, P.J., H. Steinfeld, B. Henderson, A. Mottet, C. Opio, J. Dijkman, A. Falcucci, and G. Tempio. 2013. *Tackling Climate Change through Livestock: A Global Assessment of Emissions and Mitigation Opportunities.* Rome: Food and Agriculture Organization of the United Nations.

Gerretson, F. C. 1953. *History of the Royal Dutch.* Vol. 1. Leiden: Brill.

Giles, Chris. 2017. "Why Davos 2017 Matters: 10 Things to Watch For." *Financial Times,* January 16. www.ft.com/content/576fb394-dbcd-11e6-86ac-f253db7791c6.

Glacken, Clarence J. 1967. *Traces on the Rhodian Shore: Nature and Culture in Western Thought from Ancient Times to the End of the Eighteenth Century.* Berkeley: University of California Press.

Gleeson-White, Jane. 2012. *Double Entry: How the Merchants of Venice Created Modern Finance.* London: Allen and Unwin.

Glenn, Evelyn Nakano. 1992. "From Servitude to Service Work: Historical Continuities in the Racial Division of Paid Reproductive Labor." *Signs* 18, no. 1: 1–43.

———. 2010. *Forced to Care: Coercion and Caregiving in America.* Cambridge, MA: Harvard University Press.

Gnutzmann, Hinnerk, and Piotr Śpiewanowski. 2016. "Fertilizer Fuels Food Prices: Identification through the Oil-Gas Spread." Last revised September 1. Social Science Research Network.

Gold, Mick. 1984. "A History of Nature." In *Geography Matters,* edited by Doreen Massey and John Allen, 12–33. Cambridge: Cambridge University Press.

Goldberg, Harmony. 2014. "Our Day Has Finally Come: Domestic Worker Organizing in New York City." PhD dissertation, Graduate Faculty in Anthropology, City University of New York. http://academicworks.cuny.edu/gc_etds/422/.

Goldstone, Nancy Bazelon. 2011. *Joanna: The Notorious Queen of Naples, Jerusalem and Sicily.* London: Phoenix.

Goodfriend, Glenn A., R. A. D. Cameron, and L. M. Cook. 1994. "Fossil Evidence of Recent Human Impact on the Land Snail Fauna of Madeira." *Journal of Biogeography* 21, no. 3: 309–20.

Gotzek, D., H.J. Axen, A.V. Suarez, S. Helms Cahan, and D. Shoemaker. 2015. "Global Invasion History of the Tropical Fire Ant: A Stowaway on the First Global Trade Routes." *Molecular Ecology* 24, no. 2: 374–88.

Gouge, William. 1622. *Of Domesticall Duties, Eight Treatises, Etc.* London: John Haviland, for William Bladen.

Graetz, Heinrich. (1894) 1967. *History of the Jews.* Edited and in part translated by Bella Löwy. Vol. 3. Philadelphia: Jewish Publication Society of America.

Gramsci, Antonio. 1978. *Selections from Political Writings (1921–1926).* Edited and translated by Quintin Hoare. New York: International.

Grantham, J. 2011. "Days of Abundant Resources and Falling Prices Are Over Forever." *GMO Quarterly Newsletter,* April, 1–18.

Grey, Sam, and Raj Patel. 2014. "Food Sovereignty as Decolonization: Some Contributions from Indigenous Movements to Food System and Development Politics." *Agriculture and Human Values* 32, no. 3: 431–44.

Grosfoguel, Ramón, and Eric Mielants. 2006. "The Long-Durée Entanglement between Islamophobia and Racism in the Modern / Colonial Capitalist / Patriarchal World-System: An Introduction." *Human Architecture: Journal of the Sociology of Self-Knowledge* 5, no. 1: article 2. http://scholarworks.umb.edu/humanarchitecture/vol5/iss1/2.

Grove, Richard. 1995. *Green Imperialism: Colonial Expansion, Tropical Island Edens, and the Origins of Environmentalism, 1600–1860.* Cambridge: Cambridge University Press.

Gunaratne, Shelton A. 2001. "Paper, Printing and the Printing Press: A Horizontally Integrative Macrohistory Analysis." *International Communication Gazette* 63, no. 6: 459–79.

Gurian-Sherman, Doug. 2009. "Failure to Yield: Evaluating the Performance of Genetically Engineered Crops." Cambridge, MA: Union of Concerned Scientists. www.ucsusa.org/sites/default/files/legacy/assets/documents/food_and_agriculture/failure-to-yield.pdf.

Gylfason, Thorvaldur, and Gylfi Zoega. 2002. *Inequality and Economic Growth: Do Natural Resources Matter?* Munich: Center for Economic Studies and Ifo Institute for Economic Research.

Häberlein, Mark. 2012. *The Fuggers of Augsburg: Pursuing Wealth and Honor in Renaissance Germany.* Charlottesville: University of Virginia Press.

Habermann, Friederike. 2016. *Ecommony: UmCARE zum Miteinander.* Sulzbach: Ulrike Helmer.

Haensch, S., R. Bianucci, M. Signoli, M. Rajerison, M. Schultz, S. Kacki, M. Vermunt, D. A. Weston, D. Hurst, M. Achtman, E. Carniel, and B. Bramanti. 2010. "Distinct Clones of *Yersinia pestis* Caused the Black Death." *PLOS Pathogens* 6, no. 10: e1001134.

Hall, Kim F. 1996. "Culinary Spaces, Colonial Spaces: The Gendering of Sugar in the Seventeenth Century." In *Feminist Readings of Early Modern Culture: Emerging Subjects,* edited by Valerie Traub, M. Lindsay Kaplan, and Dympna Callaghan, 168–90. Cambridge: Cambridge University Press.

Hall, Robert G. 1989. "Tyranny, Work and Politics: The 1818 Strike Wave in the English Cotton District." *International Review of Social History* 34, no. 3: 433–70.

Hall, Ruth, Marc Edelman, Saturnino M. Borras, Ian Scoones, Ben White, and Wendy Wolford. 2015. "Resistance, Acquiescence or Incorporation? An Introduction to Land Grabbing and Political Reactions 'From Below.'" *Journal of Peasant Studies* 42, nos. 3–4: 467–88.

Hall, Stuart. 1996. "Race, Articulation and Societies Structured in Dominance." In *Black British Cultural Studies,* edited by Houston A. Baker, Manthia Diawara, and Ruth H. Lindeborg, 16–60. Chicago: University of Chicago Press.

Halperin, Sandra. 2013. *Re-envisioning Global Development: A Horizontal Perspective.* London: Routledge.

Handy, Jim. 2009. "'Almost Idiotic Wretchedness': A Long History of Blaming Peasants." *Journal of Peasant Studies* 36, no. 2: 325–44.

Hannaford, Ivan. 1996. *Race: The History of an Idea in the West.* Washington DC: Woodrow Wilson Center Press; Baltimore: John Hopkins University Press.

Hansen, James E., and Makiko Sato. 2012. "Paleoclimate Implications for Human-Made Climate Change." In *Climate Change: Inferences from Paleoclimate and Regional Aspects,* edited by André Berger, Fedor Mesinger, and Djordje Šijački, 21–47. New York: Springer.

Harding, Sandra G. 1991. *Whose Science? Whose Knowledge? Thinking from Women's Lives.* Ithaca, NY: Cornell University Press.

Hardoon, Deborah, Sophia Ayele, and Ricardo Fuentes-Nieva. 2016. "An Economy for the 1%." Oxford: Oxfam GB. Available at www.oxfam.org/en/research/economy-1.

Harris, David R. 1978. "Adaptation to a Tropical Rain-Forest Environment: Aboriginal Subsistence in Northeastern Queensland." In *Human Behavior and Adaptation*, edited by N. Blurton Jones and V. Reynolds, 113–34. London: Taylor and Francis.

Harrison, Peter. 1992. "Descartes on Animals." *Philosophical Quarterly* 42, no. 167: 219–27.

Harrisse, Henry. 1888. *Christopher Columbus and the Bank of Saint George (Ufficio di San Giorgio in Genoa): Two Letters Addressed to Samuel L. M. Barlow, Esquire.* New York: privately printed.

Hart, Gillian. 1991. "Engendering Everyday Resistance: Gender, Patronage and Production Politics in Rural Malaysia." *Journal of Peasant Studies* 19, no. 1: 93–121.

Harvey, David. 1993. "From Space to Place and Back Again: Reflections on the Condition of Postmodernity." In *Mapping the Futures: Local Cultures, Global Change,* edited by John Bird, Barry Curtis, Tim Putnam, and Lisa Tickner, 3–29. London: Routledge.

———. 2005. *A Brief History of Neoliberalism.* Oxford: Oxford University Press.

Headrick, Daniel R. 1988. *The Tentacles of Progress: Technology Transfer in the Age of Imperialism, 1850–1940.* New York: Oxford University Press.

Heers, Jacques. 1961. *Gênes au XVe siècle: Activité économique et problèmes sociaux.* Paris: SEVPEN.

Heizer, Robert F. 1963. "Domestic Fuel in Primitive Society." *Journal of the Royal Anthropological Institute of Great Britain and Ireland* 93, no. 2: 186–94.

Helgerson, Richard. 1992. *Forms of Nationhood: The Elizabethan Writing of England.* Chicago: University of Chicago Press.

Herdt, Gilbert. 1994. *Third Sex, Third Gender: Beyond Sexual Dimorphism in Culture and History.* New York: Zone.

Herlihy, David, and Christiane Klapisch-Zuber. 1985. *Tuscans and Their Families: A Study of the Florentine Catasto of 1427.* New Haven, CT: Yale University Press.

Herodotus. 1945. *The History of Herodotus.* Translated by G. Rawlinson. Vol. 1. Everymans Library. London: Dent.

Herrero, Mario, Philip K. Thornton, Brendan Power, Jessica R. Bogard, Roseline Remans, Steffen Fritz, James S. Gerber, et al. 2017. "Farming and the Geography of Nutrient Production for Human Use: A Transdisciplinary Analysis." *Lancet Planetary Health* 1, no. 1: e33–e42.

Hewitt de Alcántara, Cynthia. 1973. "The 'Green Revolution' as History: The Mexican Experience." *Development and Change* 4, no. 2: 25–44.

Hildyard, Nicholas. 2016. *Licensed Larceny: Infrastructure, Financial Extraction and the Global South*. Manchester: Manchester University Press.

Hill, Bridget. 1989. *Women, Work and Sexual Politics in Eighteenth-Century England*. Oxford: Basil Blackwell.

Hills, Sally, Ryland Thomas, and Nicholas Dimsdale. 2010. "The UK Recession in Context—What Do Three Centuries of Data Tell Us?" *Bank of England Quarterly Bulletin*, Q4, 277–91.

Hilton, R.H. 1951. "Y eut-il une crise générale de la féodalité?" *Annales: Histoire, Sciences Sociales* 6, no. 1: 23–30.

———. 2003. *Bond Men Made Free: Medieval Peasant Movements and the English Rising of 1381*. London: Routledge.

Hinshelwood, Brad. 2013. "The Carolinian Context of John Locke's Theory of Slavery." *Political Theory* 41, no. 4: 562–90.

Hirway, Indira, and Sunny Jose. 2011. "Understanding Women's Work Using Time-Use Statistics: The Case of India." *Feminist Economics* 17, no. 4: 67–92.

Hobsbawm, E.J., and G. Rude. 1969. *Captain Swing*. London: Lawrence and Wishart.

Hoffmann, Richard. 2014. *An Environmental History of Medieval Europe*. Cambridge: Cambridge University Press.

Holborn, Hajo. 1982. *A History of Modern Germany*. Vol. 1, *The Reformation*. Princeton, NJ: Princeton University Press.

Holt-Giménez, Eric, and Raj Patel. 2009. *Food Rebellions! Crisis and the Hunger for Justice*. Oxford: Fahamu.

Homer, Sidney, and Richard Eugene Sylla. 1996. *A History of Interest Rates*. New Brunswick, NJ: Rutgers University Press.

Honeyman, Katrina, and Jordan Goodman. 1991. "Women's Work, Gender Conflict, and Labour Markets in Europe, 1500–1900." *Economic History Review* 44, no. 4: 608–28.

Hornborg, Alf. 2006. "Footprints in the Cotton Fields: The Industrial Revolution as Time-Space Appropriation and Environmental Load Displacement." *Ecological Economics* 59, no. 1: 74–81.

Hörning, Karl H., Anette Gerhard, and Matthias Michailow. 1995. *Time Pioneers: Flexible Working Time and New Lifestyles*. Translated by Anthony Williams. Cambridge: Polity.

Howell, Martha C. 2010. *Commerce before Capitalism in Europe, 1300–1600*. Cambridge: Cambridge University Press.

Huber, Matthew T. 2009. "Energizing Historical Materialism: Fossil Fuels, Space and the Capitalist Mode of Production." *Geoforum* 40, no. 1: 105–15.

———. 2013. *Lifeblood: Oil, Freedom, and the Forces of Capital*. Minneapolis: University of Minnesota Press.

Hudson, Kenneth, and Andrea Coukos. 2005. "The Dark Side of the Protestant Ethic: A Comparative Analysis of Welfare Reform." *Sociological Theory* 23, no. 1: 1–24.

Hufton, Olwen. 1971. "Women in Revolution, 1789–1796." *Past and Present* 53: 90–108.

———. 1983. "Social Conflict and the Grain Supply in Eighteenth-Century France." *Journal of Interdisciplinary History* 14, no. 2: 303–31.

Hurtado, Albert L. 1988. *Indian Survival on the California Frontier*. New Haven, CT: Yale University Press.

IEA (International Energy Agency). 2008. *Energy Technology Perspectives*. Paris: International Energy Agency.

———. 2016. *Medium-Term Renewable Energy Market Report 2016: Market Analysis and Forecasts to 2021*. Paris: International Energy Agency.

ILO (International Labour Office). 2014. *Profits and Poverty: The Economics of Forced Labour*. Geneva: International Labour Office. www.ilo.org/wcmsp5/groups/public/---ed_norm/---declaration/documents/publication/wcms_243391.pdf.

———. 2015. *World Employment and Social Outlook: Trends 2015*. Geneva: International Labour Office. www.ilo.org/wcmsp5/groups/public/---dgreports/---dcomm/---publ/documents/publication/wcms_337069.pdf.

IMF (International Monetary Fund). 2008. *World Economic Outlook, October 2008: Financial Stress, Downturns, and Recoveries*. Washington DC: International Monetary Fund.

———. 2014. *Global Financial Stability Report, April 2014: Moving from Liquidity- to Growth-Driven Markets*. Washington DC: International Monetary Fund.

———. 2015. *Greece: An Update of IMF Staff's Preliminary Public Debt Sustainability Analysis*. Washington DC: International Monetary Fund.

Inani, Rohit. 2015. "More Than 2,300 People Have Now Died in India's Heat Wave." *Time,* June 2. http://time.com/3904590/india-heatwave-monsoon-delayed-weather-climate-change/.

Inglehart, Ronald, and Pippa Norris. 2003. *Rising Tide: Gender Equality and Cultural Change around the World.* Cambridge: Cambridge University Press.

Ingold, Tim. 1993. "The Temporality of the Landscape." *World Archaeology* 25, no. 2: 152–74.

International Rivers Network. 2011. "Wrong Climate for Big Dams: Fact Sheet—Destroying Rivers Will Worsen Climate Crisis." www.internationalrivers.org/resources/wrong-climate-for-big-dams-fact-sheet-3373.

IPCC (Intergovernmental Panel on Climate Change). 2007. *Climate Change 2007: Synthesis Report.* Geneva: Intergovernmental Panel on Climate Change. www.ipcc.ch/pdf/assessment-report/ar4/syr/ar4_syr_full_report.pdf.

———. 2014. *Climate Change 2014: Mitigation of Climate Change.* Geneva: Intergovernmental Panel on Climate Change. www.ipcc.ch/report/ar5/wg3/.

Jackson, J. B. C. 1997. "Reefs since Columbus." *Coral Reefs* 16, no. 1: S23–S32.

Jackson, R. V. 1985. "Growth and Deceleration in English Agriculture, 1660–1790." *Economic History Review* 38, no. 3: 333–51.

Jameson, Fredric. 1998. *The Cultural Turn: Selected Writings on the Postmodern, 1983–1998.* London: Verso.

Johnson, Walter. 2013. *River of Dark Dreams.* Cambridge, MA: Harvard University Press.

Jones, Grant D. 1989. *Maya Resistance to Spanish Rule: Time and History on a Colonial Frontier.* Albuquerque: University of New Mexico Press.

Jones, W. R. 1971. "The Image of the Barbarian in Medieval Europe." *Comparative Studies in Society and History* 13, no. 4: 376–407.

Jordan, William Chester. 1997. *The Great Famine: Northern Europe in the Early Fourteenth Century.* Princeton, NJ: Princeton University Press.

Josephson, Paul R. 2013. *An Environmental History of Russia.* Cambridge: Cambridge University Press.

Jowett, Benjamin. 1914. *The Dialogues of Plato.* Vol. 4. New York: Hearst's International Libary.

Kagarlitsky, Boris. 2008. *Empire of the Periphery: Russia and the World System.* London: Pluto.

Kaimowitz, David, and Joyotee Smith. 2001. "Soybean Technology and the Loss of Natural Vegetation in Brazil and Bolivia." In *Agricultural Technologies and Tropical Deforestation*, edited by Arild Angelsen and David Kaimowitz, 195–212. Wallingford, Oxford: CABI.

Kain, Roger J. P., and Elizabeth Baigent. 1992. *The Cadastral Map in the Service of the State: A History of Property Mapping.* Chicago: University of Chicago Press.

Kander, Astrid, Paolo Malanima, and Paul Warde. 2013. *Power to the People: Energy in Europe over the Last Five Centuries.* Princeton, NJ: Princeton University Press.

Kaplan, Mitchell. 2010. "Columbus' Forgotten Patron." *Daily Beast,* October 11. www.thedailybeast.com/articles/2010/10/11/columbus-forgotten-patron.html.

Katzew, Ilona. 2004. *Casta Painting: Images of Race in Eighteenth-Century Mexico.* New Haven, CT: Yale University Press.

Keating, Christine, Claire Rasmussen, and Pooja Rishi. 2010. "The Rationality of Empowerment: Microcredit, Accumulation by Dispossession, and the Gendered Economy." *Signs* 36, no. 1: 153–76.

Keller, Catherine. 1994. "The Breast, the Apocalypse, and the Colonial Journey." *Journal of Feminist Studies in Religion* 10, no. 1: 53–72.

Kenyon, Susan. 2010. "What Do We Mean by Multitasking? Exploring the Need for Methodological Clarification in Time Use Research." *Electronic International Journal of Time Use Research* 7, no. 1: 42–60.

Kicza, John E. 1992. "Patterns in Early Spanish Overseas Expansion." *William and Mary Quarterly* 49, no. 2: 229–53.

Kino-nda-niimi Collective, ed. 2014. *The Winter We Danced: Voices from the Past, the Future, and the Idle No More Movement.* Winnipeg: ARP.

Kinsbruner, Jay. 2005. *The Colonial Spanish-American City: Urban Life in the Age of Atlantic Capitalism.* Austin: University of Texas Press.

Klein, Herbert. 2004. "The Atlantic Slave Trade to 1650." In *Tropical Babylons: Sugar and the Making of the Atlantic World, 1450–1680,* edited by Stuart B. Schwartz, 201–36. Chapel Hill: University of North Carolina.

Klein, Naomi. 2007. *The Shock Doctrine: The Rise of Disaster Capitalism.* New York: Metropolitan Books / Henry Holt.

———. 2014. *This Changes Everything: Capitalism vs. the Climate.* New York: Simon and Schuster.

Knox, James C. 1993. "Large Increases in Flood Magnitude in Response to Modest Changes in Climate." *Nature* 361, no. 6411: 430–32.

Koenigsberger, H. G., and George L. Mosse. 1968. *Europe in the Sixteenth Century*. New York: Holt, Rinehart and Winston.

Koning, Hans. 1976. *Columbus: His Enterprise*. New York: Monthly Review Press.

Kucharik, Christopher J., and Shawn P. Serbin. 2008. "Impacts of Recent Climate Change on Wisconsin Corn and Soybean Yield Trends." *Environmental Research Letters* 3, no. 3: 1–10.

Kumar, Avneesh, and Anuj Kumar. 2016. "Black Face of Green Revolution in Malwa Region of Punjab." *Biological Insights* 1: 3–4.

La Berge, Leigh Claire. 2014. "The Rules of Abstraction Methods and Discourses of Finance." *Radical History Review* 118: 93–112.

LaDuke, Winona. 1994. "Traditional Ecological Knowledge and Enviromental Futures." *Colorado Journal of International Environmental Law and Policy* 5: 127–48.

Lamb, Hubert H. 2002. *Climate, History and the Modern World*. London: Routledge.

Langley, Paul. 2002. *World Financial Orders: An Historical International Political Economy*. New York: Routledge.

Lappé, Frances Moore, Jennifer Clapp, Molly Anderson, Robin Broad, Ellen Messer, Thomas Pogge, and Timothy Wise. 2013. "How We Count Hunger Matters." *Ethics and International Affairs* 27, no. 3: 251–59.

Latimer, Jeff, Craig Dowden, and Danielle Muise. 2005. "The Effectiveness of Restorative Justice Practices: A Meta-analysis." *Prison Journal* 85, no. 2: 127–44.

La Vega, Garcilasso de. 1688. *The Royal Commentaries of Peru, in Two Parts. . . .* Translated by Paul Rycaut. London: Miles Flesher.

La Via Campesina. 2009. "Via Campesina Campaign to End Violence against Women." https://viacampesina.org/en/index.php/main-issues-mainmenu-27/women-mainmenu-39/643-via-campesina-campaign-to-end-violence-against-women.

Leach, Gerald. 1987. *Household Energy in South Asia*. London: Elsevier Applied Science.

Le Grange, Lesley. 2012. "*Ubuntu, Ukama* and the Healing of Nature, Self and Society." *Educational Philosophy and Theory* 44: 56–67.

Lenin, Vladimir I. 1965. "The Taylor System—Man's Enslavement by the Machine." In *Collected Works*. Vol. 20, *December 1913–August 1914*, 152–54. London: Lawrence and Wishart.

———. 1987. *Essential Works of Lenin: "What Is to Be Done?" and Other Writings*. Edited by Henry M. Christman. New York: Dover.

Levine, David. 2001. *At the Dawn of Modernity: Biology, Culture, and Material Life in Europe after the Year 1000*. Berkeley: University of California Press.

Levins, Richard, and Richard C. Lewontin. 1985. *The Dialectical Biologist*. Cambridge, MA: Harvard University Press.

Lewis, Percival. 1811. *Historical Inquiries concerning Forests and Forest Laws with Topological Remarks upon the Ancient and Modern State of New Forest*. London: T. Payne.

Lewis, Simon L., and Mark A. Maslin. 2015. "Defining the Anthropocene." *Nature* 519, no. 7542: 171–80.

Li, Xia, Weihua Li, Hong Wang, Jie Cao, Kenji Maehashi, Liquan Huang, Alexander A. Bachmanov, Danielle R. Reed, Véronique Legrand-Defretin, and Gary K. Beauchamp. 2005. "Pseudogenization of a Sweet-Receptor Gene Accounts for Cats' Indifference toward Sugar." *PLoS Genetics* 1, no. 1: e3.

Lichtenstein, Nelson. 2002. *State of the Union: A Century of American Labor*. Princeton, NJ: Princeton University Press.

Lieberman, Victor. 2009. *Mainland Mirrors: Europe, Japan, China, South Asia, and the Islands*. Vol. 2 of *Strange Parallels: Southeast Asia in Global Context, c. 800–1830*. Cambridge: Cambridge University Press.

Linebaugh, Peter. 2008. *The Magna Carta Manifesto: Liberties and Commons for All*. Berkeley: University of California Press.

Linebaugh, Peter, and Marcus Rediker. 2000. *The Many-Headed Hydra: Sailors, Slaves, Commoners, and the Hidden History of the Revolutionary Atlantic*. Boston: Beacon.

Linné, Carl von [Linnaeus]. 1806. *A General System of Nature. . . .* Translated and edited by William Turton. Vol. 1. London: Lackington, Allen.

Lipsett-Rivera, Sonya. 1990. "Puebla's Eighteenth-Century Agrarian Decline: A New Perspective." *Hispanic American Historical Review* 70, no. 3: 463–81.

Liu, Yi-Ping, Gui-Sheng Wu, Yong-Gang Yao, Yong-Wang Miao, Gordon Luikart, Mumtaz Baig, Albano Beja-Pereira, Zhao-Li Ding, Malliya

Gounder Palanichamy, and Ya-Ping Zhang. 2006. "Multiple Maternal Origins of Chickens: Out of the Asian Jungles." *Molecular Phylogenetics and Evolution* 38, no. 1: 12–19.

Livingston, James. 2016. *No More Work: Why Full Employment Is a Bad Idea.* Chapel Hill: University of North Carolina Press.

Lo, Jung-Pang. 1955. "The Emergence of China as a Sea Power during the Late Sung and Early Yüan Periods." *Far Eastern Quarterly* 14, no. 4: 489–503.

Lobell, David, and Christopher B. Field. 2007. "Global Scale Climate-Crop Yield Relationships and the Impacts of Recent Warming." *Environmental Research Letters* 2, no. 1: 014002.

Lobell, David B., Wolfram Schlenker, and Justin Costa-Roberts. 2011. "Climate Trends and Global Crop Production since 1980." *Science* 333, no. 6042: 616–20.

Locke, John. 1997. *Political Essays.* Edited by Mark Goldie. Cambridge: Cambridge University Press.

———. 2003. *Two Treatises of Government and A Letter concerning Toleration.* Edited by Ian Shapiro. New Haven, CT: Yale University Press.

Lohmann, Larry. 2008. "Carbon Trading, Climate Justice and the Production of Ignorance: Ten Examples." *Development* 51, no. 3: 359–65.

Lopez, Robert Sabatino. 1964. "Market Expansion: The Case of Genoa." *Journal of Economic History* 24, no. 4: 445–64.

Louys, Julien, Darren Curnoe, and Haowen Tong. 2007. "Characteristics of Pleistocene Megafauna Extinctions in Southeast Asia." *Palaeogeography, Palaeoclimatology, Palaeoecology* 243, no. 1: 152–73.

Lovell, Julia. 2012. *The Opium War: Drugs, Dreams and the Making of China.* London: Picador.

Lucashenko, Melissa. 1996. "Violence against Indigenous Women: Public and Private Dimensions." *Violence against Women* 2, no. 4: 378–90.

Lugones, Maria. 2007. "Heterosexualism and the Colonial/Modern Gender System." *Hypatia* 22, no. 1: 186–209.

Lustick, Ian. 1985. *State-Building Failure in British Ireland and French Algeria.* Berkeley: Institute of International Studies, University of California, Berkeley.

Lutz, Helma. 2002. "At Your Service Madam! The Globalization of Domestic Service." *Feminist Review* 70: 89–104.

Luxemburg, Rosa. (1913) 2003. *The Accumulation of Capital.* Translated by Agnes Schwarzschild. London: Routledge.

Lynch, John. 1964. *Spain under the Habsburgs.* Vol. 2. Oxford: Blackwell.

Macdonald, Isabel. 2010. "France's Debt of Dishonour to Haiti." *Guardian,* August 16. www.theguardian.com/commentisfree/cifamerica/2010/aug/16/haiti-france.

Maddison, Angus. 2007. *Contours of the World Economy, 1–2030 AD: Essays in Macro-economic History.* Oxford: Oxford University Press.

Majid, Anouar. 2009. *We Are All Moors: Ending Centuries of Crusades against Muslims and Other Minorities.* Minneapolis: University of Minnesota Press.

Malanima, Paolo. 2009. *Pre-modern European Economy: One Thousand Years (10th–19th Centuries).* Leiden: Brill.

Malthus, Thomas Robert. 1798. *An Essay on the Principle of Population, as It Affects the Future Improvement of Society, with Remarks on the Speculations of Mr. Godwin, M. Condorcet, and Other Writers.* London: J. Johnson.

Mamdani, Mahmood. 1996. *Citizen and Subject: Contemporary Africa and the Legacy of Late Colonialism.* Princeton, NJ: Princeton University Press.

———. 2012. *Define and Rule: Native as Political Identity.* Cambridge, MA: Harvard University Press.

Manning, Richard. 2004. "The Oil We Eat: Following the Food Chain Back to Iraq." *Harpers,* February.

Mantena, Karuna. 2010. *Alibis of Empire: Henry Maine and the Ends of Liberal Imperialism.* Princeton, NJ: Princeton University Press.

Mantoux, Paul. 1961. *The Industrial Revolution in the Eighteenth Century: An Outline of the Beginnings of the Modern Factory System in England.* Rev. ed. New York: Macmillan.

Marçal, Katrine. 2015. *Who Cooked Adam Smith's Dinner? A Story about Women and Economics.* Translated by Saskia Vogel. London: Portobello.

Mariana-Costantini, Alda, and Giancarlo Ligabue. 1992. "Did Columbus Also Open the Exploration of the Modern Diet?" *Nutrition Reviews* 50, no. 11: 313–19.

Martínez, María Elena. 2011. *Genealogical Fictions: Limpieza de sangre, Religion, and Gender in Colonial Mexico.* Stanford, CA: Stanford University Press.

Martinez-Alier, Joan. 2014. "The Environmentalism of the Poor." *Geoforum* 54: 239–41.

Marx, Karl. 1967a. *Capital: A Critique of Political Economy.* Edited by F. Engels. Vol. 3, *Process of Capitalist Production as a Whole.* New York: International.

———. 1967b. *Capital: A Critique of Political Economy.* Edited by F. Engels. Vol. 2, *Process of Circulation of Capital.* New York: International.

———. 1973a. "Critique of the Gotha Programme." In *Marx/Engels Selected Works,* vol. 3, 13–30. Moscow: International.

———. 1973b. *Grundrisse.* Translated by Martin Nicolaus. London: Penguin / New Left.

———. 1976. *Capital: A Critique of Political Economy.* Translated by Ben Fowkes. London: Pelican.

———. 2000. "On the Jewish Question." In *Karl Marx: Selected Writings,* edited by David McLellan, 46–74. New York: Oxford University Press.

Matuschke, Ira, Ritesh R. Mishra, and Matin Qaim. 2007. "Adoption and Impact of Hybrid Wheat in India." *World Development* 35, no. 8: 1422–35.

Maxwell, John Francis. 1975. *Slavery and the Catholic Church: The History of Catholic Teaching concerning the Moral Legitimacy of the Institution of Slavery.* Chichester: Barry Rose.

Maybud, Susan. 2015. "Women and the Future of Work—Taking Care of the Caregivers." ILO's Work in Progress. Geneva: International Labour Office. www.ilo.org/wcmsp5/groups/public/---ed_protect/---protrav/---travail/documents/publication/wcms_351297.pdf.

Mayhew, N.J. 2013. "Prices in England, 1170–1750." *Past and Present* 219, no. 1: 3–39.

McCarthy, Charles H. 1915. "Columbus and the Santa Hermandad in 1492." *Catholic Historical Review* 1, no. 1: 38–50.

McClintock, Anne. 1995. *Imperial Leather: Race, Gender and Sexuality in the Colonial Context.* London: Routledge.

Mcglone, Matt S., and Janet M. Wilmshurst. 1999. "A Holocene Record of Climate, Vegetation Change and Peat Bog Development, East Otago, South Island, New Zealand." *Journal of Quaternary Science* 14, no. 3: 239–54.

McKeon, Michael. 1995. "Historicizing Patriarchy: The Emergence of Gender Difference in England, 1660–1760." *Eighteenth-Century Studies* 28, no. 3: 295–322.

McMichael, Philip. 1998. "Global Food Politics." *Monthly Review* 50, no. 3: 97.

———. 2000. "World-Systems Analysis, Globalization, and Incorporated Comparison." *Journal of World-Systems Research* 6, no. 3: 668–90.

———. 2009. "A Food Regime Analysis of the 'World Food Crisis.'" *Agriculture and Human Values* 26, no. 4: 281–95.

———. 2017. *Development and Social Change: A Global Perspective.* 6th ed. Los Angeles: Sage.

McNally, David. 2014. "The Blood of the Commonwealth." *Historical Materialism* 22, no. 2: 3–32.

McNeill, William Hardy. 1976. *Plagues and Peoples.* Garden City, NY: Anchor.

McRuer, Robert. 2006. *Crip Theory: Cultural Signs of Queerness and Disability.* New York: New York University Press; London: Eurospan.

McWhorter, L. 2005. "Where Do White People Come From? A Foucaultian Critique of Whiteness Studies." *Philosophy and Social Criticism* 31, nos. 5–6: 533–56.

Meade, J. E. 1952. "External Economies and Diseconomies in a Competitive Situation." *Economic Journal* 62, no. 245: 54–67.

Meade, Teresa A., and Merry E. Wiesner. 2004. *A Companion to Gender History.* Malden, MA: Wiley-Blackwell.

Melillo, Edward Dallam. 2015. *Strangers on Familiar Soil: Rediscovering the Chile-California Connection.* New Haven, CT: Yale University Press.

Merchant, Carolyn. 1980. *The Death of Nature: Women, Ecology, and the Scientific Revolution.* San Francisco: Harper and Row.

———. 1987. "The Theoretical Structure of Ecological Revolutions." *Environmental Review* 11, no. 4: 265–74.

———. 2006. "The Scientific Revolution and the Death of Nature." *Isis* 97, no. 3: 513–33.

———. 2008. "Secrets of Nature: The Bacon Debates Revisited." *Journal of the History of Ideas* 69, no. 1: 147–62.

———. 2013. "Francis Bacon and the 'Vexations of Art': Experimentation as Intervention." *British Journal for the History of Science* 46, no. 4: 551–99.

Mielants, Eric. 2002. "Europe and China Compared." *Review (Fernand Braudel Center)* 25, no. 4: 401–49.

———. 2008. *The Origins of Capitalism and the "Rise of the West."* Philadelphia: Temple University Press.

Mies, Maria. 1986. *Patriarchy and Accumulation on a World Scale: Women in the International Division of Labour.* London: Zed.

Miller, Owen. 2007. "The Myonjujon Documents: Accounting Methods and Merchants' Organisations in Nineteenth Century Korea." *Sungkyun Journal of East Asian Studies* 7, no. 1: 87–114.

Miller, Victoria, Salim Yusuf, Clara K. Chow, Mahshid Dehghan, Daniel J. Corsi, Karen Lock, Barry Popkin, et al. 2016. "Availability, Affordability, and Consumption of Fruits and Vegetables in 18 Countries across Income Levels: Findings from the Prospective Urban Rural Epidemiology (PURE) Study." *Lancet Global Health* 4, no. 10: e695–e703.

Minge-Klevana, Wanda, Kwame Arhin, P. T. W. Baxter, T. Carlstein, Charles J. Erasmus, Michael P. Freedman, Allen Johnson, et al. 1980. "Does Labor Time Decrease with Industrialization? A Survey of Time-Allocation Studies [and Comments and Reply]." *Current Anthropology* 21, no. 3: 279–98.

Mink, Gwendolyn. 1990. "The Lady and the Tramp: Gender, Race, and the Origins of the American Welfare State." In *Women, the State, and Welfare,* edited by Linda Gordon, 92–111. Madison: University of Wisconsin.

Mintz, Sidney Wilfred. 1985. *Sweetness and Power: The Place of Sugar in Modern History.* New York: Penguin.

Mitchell, Timothy. 2011. *Carbon Democracy: Political Power in the Age of Oil.* London: Verso.

Modest, Wayne. 2012. "We Have Always Been Modern: Museums, Collections, and Modernity in the Caribbean." *Museum Anthropology* 35, no. 1: 85–96.

Mohawk, John. 1992. "Discovering Columbus: The Way Here." In *Confronting Columbus: An Anthology,* edited by John Yewell, Chris Dodge, and Jan DeSirey, 15–29. Jefferson, NC: McFarland.

Moloney, Pat. 2011. "Hobbes, Savagery, and International Anarchy." *American Political Science Review* 105, no. 1: 189–204.

Monbiot, George. 2012. "We Were Wrong on Peak Oil: There's Enough to Fry Us All." *Guardian,* July 2. www.theguardian.com/commentisfree/2012/jul/02/peak-oil-we-we-wrong.

Montaño, John Patrick. 2011. *The Roots of English Colonialism in Ireland.* Cambridge: Cambridge University Press.

Moody, Kim. 1988. *An Injury to All: The Decline of American Unionism.* London: Verso.

Moore, Jason W. 2003a. "*The Modern World-System* as Environmental History? Ecology and the Rise of Capitalism." *Theory and Society* 32, no. 3: 307–77.

———. 2003b. "Nature and the Transition from Feudalism to Capitalism." *Review (Fernand Braudel Center)* 26, no. 2: 97–172.

———. 2007. "Ecology and the Rise of Capitalism." PhD dissertation, Department of Geography, University of California, Berkeley.

———. 2009. "Madeira, Sugar, and the Conquest of Nature in the 'First' Sixteenth Century, Part I: From 'Island of Timber' to Sugar Revolution, 1420–1506." *Review (Fernand Braudel Center)* 32, no. 4: 345–90.

———. 2010a. "'Amsterdam Is Standing on Norway,' Part I: The Alchemy of Capital, Empire and Nature in the Diaspora of Silver, 1545–1648." *Journal of Agrarian Change* 10, no. 1: 33–68.

———. 2010b. "'Amsterdam Is Standing on Norway,' Part II: The Global North Atlantic in the Ecological Revolution of the Long Seventeenth Century." *Journal of Agrarian Change* 10, no. 2: 188–227.

———. 2010c. "The End of the Road? Agricultural Revolutions in the Capitalist World-Ecology, 1450–2010." *Journal of Agrarian Change* 10, no. 3: 389–413.

———. 2010d. "'This Lofty Mountain of Silver Could Conquer the Whole World': Potosí and the Political Ecology of Underdevelopment, 1545–1800." *Journal of Philosophical Economics* 4, no. 1: 58–103.

———. 2010e. "Madeira, Sugar, and the Conquest of Nature in the 'First' Sixteenth Century, Part II: From Local Crisis to Commodity Frontier, 1506–1530." *Review (Fernand Braudel Center)* 33, no. 1: 1–24.

———. 2011. "Transcending the Metabolic Rift: A Theory of Crises in the Capitalist World-Ecology." *Journal of Peasant Studies* 38, no. 1: 1–46.

———. 2014. "The End of Cheap Nature, or How I Learned to Stop Worrying about 'the' Environment and Love the Crisis of Capitalism." In *Structures of the World Political Economy and the Future of Global Conflict and Cooperation*, edited by Christopher Chase-Dunn and Christian Suter, 285–314. Berlin: Lit.

———. 2015. *Capitalism in the Web of Life: Ecology and the Accumulation of Capital.* London: Verso.

———, ed. 2016. *Anthropocene or Capitalocene? Nature, History, and the Crisis of Capitalism.* Oakland, CA: PM Press.

———. 2017a. "The Capitalocene, Part I: On the Nature and Origins of Our Ecological Crisis." *Journal of Peasant Studies* 44, no. 3: 594–630.

———. 2017b. "The Capitalocene, Part II: Accumulation by Appropriation and the Centrality of Unpaid Work/Energy." *Journal of Peasant Studies* (in press).

Moore, Jason, Sharae Deckard, Michael Niblett, and Diana C. Gildea, eds. 2017. *Capitalism's Ecologies: Culture, Power, and Crisis in the 21st Century.* Oakland, CA: PM Press.

Morgan, Jennifer L. 1997. "'Some Could Suckle over Their Shoulder': Male Travelers, Female Bodies, and the Gendering of Racial Ideology, 1500–1770." *William and Mary Quarterly* 54, no. 1: 167–92.

———. 2004. *Laboring Women: Reproduction and Gender in New World Slavery.* Philadelphia: University of Pennsylvania Press.

Morison, Samuel Eliot, ed. and trans. 1963. *Journals and Other Documents on the Life and Voyages of Christopher Columbus.* New York: Heritage.

Moshenberg, Daniel. 2015. Interview by Rebecca McInroy, Tom Philpott, Raj Patel. "Prison Food," episode of *The Secret Ingredient* (podcast). August 14. http://thesecretingredient.org/prison-food-daniel-moshenberg/.

Mosse, George L. 1988. *Nationalism and Sexuality: Middle-Class Morality and Sexual Norms in Modern Europe.* Madison: University of Wisconsin Press.

Movement for Black Lives. n.d. "Reparations." https://policy.m4bl.org/reparations/.

Mumford, Lewis. 1934. *The Golden Day: A Study in American Literature and Culture.* New York: W. W. Norton.

———. (1934) 2010. *Technics and Civilization.* Chicago: University of Chicago Press.

Munro, John H. 2003. "The Monetary Origins of the 'Price Revolution': South German Silver Mining, Merchant-Banking, and Venetian Commerce, 1470–1540." Working paper no. 8, Department of Economics, University of Toronto.

Münzer, Thomas. 1524. *Hochverursachte Schutzrede und Antwort wider das geistlose, sanftlebende Fleisch zu Wittenberg, welches mit verkehrter Weise durch den Diebstahl der heiligen Schrift die erbärmliche Christenheit also ganz jämmerlich besudelt hat.* Nuremburg: Hieronymus Höltzel.

Murali, Atluri. 1995. "Whose Trees? Forest Practices and Local Communities in Andhra, 1600–1922." In *Nature, Culture, Imperialism: Essays on Envi-*

ronmental History of South Asia, edited by David Arnold and Ramachandra Guha, 50–86. New Delhi: Oxford University Press.

Nader, Helen. 2002. "Desperate Men, Questionable Acts: The Moral Dilemma of Italian Merchants in the Spanish Slave Trade." *Sixteenth Century Journal* 33, no. 2: 401–22.

Nairn, I.A., P.R. Shane, J.W. Cole, G.J. Leonard, S. Self, and N. Pearson. 2004. "Rhyolite Magma Processes of the ~AD 1315 Kaharoa Eruption Episode, Tarawera Volcano, New Zealand." *Journal of Volcanology and Geothermal Research* 131, nos. 3–4: 265–94.

Nairn, Tom. 1977. *The Break-up of Britain: Crisis and Neo-nationalism.* London: New Left.

Nanni, Giordano. 2011. "Time, Empire and Resistance in Settler-Colonial Victoria." *Time and Society* 20, no. 1: 5–33.

Nathan, Dev, and Govind Kelkar. 1997. "Wood Energy: The Role of Women's Unvalued Labor." *Gender, Technology and Development* 1, no. 2: 205–24.

National Nutrition Monitoring Bureau. 2012. *Diet and Nutritional Status of Rural Population, Prevalence of Hypertension and Diabetes among Adults and Infant and Young Child Feeding Practices—Report of Third Repeat Survey.* Hyderabad: National Institute of Nutrition, Indian Council of Medical Research.

National Research Council. 2011. "Warming World: Impacts by Degree." New York: National Research Council. http://dels.nas.edu/resources/static-assets/materials-based-on-reports/booklets/warming_world_final.pdf.

Naylor, Hugh. 2016. "An Epic Middle East Heat Wave Could Be Global Warming's Hellish Curtain-Raiser." *Washington Post,* August 10. www.washingtonpost.com/world/middle_east/an-epic-middle-east-heat-wave-could-be-global-warmings-hellish-curtain-raiser/2016/08/09/c8c717d4-5992-11e6-8b48-0cb344221131_story.html.

Neal, Larry. 2015. *A Concise History of International Finance: From Babylon to Bernanke.* Cambridge: Cambridge University Press.

Nef, John U. 1934. "The Progress of Technology and the Growth of Large Scale Industry in Great Britain, 1540–1640." *Economic History Review* 5, no. 1: 3–24.

———. 1941. "Silver Production in Central Europe, 1450–1618." *Journal of Political Economy* 49, no. 4: 575–91.

———. 1964. *The Conquest of the Material World: Essays on the Coming of Industrialism.* New York: Meridian.

Nelson, Diane M. 2009. *Reckoning: The Ends of War in Guatemala.* Durham, NC: Duke University Press.

Neocleous, Mark. 2014. *War Power, Police Power.* Edinburgh: Edinburgh University Press.

Nguyen, Dan Thu. 1992. "The Spatialization of Metric Time: The Conquest of Land and Labour in Europe and the United States." *Time and Society* 1, no. 1: 29–50.

Nietzsche, Friedrich. 2001. *The Gay Science: With a Prelude in German Rhymes and an Appendix of Songs.* Edited by Bernard Williams. Translated by Josefine Nauckhoff and Adrian Del Caro. Cambridge: Cambridge University Press.

Nove, Alec. 1992. *An Economic History of the USSR, 1917–1991.* 3rd ed. London: Penguin.

O'Connell, Sanjida. 2004. *Sugar: The Grass That Changed the World.* London: Virgin.

O'Connor, James. 1988. "Capitalism, Nature, Socialism: A Theoretical Introduction." *Capitalism Nature Socialism* 1, no. 1: 11–38.

Offer, Avner. 1991. *The First World War: An Agrarian Interpretation.* Oxford: Clarendon.

Offer, Shira, and Barbara Schneider. 2011. "Revisiting the Gender Gap in Time-Use Patterns." *American Sociological Review* 76, no. 6: 809–33.

Ohlmeyer, Jane. 2016. "Conquest, Civilization, Colonization." In *The Princeton History of Modern Ireland,* edited by Richard Bourke and Ian McBride, 21–47. Princeton, NJ: Princeton University Press.

Olson-Sawyer, Kai. 2013. "Meat's Large Water Footprint: Why Raising Livestock and Poultry for Meat Is So Resource-Intensive." Food Tank, December 16. http://foodtank.com/news/2013/12/why-meat-eats-resources.

Oram, Richard. 2013. "Arrested Development? Energy Crises, Fuel Supplies, and the Slow March to Modernity in Scotland, 1450–1850." In *Energy Transitions in History: Global Cases of Continuity and Change,* edited by Richard W. Unger, 17–24. Munich: Rachel Carson Centre.

Ormrod, David. 2003. *The Rise of Commercial Empires: England and the Netherlands in the Age of Mercantilism, 1650–1770.* Cambridge: Cambridge University Press.

Orren, Karen. 1991. *Belated Feudalism: Labor, the Law, and Liberal Development in the United States.* Cambridge: Cambridge University Press.

Overton, Mark. 1996. *The Agricultural Revolution.* Cambridge: Cambridge University Press.

Oxfam America. 2015. *Lives on the Line: The Human Cost of Cheap Chicken.* Washington DC: Oxfam America. www.oxfamamerica.org/static/media/files/Lives_on_the_Line_Full_Report_Final.pdf.

Oyěwùmí, Oyèrónkẹ́. 1997. *The Invention of Women: Making an African Sense of Western Gender Discourses.* Minneapolis: University of Minnesota Press.

Page, Brian, and Richard Walker. 1991. "From Settlement to Fordism: The Agro-industrial Revolution in the American Midwest." *Economic Geography* 67, no. 4: 281–315.

Painter, David S. 2014. "Oil and Geopolitics: The Oil Crises of the 1970s and the Cold War." *Historical Social Research* 39, no. 4: 186–208.

Pal, Jeremy S., and Elfatih A.B. Eltahir. 2016. "Future Temperature in Southwest Asia Projected to Exceed a Threshold for Human Adaptability." *Nature Climate Change* 6, no. 2: 197–200.

Palmer, G. 1974. "The Emergence of Modern Finance in Europe, 1500–1750." In *The Fontana Economic History of Europe,* edited by Carlo M. Cipolla. Vol. 2, *The Sixteenth and Seventeenth Centuries,* 527–94. London: Collins/Fontana.

Panitch, Leo, and Sam Gindin. 2012. *The Making of Global Capitalism.* London: Verso.

Parenti, Christian. 2016. "Environment-Making in the Capitalocene." In *Anthropocene or Capitalocene? Nature, History, and the Crisis of Capitalism,* edited by Jason W. Moore, 166–84. Oakland, CA: PM Press.

Parise, Agustín. 2008. "The Valladolid Controversy Revisited: Looking Back at the Sixteenth-Century Debate on Native Americans While Facing the Current Status of Human Embryos." *Journal of Civil Law Studies* 1, no. 1: article 7.

Parker, Geoffrey. 1976. "The 'Military Revolution,' 1560–1660—a Myth?" *Journal of Modern History* 48, no. 2: 196–214.

———. 1996. *The Military Revolution: Military Innovation and the Rise of the West, 1500–1800.* Cambridge: Cambridge University Press.

———. 2014. *Global Crisis: War, Climate Change and Catastrophe in the Seventeenth Century.* New Haven, CT: Yale University Press.

Patel, Raj. 2007. *Stuffed and Starved: Markets, Power and the Hidden Battle for the World Food System*. London: Portobello.

———. 2013. "The Long Green Revolution." *Journal of Peasant Studies* 40, no. 1: 1–63.

Patel, Raj, Rachel Bezner Kerr, Lizzie Shumba, and Laifolo Dakishoni. 2014. "Cook, Eat, Man, Woman: Understanding the New Alliance for Food Security and Nutrition, Nutritionism, and Its Alternatives from Malawi." *Journal of Peasant Studies* 42, no. 1: 21–44.

Patel, Raj, and Philip McMichael. 2004. "Third Worldism and the Lineages of Global Fascism: The Regrouping of the Global South in the Neoliberal Era." *Third World Quarterly* 25, no. 1: 231–54.

———. 2009. "A Political Economy of the Food Riot." *Review (Fernand Braudel Center)* 32, no. 1: 9–35.

Patterson, Clair C. 1972. "Silver Stocks and Losses in Ancient and Medieval Times." *Economic History Review* 25, no. 2: 205–33.

Patterson, Orlando. 1982. *Slavery and Social Death: A Comparative Study*. Cambridge, MA: Harvard University Press.

Paul, Diane. 1981. "'In the Interests of Civilization': Marxist Views of Race and Culture in the Nineteenth Century." *Journal of the History of Ideas* 42, no. 1: 115–38.

Paul-Majumder, Pratima, and Anwara Begum. 2000. "The Gender Imbalances in the Export Oriented Garment Industry in Bangladesh." Policy Research Report on Gender and Development Working Paper Series No. 12, Development Research Group / Poverty Reduction and Economic Management Network, World Bank, Washington DC. Available at www.atria.nl/epublications/2000/Gender_Imbalances.pdf.

Payne, Chris S. 2016. "Changes in the Value and Division of Unpaid Care Work in the UK: 2000 to 2015." November 10. London: Office for National Statistics. www.ons.gov.uk/economy/nationalaccounts/satelliteaccounts/articles/changesinthevalueanddivisionofunpaidcareworkintheuk/2000to2015.

Pearson, M.N. 1987. *The Portuguese in India*. Cambridge: Cambridge University Press.

Peet, Richard, and Michael Watts. 2004. *Liberation Ecologies: Environment, Development, Social Movements*. 2nd ed. London: Routledge.

Peng, Shaobing, Jianliang Huang, John E. Sheehy, Rebecca C. Laza, Romeo M. Visperas, Xuhua Zhong, Grace S. Centeno, Gurdev S. Khush, and Kenneth G. Cassman. 2004. "Rice Yields Decline with Higher Night Temperature from Global Warming." *Proceedings of the National Academy of Sciences of the United States of America* 101, no. 27: 9971–75.

PennState Extension. 2015. "Modern Meat Chicken Industry." http://extension.psu.edu/animals/poultry/topics/general-educational-material/the-chicken/modern-meat-chicken-industry.

Pew Research Center. 2010. "Global Indicators Database." www.pewglobal.org/database/.

Phillips, Kevin. 2009. *Bad Money: Reckless Finance, Failed Politics, and the Global Crisis of American Capitalism.* New York: Penguin.

Phillips, Ulrich Bonnell. 1929. *Life and Labor in the Old South.* New York: Little, Brown.

Phillips, William D., Jr. 2004. "Sugar in Iberia." In *Tropical Babylons: Sugar and the Making of the Atlantic World, 1450–1680,* edited by Stuart B. Schwartz, 27–41. Chapel Hill: University of North Carolina Press.

———. 2013. *Slavery in Medieval and Early Modern Iberia.* Philadelphia: University of Pennsylvania Press.

Pigou, A.C. 1920. *The Economics of Welfare.* London: Macmillan.

Piketty, Thomas. 2014. *Capital in the Twenty-First Century.* Translated by Arthur Goldhammer. Cambridge, MA: Belknap Press of Harvard University Press.

Pitts, Jennifer. 2010. "Political Theory of Empire and Imperialism." *Annual Review of Political Science* 13: 211–35.

Piven, Frances Fox. 1990. "Ideology and the State: Women, Power, and the Welfare State." In *Women, the State, and Welfare,* edited by Linda Gordon, 250–64. Madison: University of Wisconsin Press.

Planning Commission. 2012. *India Human Development Report 2011: Towards Social Inclusion.* Oxford: Oxford University Press for the Government of India.

Platter, Thomas. 1937. *Thomas Platter's Travels in England, 1599.* Translated by Clare Williams. London: Cape.

Plumwood, Val. 1993. *Feminism and the Mastery of Nature.* London: Routledge.

Pollin, Robert. 1996. "Contemporary Economic Stagnation in World Historical Perspective." *New Left Review* I/219: 109–18.

Pomeranz, Kenneth. 2000. *The Great Divergence: China, Europe, and the Making of the Modern World Economy.* Princeton, NJ: Princeton University Press.

———. 2002. "Political Economy and Ecology on the Eve of Industrialization: Europe, China, and the Global Conjuncture." *American Historical Review* 107, no. 2: 425–46.

Postle, Martin. 2002. *Thomas Gainsborough.* Princeton, NJ: Princeton University Press.

Potter, Will. 2013. *Green Is the New Red: An Insider's Account of a Social Movement under Siege.* San Francisco: City Lights.

Prashad, Vijay. 2012. *The Poorer Nations: A Possible History of the Global South.* London: Verso.

Price, Brian. 1992. "Frank and Lillian Gilbreth and the Motion Study Controversy, 1907–1930." In *A Mental Revolution: Scientific Management since Taylor,* edited by Daniel Nelson, 58–76. Columbus: Ohio State University Press.

Prince, Hugh C. 1988. "Art and Agrarian Change, 1710–1815." In *The Iconography of Landscape,* edited by D. Cosgrove and S.J. Daniels, 98–118. Cambridge: Cambridge University Press.

Quaglia, Lucia, and Sebastián Royo. 2015. "Banks and the Political Economy of the Sovereign Debt Crisis in Italy and Spain." *Review of International Political Economy* 22, no. 3: 485–507.

Quijano, Aníbal. 2000. "Coloniality of Power and Eurocentrism in Latin America." *International Sociology* 15, no. 2: 215–32.

Quirk, Robert E. 1954. "Some Notes on a Controversial Controversy: Juan Ginés de Supúlveda [*sic*] and Natural Servitude." *Hispanic American Historical Review* 34, no. 3: 357–64.

Rachleff, Peter J. 1993. *Hard-Pressed in the Heartland: The Hormel Strike and the Future of the Labor Movement.* Boston: South End.

Rae, John M.A. 1895. *Life of Adam Smith.* London: Macmillan.

Rai, Milan. 1993. "Columbus in Ireland." *Race and Class* 34, no. 4: 25–34.

Ramsey, L. F. 1920. "Levada-Walking in Madeira." *Living Age,* 8th ser., vol. 20: 656–63.

Ranelagh, John O'Beirne. 1999. *A Short History of Ireland.* 2nd ed. Cambridge: Cambridge University Press.

Ratekin, Mervyn. 1954. "The Early Sugar Industry in Española." *Hispanic American Historical Review* 34, no. 1: 1–19.

Raworth, Kate. 2014. "Must the Anthropocene Be a Manthropocene?" *Guardian,* October 20. www.theguardian.com/commentisfree/2014/oct/20/anthropocene-working-group-science-gender-bias.

Registered Nurse Response Network. 2016. "Registered Nurse Response Network Sends Nurse Volunteers on Second Deployment to Standing Rock." Press release, November 7. www.nationalnursesunited.org/press/entry/registered-nurse-response-network-sends-nurse-volunteers-on-2nd-deployment/.

Reis, João José. 1993. *Slave Rebellion in Brazil: The Muslim Uprising of 1835 in Bahia.* Translated by Arthur Brakel. Baltimore: Johns Hopkins University Press.

Renda, Mary A. 2001. *Taking Haiti: Military Occupation and the Culture of U.S. Imperialism, 1915–1940.* Chapel Hill: University of North Carolina Press.

Reséndez, Andrés. 2016. *The Other Slavery: The Uncovered Story of Indian Enslavement in America.* Boston: Houghton Mifflin Harcourt.

Resnick, David. 1992. "John Locke and Liberal Nationalism." *History of European Ideas* 15, nos. 4–6: 511–17.

Revette, Anna C. 2016. "This Time It's Different: Lithium Extraction, Cultural Politics and Development in Bolivia." *Third World Quarterly* 38, no. 1: 149–68.

Rivera-Batiz, L. Francisco. 1999. "Undocumented Workers in the Labor Market: An Analysis of the Earnings of Legal and Illegal Mexican Immigrants in the United States." *Journal of Population Economics* 12, no. 1: 91–116.

Roberts, Neil. 1989. *The Holocene: An Environmental History.* Oxford: Basil Blackwell.

Robinson, Jo. 2013. "Breeding the Nutrition Out of Our Food." *New York Times,* May 26. www.nytimes.com/2013/05/26/opinion/sunday/breeding-the-nutrition-out-of-our-food.html.

Rolf, David. 2016. "Life on the Homecare Front." *Generations* 40, no. 1: 82–87.

Roper, John Herbert, and Lolita G. Brockington. 1984. "Slave Revolt, Slave Debate: A Comparison." *Phylon* 45, no. 2: 98–110.

Rose, Gillian. 1993. *Feminism and Geography: The Limits of Geographical Knowledge.* Cambridge: Polity.

Rosen, Ruth. 2000. *The World Split Open: How the Modern Women's Movement Changed America.* New York: Viking.

Ross, Eric B. 2000. *The Malthus Factor: Poverty, Politics and Population in Capitalist Development.* Sturminster Newton, Dorset: Corner House.

Rosset, Peter. 2000. "Lessons from the Green Revolution." Food First / Institute for Food and Development Policy. Available at https://web.archive.org/web/20080211181547/www.foodfirst.org/media/opeds/2000/4-greenrev.html.

Rosset, Peter M., and Maria Elena Martínez-Torres. 2012. "Rural Social Movements and Agroecology: Context, Theory, and Process." *Ecology and Society* 17, no. 3.

Roy, Ananya. 2010. *Poverty Capital: Microfinance and the Making of Development.* London: Routledge.

Ruddiman, William F. 2005. *Plows, Plagues, and Petroleum: How Humans Took Control of Climate.* Princeton, NJ: Princeton University Press.

Ruddiman, W.F., D.Q. Fuller, J.E. Kutzbach, P.C. Tzedakis, J.O. Kaplan, E.C. Ellis, S.J. Vavrus, et al. 2016. "Late Holocene Climate: Natural or Anthropogenic?" *Reviews of Geophysics* 54, no. 1: 93–118.

Rudrappa, Sharmila. 2015. *Discounted Life: The Price of Global Surrogacy in India.* New York: New York University Press.

Ruggiero, Guido. 2015. *The Renaissance in Italy: A Social and Cultural History of the Rinascimento.* New York: Cambridge University Press.

Ruiz, Teofilo F. 1994. *Crisis and Continuity: Land and Town in Late Medieval Castile.* Philadelphia: University of Pennsylvania Press.

Safri, Maliha, and Julie Graham. 2010. "The Global Household: Toward a Feminist Postcapitalist International Political Economy." *Signs* 36, no. 1: 99–125.

Sahlins, Marshall David. 1972. *Stone Age Economics.* Chicago: Aldine-Atherton.

Salleh, Ariel. 1997. *Ecofeminism as Politics: Nature, Marx, and the Postmodern.* London: Zed.

———. 2010. "From Metabolic Rift to 'Metabolic Value': Reflections on Environmental Sociology and the Alternative Globalization Movement." *Organization and Environment* 23, no. 2: 205–19.

Santiago-Valles, Kelvin. 2005. "World-Historical Ties among 'Spontaneous' Slave Rebellions in the Atlantic." *Review (Fernand Braudel Center)* 28, no. 1: 51–83.

Sayre, Nathan F. 2008. "The Genesis, History, and Limits of Carrying Capacity." *Annals of the Association of American Geographers* 98, no. 1: 120–34.

Scarth, David Todd. 2010. "Sovereignty, Property, and Indigeneity: The Relationship between Aboriginal North America and the Modern State in Historical and Geographical Context." PhD thesis, University of Sussex. http://sro.sussex.ac.uk/45251/.

Schlozman, Kay Lehman, Nancy Burns, and Sidney Verba. 1999. "'What Happened at Work Today?': A Multistage Model of Gender, Employment, and Political Participation." *Journal of Politics* 61, no. 1: 29–53.

Schneider, Mindi, and Philip McMichael. 2010. "Deepening, and Repairing, the Metabolic Rift." *Journal of Peasant Studies* 37, no. 3: 461–84.

Schumpeter, Joseph Alois. 1961. *The Theory of Economic Development: An Inquiry into Profits, Capital, Credit, Interest, and the Business Cycle.* Translated by Redvers Opie. Oxford: Oxford University Press.

———. 1976. *Capitalism, Socialism and Democracy.* 5th ed. London: Allen and Unwin.

Schwartz, Stuart B. 1978. "Indian Labor and New World Plantations: European Demands and Indian Responses in Northeastern Brazil." *American Historical Review* 83, no. 1: 43–79.

———. 1985. *Sugar Plantations in the Formation of Brazilian Society: Bahia, 1550–1835.* Cambridge: Cambridge University Press.

———. 2004. "A Commonwealth within Itself: The Early Brazilian Sugar Industry, 1550–1670." In *Tropical Babylons: Sugar and the Making of the Atlantic World, 1450–1680,* edited by Schwartz, 158–200. Chapel Hill: University of North Carolina Press.

Scott, James C. 1985. *Weapons of the Weak: Everyday Forms of Peasant Resistance.* New Haven, CT: Yale University Press.

Scott, Joan Wallach. 1999. *Gender and the Politics of History.* Rev. ed. New York: Columbia University Press.

Seabrook, Jeremy. 2003. "The Language of Labouring Reveals Its Tortured Roots." *Guardian,* January 14. www.theguardian.com/commentisfree/2013/jan/14/language-labouring-reveals-tortured-roots1.

Seabury, Seth A., Ethan Scherer, Paul O'Leary, Al Ozonoff, and Leslie Boden. 2014. "Using Linked Federal and State Data to Study the Adequacy of Workers' Compensation Benefits." *American Journal of Industrial Medicine* 57, no. 10: 1165–73.

Seccombe, Wally. 1992. *A Millennium of Family Change: Feudalism to Capitalism in Northwestern Europe.* London: Verso.

Segato, Rita Laura. 2014. "Las nuevas formas de la guerra y el cuerpo de las mujeres." *Sociedade e Estado* 29: 341–71.

Select Committee of the Legislative Council on the Aborigines. 1859. *Report of the Select Committee of the Legislative Council on the Aborigines.* Melbourne: Government Printer.

Shaikh, Anwar. 2011. "The First Great Depression of the 21st Century." *Socialist Register* 47: 44–63.

Sheiham, Aubrey, and W. Philip T. James. 2014. "A New Understanding of the Relationship between Sugars, Dental Caries and Fluoride Use: Implications for Limits on Sugars Consumption." *Public Health Nutrition* 17, no. 10: 2176–84.

Sherwood, Steven C., and Matthew Huber. 2010. "An Adaptability Limit to Climate Change Due to Heat Stress." *Proceedings of the National Academy of Sciences* 107, no. 21: 9552–55.

Shindell, Drew T. 2016. "Crop Yield Changes Induced by Emissions of Individual Climate-Altering Pollutants." *Earth's Future* 4, no. 8: 373–80.

Sigal, Peter Herman. 2000. *From Moon Goddesses to Virgins: The Colonization of Yucatecan Maya Sexual Desire.* Austin: University of Texas Press.

Silver, Beverly J. 2003. *Forces of Labor: Workers' Movements and Globalization since 1870.* Cambridge: Cambridge University Press.

Simpson, J. A., and E. S. C. Weiner, eds. 1989. *The Oxford English Dictionary.* 2nd ed. 20 vols. Oxford: Clarendon.

Sinclair, Upton. 1906. *The Jungle.* New York: Doubleday, Page.

Slaughter, Thomas P. 1986. *The Whiskey Rebellion: Frontier Epilogue to the American Revolution.* Oxford: Oxford University Press.

Slicher van Bath, Bernard Hendrik, and O. Ordish. 1963. *The Agrarian History of Western Europe, A.D. 500–1850.* London: Arnold.

Smil, Vaclav. 1999. "Detonator of the Population Explosion." *Nature* 400, no. 6743: 415.

———. 2010. *Energy Transitions: History, Requirements, Prospects.* Santa Barbara, CA: Praeger.

Smith, Adam. (1759) 1976. *The Theory of Moral Sentiments.* Oxford: Clarendon.

Smith, Daniel Scott. 1993. "The Curious History of Theorizing about the History of the Western Nuclear Family." *Social Science History* 17, no. 3: 325–53.

Smith, William D. 1973. "New Rises Are Feared; Price Quadruples for Iranian Crude Oil at Auction." *New York Times,* December 12, 1.

Snell, Keith D. M. 1987. *Annals of the Labouring Poor: Social Change and Agrarian England, 1660–1900.* Cambridge: Cambridge University Press.

Soble, Alan. 1995. "In Defense of Bacon." *Philosophy of the Social Sciences* 25, no. 2: 192–215.

Sohn-Rethel, Alfred. 1978. *Intellectual and Manual Labour: A Critique of Epistemology.* Atlantic Highlands, NJ: Humanities.

Solar, Peter M. 2012. "The Triumph of Cotton in Europe." https://pdfs.semanticscholar.org/5550/0d2a0b8483b53f798f537b0370b0316750f7.pdf.

Solow, Barbara L. 1987. "Capitalism and Slavery in the Exceedingly Long Run." *Journal of Interdisciplinary History* 17, no. 4: 711–37.

Sonn, Hochul. 1997. "The 'Late Blooming' of the South Korean Labor Movement." *Monthly Review* 49, no. 3: 117–29.

Specter, Michael. 2014. "Seeds of Doubt: An Activist's Controversial Crusade against Genetically Modified Crops." *New Yorker,* August 25.

Spence, O. M. 1870. "The Bank of St. George, Genoa." *Harper's New Monthly Magazine,* vol. 42, 392–400.

Spinden, Herbert J. 1920. "Central American Calendars and the Gregorian Day." *Proceedings of the National Academy of Sciences* 6, no. 2: 56–59.

Spínola, H., A. Brehm, F. Williams, J. Jesus, and D. Middleton. 2002. "Distribution of HLA Alleles in Portugal and Cabo Verde: Relationships with the Slave Trade Route." *Annals of Human Genetics* 66, no. 4: 285–96.

Srnicek, Nick. 2017. *Platform Capitalism.* Malden, MA: Polity.

Srnicek, Nick, and Alex Williams. 2015. *Inventing the Future: Postcapitalism and a World without Work.* Brooklyn: Verso.

Standing, Guy. 2016. *The Precariat: The New Dangerous Class.* Rev. ed. New York: Bloomsbury Academic.

Stavig, Ward. 2000. "Ambiguous Visions: Nature, Law, and Culture in Indigenous-Spanish Land Relations in Colonial Peru." *Hispanic American Historical Review* 80, no. 1: 77–111.

Stedman, John Gabriel. 1796. *Narrative of a Five Years' Expedition against the Revolted Negroes of Surinam in Guyana on the Wild Coast of South America; from the Year 1772 to 1777.* Vol. 2. London: J. Johnson.

Stein, Robert L. 1984. "From Saint Domingue to Haiti, 1804–1825." *Journal of Caribbean History* 19, no. 2: 189–226.

Steinmetz, Greg. 2016. *The Richest Man Who Ever Lived: The Life and Times of Jacob Fugger.* New York: Simon and Schuster.

Stevens-Arroyo, Anthony M. 1993. "The Inter-Atlantic Paradigm: The Failure of Spanish Medieval Colonization of the Canary and Caribbean Islands." *Comparative Studies in Society and History* 35, no. 3: 515–43.

Stoler, Ann L. 1989. "Making Empire Respectable: The Politics of Race and Sexual Morality in 20th-Century Colonial Cultures." *American Ethnologist* 16, no. 4: 634–60.

———. 2010. *Carnal Knowledge and Imperial Power: Race and the Intimate in Colonial Rule.* Berkeley: University of California Press.

Stone, Irving. 1999. *The Global Export of Capital from Great Britain, 1865–1914: A Statistical Survey.* Basingstoke: Macmillan.

Stoneman, Adam. 2015. "The New Conspicuous Consumption." *Jacobin*, June 8.

Stotsky, Janet G., Sakina Shibuya, Lisa Kolovich, and Suhaib Kebhaj. 2016. "Trends in Gender Equality and Women's Advancement." IMF Working Paper. Washington DC: International Monetary Fund.

Strasser, Ulrike, and Heidi Tinsman. 2010. "It's a Man's World? World History Meets the History of Masculinity, in Latin American Studies, for Instance." *Journal of World History* 21, no. 1: 75–96.

Studnicki-Gizbert, Daviken, and David Schecter. 2010. "The Environmental Dynamics of a Colonial Fuel-Rush: Silver Mining and Deforestation in New Spain, 1522 to 1810." *Environmental History* 15, no. 1: 94–119.

Suárez de Figueroa, Cristóbal. (1617) 1914. *El passagero.* Madrid: Sociedad de Bibliófilos Españoles.

Sudarkasa, Niara. 1986. "'The Status of Women' in Indigenous African Societies." *Feminist Studies* 12, no. 1: 91–103.

Sued-Badillo, Jalil. 1992. "Christopher Columbus and the Enslavement of the Amerindians in the Caribbean." *Monthly Review* 44, no. 3: 71–103.

Tallett, Frank. 2010. *War and Society in Early Modern Europe: 1495–1715.* London: Routledge.

Tanumihardjo, Sherry A., Cheryl Anderson, Martha Kaufer-Horwitz, Lars Bode, Nancy J. Emenaker, Andrea M. Haqq, Jessie A. Satia, Heidi J. Silver, and Diane D. Stadler. 2007. "Poverty, Obesity, and Malnutrition: An International Perspective Recognizing the Paradox." *Journal of the American Dietetic Association* 107, no. 11: 1966–72.

Taylor, Andrew. 2004. *The World of Gerard Mercator: The Mapmaker Who Revolutionized Geography.* New York: Walker.

Teng, Shu-Chun. 1927. "The Early History of Forestry in China." *Journal of Forestry* 25, no. 5: 564–70.

Teschke, Benno Gerhard. 1999. "The Making of the Westphalian State System: Social Property Relations, Geopolitics and the Myth of 1648." PhD thesis, London School of Economics and Political Science. http://etheses.lse.ac.uk/1555/.

't Hart, Marjolein, Pepijn Brandon, and Thomas Goossens. 2008. "The Commercialization of Warfare as a Strategy for Hegemonial Powers: The Dutch Case Compared." Paper presented at the Second European Congress of World and Global History, Dresden, July 3–5.

Theodorou, Angelina E. 2014. "64 Countries Have Religious Symbols on Their National Flags." November 25. Pew Research Center. www.pewresearch.org/fact-tank/2014/11/25/64-countries-have-religious-symbols-on-their-national-flags/.

Thirsk, Joan. 1964. "The Common Fields." *Past and Present* 29: 3–25.

———. 1987. *Agricultural Regions and Agrarian History in England, 1500–1750.* London: Macmillan.

Thomas, Hugh. 1997. *The Slave Trade: The Story of the Atlantic Slave Trade, 1440–1870.* New York: Simon and Schuster.

———. 2013. *Rivers of Gold: The Rise of the Spanish Empire, from Columbus to Magellan.* New York: Random House.

Thompson, Edward P. 1967. "Time, Work-Discipline, and Industrial Capitalism." *Past and Present* 38: 56–97.

Tilly, Charles. 1992. *Coercion, Capital, and European States, AD 990–1992.* Oxford: Blackwell.

Timmermann, Cristian, and Georges F. Félix. 2015. "Agroecology as a Vehicle for Contributive Justice." *Agriculture and Human Values* 32, no. 3: 523–38.

Tinker, George E. 1993. *Missionary Conquest: The Gospel and Native American Cultural Genocide.* Minneapolis: Fortress.

Tiwana, N.S., Neelima Jerath, Gurharminder Singh, and Ravleen Singh. 2009. "Pesticide Pollution in Punjab: A Review." *Asian Journal of Water, Environment and Pollution* 6, no. 1: 89–96.

Tomich, Dale W. 1990. *Slavery in the Circuit of Sugar: Martinique and the World Economy, 1830–1848.* Baltimore: Johns Hopkins University Press.

Topolski, Jerzy. 1962. "La regression économique en Pologne du XVIe au XVIIIe siècle." *Acta poloniae historica* 7: 28–49.

Toscano, Alberto. 2008. "The Open Secret of Real Abstraction." *Rethinking Marxism* 20, no. 2: 273–87.

———. 2016. "A Structuralism of Feeling?" *New Left Review* 97: 73–93.

Trexler, Richard C. 1995. *Sex and Conquest: Gendered Violence, Political Order and the European Conquest of the Americas.* Cambridge: Polity.

Tronto, Joan C. 2002. "The 'Nanny' Question in Feminism." *Hypatia* 17, no. 2: 34–51.

Tsing, Anna Lowenhaupt. 2015. *The Mushroom at the End of the World: On the Possibility of Life in Capitalist Ruins.* Princeton, NJ: Princeton University Press.

Tuck, Richard. 1999. *The Rights of War and Peace: Political Thought and the International Order from Grotius to Kant.* Oxford: Oxford University Press.

Ulrich, Laurel. 1991. *Good Wives: Image and Reality in the Lives of Women in Northern New England, 1650–1750.* New York: Vintage.

UNDP (United Nations Development Programme). 1995. *Human Development Report 1995: Gender and Human Development.* New York: Oxford University Press.

Unger, Richard W. 1984. "Energy Sources for the Dutch Golden Age: Peat, Wind, and Coal." *Research in Economic History* 9: 221–53.

USBC (United States Bureau of the Census). 1909. *A Century of Population Growth: From the First Census of the United States to the Twelfth, 1790–1900.* Washington DC: Government Printing Office.

USDA (United States Department of Agriculture). 2017a. "Food Expenditures." Last modified February 28. www.ers.usda.gov/data-products/food-expenditures.aspx.

———. 2017b. "Sugar and Sweeteners Yearbook Tables." Last modified March 6. www.ers.usda.gov/data-products/sugar-and-sweeteners-yearbook-tables.aspx.

van Dam, Petra J. E. M. 2001. "Sinking Peat Bogs: Environmental Change in Holland, 1350–1550." *Environmental History* 6, no. 1: 32–45.

———. 2002. "Ecological Challenges, Technological Innovations: The Modernization of Sluice Building in Holland, 1300–1600." *Technology and Culture* 43, no. 3: 500–520.

van de Pol, Lotte, and Erika Kuijpers. 2005. "Poor Women's Migration to the City: The Attraction of Amsterdam Health Care and Social Assistance in Early Modern Times." *Journal of Urban History* 32, no. 1: 44–60.

van der Woude, Ad. 2003. "Sources of Energy in the Dutch Golden Age: The Case of Holland." *NEHA-Jaarboek* 66: 64–84.

van Dillewijn, C. 1952. *Botany of Sugarcane.* Waltham, MA: Chronica Botanica.

Van Kirk, Sylvia. 1983. *Many Tender Ties: Women in Fur-Trade Society, 1670–1870.* Norman: University of Oklahoma Press.

van Zanden, J. L. 1993. *The Rise and Decline of Holland's Economy: Merchant Capitalism and the Labour Market.* Manchester: Manchester University Press.

Varoufakis, Yanis. 2016. *And the Weak Suffer What They Must? Europe, Austerity and the Threat to Global Stability.* London: Bodley Head.

Veblen, Thorstein. (1899) 1973. *The Theory of the Leisure Class.* Boston: Houghton Mifflin.

Verlinden, Charles. 1970. *The Beginnings of Modern Colonization.* Ithaca, NY: Cornell University Press.

Vickers, Brian. 2008. "Francis Bacon, Feminist Historiography, and the Dominion of Nature." *Journal of the History of Ideas* 69, no. 1: 117–41.

Vieira, Alberto. 1996. *A escravatura na Madeira nos séculos XV a XVII: O ponto da situação.* Funchal, Madeira: Centro de Estudos de História do Atlântico. www.madeira-edu.pt/Portals/31/hm-esc-3-ponto.pdf.

———. 2004. "Sugar Islands: The Sugar Economy of Madeira and the Canaries, 1450–1650." In *Tropical Babylons: Sugar and the Making of the Atlantic World, 1450–1680,* edited by Stuart B. Schwartz, 42–84. Chapel Hill: University of North Carolina Press.

Vilar, Pierre, and Judith White. 1976. *A History of Gold and Money, 1450–1920.* London: New Left.

von der Heydt-Coca, Magda. 2005. "Andean Silver and the Rise of the Western World." *Critical Sociology* 31, no. 4: 481–513.

von Tunzelmann, G. N. 1981. "Technological Progress during the Industrial Revolution." In *The Economic History of Britain since 1700.* Vol. 1, *1700–1860,* edited by Roderick Floud and Donald McCloskey, 143–63. Cambridge: Cambridge University Press.

Voss, Barbara L. 2008. "Domesticating Imperialism: Sexual Politics and the Archaeology of Empire." *American Anthropologist* 110, no. 2: 191–203.

Vries, P. H. H. 2001. "Are Coal and Colonies Really Crucial? Kenneth Pomeranz and the Great Divergence." *Journal of World History* 12, no. 2: 407–46.

Wackernagel, Mathis, and William Rees. 1996. *Our Ecological Footprint*. Gabriola Island, British Columbia: New Society.

Wackernagel, Mathis, Niels B. Schulz, Diana Deumling, Alejandro Callejas Linares, Martin Jenkins, Valerie Kapos, Chad Monfreda, et al. 2002. "Tracking the Ecological Overshoot of the Human Economy." *Proceedings of the National Academy of Sciences* 99, no. 14: 9266–71.

Wackernagel, Mathis, and Judith Silverstein. 2000. "Big Things First: Focusing on the Scale Imperative with the Ecological Footprint." *Ecological Economics* 32, no. 3: 391–94.

Wakeman, George. 1868. *Official Proceedings of the National Democratic Convention Held at New York, July 4–9, 1868*. Boston: Rockwell and Rollins.

Walia, Harsha. 2014. "Decolonizing Together: Moving beyond a Politics of Solidarity toward a Practice of Decolonization." In *The Winter We Danced: Voices from the Past, the Future, and the Idle No More Movement*, edited by the Kino-nda-niimi Collective, 44–50. Winnipeg: ARP.

Wallerstein, Immanuel. 1974. *The Modern World-System I: Capitalist Agriculture and the Origins of the European World-Economy in the Sixteenth Century*. New York: Academic.

———. 1983. *Historical Capitalism*. London: Verso.

———. 1989. *The Modern World-System III*. San Diego: Academic.

Wang, Ting, Donna Surge, and Karen Jo Walker. 2013. "Seasonal Climate Change across the Roman Warm Period/Vandal Minimum Transition Using Isotope Sclerochronology in Archaeological Shells and Otoliths, Southwest Florida, USA." *Quaternary International* 308–9: 230–41.

Warrell, Helen 2015. "Ruthless UK Employers Trap Migrants in 'Modern-Day Slavery.'" *Financial Times*, August 12. www.ft.com/content/43daccd0-410d-11e5-9abe-5b335da3a90e.

Watts, Michael. 1983. "On the Poverty of Theory: Natural Hazards Research in Context." In *Interpretations of Calamity from the Viewpoint of Human Ecology*, edited by K. Hewitt, 231–62. Boston: Allen and Unwin.

———. 2004. "Resource Curse? Governmentality, Oil and Power in the Niger Delta, Nigeria." *Geopolitics* 9, no. 1: 50–80.

Weatherford, Jack. 2009. *The History of Money*. New York: Three Weathers.

Webber, Jeffery R. 2017. *The Last Day of Oppression, and the First Day of the Same: The Politics and Economics of the New Latin American Left.* Chicago: Haymarket.

Wei, Zhudeng, Xiuqi Fang, and Yun Su. 2014. "Climate Change and Fiscal Balance in China over the Past Two Millennia." *Holocene* 24, no. 12: 1771–84.

Weis, Tony. 2013. *The Ecological Hoofprint: The Global Burden of Industrial Livestock.* London: Zed.

Werlhof, Claudia von. 1988. "On the Concept of Nature and Society in Capitalism." In *Women: The Last Colony,* edited by Maria Mies, Veronika Bennholdt-Thomsen, and Werlhof, 95–112. London: Zed.

Westermann, Ekkehard. 1996. "Central European Forestry and Mining Industries in the Early Modern Period." In *L'uomo e la foresta: Secc. XIII–XVIII,* edited by Simonetta Cavaiocchi, 927–53. Florence: Le Monnier.

Westoby, Jack. 1989. *Introduction to World Forestry.* Oxford: Basil Blackwell.

Westra, Laura. 1998. "Development and Environmental Racism: The Case of Ken Saro-Wiwa and the Ogoni." *Race, Gender and Class* 6, no. 1: 152–62.

White, Lynn Townsend. 1962. *Medieval Technology and Social Change.* London: Oxford University Press.

White, Richard. 1996. "'Are You an Environmentalist or Do You Work for a Living?': Work and Nature." In *Uncommon Ground: Rethinking the Human Place in Nature,* edited by William Cronon, 171–85. New York: W.W. Norton.

———. 2011. *The Organic Machine: The Remaking of the Columbia River.* New York: Macmillan.

Whittle, Jane. 1998. "Individualism and the Family-Land Bond: A Reassessment of Land Transfer Patterns among the English Peasantry, c. 1270–1580." *Past and Present* 160: 25–63.

Wickham, Chris. 1994. *Land and Power: Studies in Italian and European Social History, 400–1200.* Rome: British School at Rome.

———. 2008. "Productive Forces and the Economic Logic of the Feudal Mode of Production." *Historical Materialism* 16, no. 2: 3–22.

Wiesner-Hanks, Merry E. 2008. *Women and Gender in Early Modern Europe.* 3rd ed. Cambridge: Cambridge University Press.

Wiggins, Steve, and Sharada Keats. 2015. *The Rising Cost of a Healthy Diet: Changing Relative Prices of Foods in High-Income and Emerging Economies.*

London: Overseas Development Institute. www.odi.org/sites/odi.org.uk/files/odi-assets/publications-opinion-files/9580.pdf.

Williams, Lewis. 2012. "The Human Ecologist as Alchemist: An Inquiry into Ngai Te Rangi Cosmology, Human Agency and Well-Being in a Time of Ecological Peril." In *Radical Human Ecology: Intercultural and Indigenous Approaches,* edited by Williams, Rose Roberts, and Alastair McIntosh, 91–120. New York: Routledge.

Williams, Michael. 2003. *Deforesting the Earth: From Prehistory to Global Crisis.* Chicago: University of Chicago Press.

Williams, Raymond. 1976. *Keywords: A Vocabulary of Culture and Society.* New York: Oxford University Press.

Wills, Ian R. 1972. "Projections of Effects of Modern Inputs on Agricultural Income and Employment in a Community Development Block, Uttar Pradesh, India." *American Journal of Agricultural Economics* 54, no. 3: 452–60.

Wily, Liz Alden. 2012. "Looking Back to See Forward: The Legal Niceties of Land Theft in Land Rushes." *Journal of Peasant Studies* 39, nos. 3–4: 751–75.

Wintle, Michael. 1999. "Renaissance Maps and the Construction of the Idea of Europe." *Journal of Historical Geography* 25, no. 2: 137–65.

Wish, Harvey. 1937. "American Slave Insurrections before 1861." *Journal of Negro History* 22, no. 3: 299–320.

Wittman, Hannah. 2009. "Reworking the Metabolic Rift: La Vía Campesina, Agrarian Citizenship, and Food Sovereignty." *Journal of Peasant Studies* 36, no. 4: 805–26.

Wolf, Eric R. 1982. *Europe and the People without History.* Berkeley: University of California Press.

Wood, Andy. 2007. *The 1549 Rebellions and the Making of Early Modern England.* Cambridge: Cambridge University Press.

Wood, Ellen Meiksins. 2003. *Empire of Capital.* London: Verso.

Woods, Jeremy, Adrian Williams, John K. Hughes, Mairi Black, and Richard Murphy. 2010. "Energy and the Food System." *Philosophical Transactions of the Royal Society B: Biological Sciences* 365, no. 1554: 2991–3006.

Working Group on the "Anthropocene." 2016. "What Is the 'Anthropocene'?—Current Definition and Status." Last modified January 4. http://quaternary.stratigraphy.org/workinggroups/anthropocene/.

World Economic Forum. 2012. *Energy for Economic Growth: Energy Vision Update 2012*. Geneva: World Economic Forum. http://reports.weforum.org/energy-for-economic-growth-energy-vision-update-2012/.

———. 2016. *The New Plastics Economy: Rethinking the Future of Plastics*. Geneva: World Economic Forum. http://www3.weforum.org/docs/WEF_The_New_Plastics_Economy.pdf.

Worm, Boris, Edward B. Barbier, Nicola Beaumont, J. Emmett Duffy, Carl Folke, Benjamin S. Halpern, Jeremy B.C. Jackson, et al. 2006. "Impacts of Biodiversity Loss on Ocean Ecosystem Services." *Science* 314, no. 5800: 787–90.

Wright, Melissa W. 2006. *Disposable Women and Other Myths of Global Capitalism*. New York: Routledge.

Wrigley, Edward Anthony. 1990. *Continuity, Chance and Change: The Character of the Industrial Revolution in England*. Cambridge: Cambridge University Press.

Yager, Tom. 2002. "What Was Rundale and Where Did It Come From?" *Béaloideas* 70: 153–86.

Yeates, Nicola. 2005. "A Global Political Economy of Care." *Social Policy and Society* 4, no. 2: 227–34.

———. 2009. *Globalizing Care Economies and Migrant Workers: Explorations in Global Care Chains*. Basingstoke: Palgrave Macmillan.

Yuval-Davis, Nira. 1993. "Gender and Nation." *Ethnic and Racial Studies* 16, no. 4: 621–32.

Zaid, Omar Abdullah. 2004. "Accounting Systems and Recording Procedures in the Early Islamic State." *Accounting Historians Journal* 31, no. 2: 149–70.

Zamora, Margarita. 1990. "Abreast of Columbus: Gender and Discovery." *Cultural Critique* 17: 127–49.

Zeeuw, J.W. de. 1978. "Peat and the Dutch Golden Age: The Historical Meaning of Energy Attainability." *AAG Bijdragen* 21: 3–31.

Ziegler, Philip. 2013. *The Black Death*. London: Faber and Faber.

Zinn, Howard. 2003. *A People's History of the United States: 1492–Present*. 3rd ed. London: Pearson/Longman.

Zorrilla, Marcelo Gabriel. 2006. "El acta de requerimiento y la guerra justa." *Revista del Notariado* 885: 247–55.

Index